Unemployment and Inflation

An Introduction to Macroeconomics

C. V. Brown

BASIL BLACKWELL

First published in 1984 by Basil Blackwell Ltd.,
108 Cowley Road, Oxford OX4 1JF.

British Library Cataloguing in Publication Data
Brown, C. V.
    Unemployment and Inflation.
    1. Macroeconomics
    I. Title
    339   HB172.5

ISBN 0-85520-722-1
ISBN 0-85520-723-X Pbk

Typeset by Stephen Austin/Hertford England
Printed and bound in Great Britain by Bell and Bain, Glasgow

Contents

Part I The basic framework

Part II Extending the basic framework

Part III   The open economy

To the Student

The primary purpose of this book is to help you to understand the causes of unemployment and inflation and what can be done about them. I am not of course claiming to provide simple solutions to these major problems but I do believe that both causes and cures can be better understood with the framework of this book, rather than with the theory used in most introductory texts.

The basic framework of the book is the use of aggregate supply and demand curves to explain both the level of output in our economy and the level of prices. This framework is preferable to the standard 'Keynesian-cross' framework, not because it is more difficult than that framework but because it is more suited to explaining output employment and price level changes in a unified way.

The book is almost totally free of mathematics. Some very simple algebra is used in Chapter 3 to explain the multiplier but the multiplier is also explained in words, with a numerical example and with a figure. I have used a few symbols — mainly to label the figures — and for your convenience I have brought all these together in a list of symbols.

HOW TO USE THIS BOOK

When you come to a chapter, I suggest you first read it through very quickly so that you get a general idea of what the chapter is about. Don't worry about following all the details of the argument. Second, go back and read the chapter carefully, trying to follow the argument at each stage. Occasionally you will find a question in the text or a short exercise to test your understanding. Try this before going on. Third, test yourself. Can you follow the argument from the summary underneath each figure? If so, go on; if not re-read the section. Then look at the concepts for review. Can you remember what each means? If not go back to the text. To help you find the correct sections **these concepts have been put in bold type** in the main text. Finally test your understanding by thinking through the answers to the questions for discussion. When you review for your exams use the same self-test procedures – the captions under the figures, the concepts for review and the questions for discussion.

You will have noted that if you followed the advice you will go over the material several times – especially if it is also covered in lectures or classes. This is deliberate advice. Repetition is an important part of the learning process. If you have 5 hours in all to spend on a chapter you will learn more from five sessions of 1 hour each than from one session of 5 hours.

Most people who study this book will have already done a course in microeconomics. If you haven't you may find it helpful to consult the microeconomic glossary which explains the micro concepts you need to know.

UNEMPLOYMENT AND INFLATION

Unemployment and inflation are important. They are important partly because they may affect our own standard of living very profoundly. Even if you are lucky enough to be protected against the worst effects of unemployment and inflation other members of society may not be. Unemployment and inflation are also important in an indirect sense because governments' chances of re-election depend in part on their economic record in dealing with these two main issues.

Because unemployment and inflation are very important it can be interesting to learn about their causes and about various views on what to do about them. I hope you will find it interesting to learn about these two major economic problems facing industrialized countries.

July, 1984

To the Teacher

I have written this book because of the unsatisfactory treatment of macroeconomics in introductory economics texts. These typically have models in which the level of output is explained by aggregate demand using a Keynesian cross or a Hicksian cross. These models have no price changes and thus have in effect implicit aggregate supply curves which are *perfectly elastic.*

The explanation of inflation is in terms of the quantity theory of money and the expectations-augmented Phillips curve which imply aggregate supply curves which are *perfectly inelastic.* Students must end up thoroughly confused about aggregate supply and yet a great deal of the current debate about macroeconomic policy is best understood as a debate about the shape and position of the aggregate supply curve. The conventional introductory text introduces financial markets as its second market (after the goods market) and very often says virtually nothing about the labour market despite the use of Phillips curves.

In view of this unsatisfactory state of affairs it will be no surprise that this book contains an unconventional introduction to macroeconomics. It is unconventional both in some of the topics that are covered and in the analytical techniques used. Like the macroeconomic chapters of conventional introductory texts it provides an introduction to economists' thinking on levels of employment and unemployment, the determination of national income, the role of the banking system and the influence of money on the economy, the balance of payments, and economic growth.

Most introductory texts focus very largely on aggregate demand in explaining these issues. Without neglecting the importance of demand this text places much more emphasis on supply: capital, labour and their interaction. The basic theoretical framework is the use of aggregate supply and aggregate demand curves. To enable students to see where I am going I have introduced these (without explanation) in Chapter 1 but they are carefully derived during the course of Part I. The position of the aggregate demand curve is determined by the equality of desired leakages and injections at constant prices (see Figure 3.6 in Chapter 3, which assumes a perfectly elastic aggregate supply curve). The downward slope of the aggregate demand curve is explained (in Chapter 5) by a combination of (1) real wage, (2) share of profits, (3) real balance and (4) foreign trade effects (see Figure 5.2). These are shown to the shift leakages or injections functions if the price level changes. This avoids the complexities of IS/LM analysis in explaining the shape of the aggregate demand curve.

The shape of the aggregate supply curve is determined in the labour market. The demand for labour is treated as a function of the real wage throughout. If the only determinant of the supply of labour is the real wage, and if the labour market is competitive, this gives a 'classical' vertical aggregate supply curve (see Figure 4.4). Positively sloped aggregate curves are explained in terms of (1) interest rate effects, (2) real balance effects, (3) and money illusion (see Figure 4.8) and (4) sticky wages (see Appendix to Chapter 4 and verbal explanation in section A of Chapter 5). Some of these explanations are not part of the standard introductory syllabus but the use of supply and demand analysis enables them to be introduced simply. It is my belief that the analysis is no more difficult than the Keynesian cross plus expectations-augmented Phillips curve, and is both simpler and more relevant than IS/LM analysis which is now taught in some schools. (I do not mean to imply that IS/LM analysis should not be taught – rather that it should come at an intermediate level where it can be used to explain the nature of the aggregate demand curve more rigorously).

Does my use of aggregate supply curve mean this is a book on supply-side economics? In one sense the answer to that question is 'yes, in part', but in another sense the answer is 'No', because the term supply-side economics has become associated in many people's minds with the oversimplified idea that supply can be greatly increased by cuts in taxes (the Laffer curve argument).

You may care to note that I have used diagrams (such as Figure 4.4) in which it is implied that employment is proportional to output. It is of course more conventional to assume that the relationship is non-proportional because of the diminishing marginal productivity of labour (as in the Appendix to Chapter 4). I believe the advantages to be gained from integrating the labour market in a simple way outweigh the disadvantages.[1]

The book assumes familiarity with the tools of supply and demand. When macro is taught after micro there is clearly no problem, nor is there a problem at university for students who have done economics at school. In other cases

1. In practice the relationship between employment and output is as much determined by movements away from and towards the marginal product curve as by movement along it – i.e. by changes in labour productivity (slack). It has frequently been the case that when output has fallen, employment has fallen less than proportionately but in the most recent recession employment has fallen.

teachers who prefer to teach macro first may find it an advantage to teach the basic elements of supply and demand before using this book. A glossary of microeconomic concepts is included. These introduce the concepts at a sufficiently technical level for the purposes of this book.

One of the most important decisions to be made in writing an economics text is to decide the order of theoretical and applied material. One view is that the theory appropriate to a particular level should precede discussions of policy. The advantages of this approach in terms of clear layout of material are obvious. The disadvantage is that students cannot see how the theory can be used for policy purposes and they can lose interest. The approach that I have adopted is to try to ensure that the student is kept fully aware of the purposes of the theory – to provide from the outset a framework for understanding the causes of macroeconomic problems such as unemployment and inflation, and to use this framework to explore various policy options. For this reason I try to relate theory to policy at frequent intervals.

Views differ about rational expectations. In part the differences are about how useful the approach is. Both those who think the approach important and those who think it unimportant can differ on whether it is an appropriate topic for an introductory text. I have included rational expectations as a separate chapter. It can be omitted with no loss of continuity to the argument in the other chapters.

Acknowledgements

Textbook writers are always conscious of the vast unacknowledged debt that they have to the literature of their subject, to their teachers, their colleagues and their students, and certainly I am indebted to all these groups.

I am grateful to Paul Hare, Eric Levin and Ron Shone, and an anonymous referee, for very helpful comments on parts of the book. Mark Casson and David Ulph read the whole of the first draft and both provided quite exceptionally valuable sets of comments. I am also indebted to Shirley Hewitt for drawing the figures and to Catherine McIntosh for typing the text. The latter had an even more difficult job than the usual one of coping with handwriting. In this case she had to cope with an unexpectedly difficult change of word processors between drafts. I am of course responsible for all remaining errors and omissions.

I am also grateful to the following for permission to make use of previously published material: Bank of England, Cambridge University Press, Controller of Her Majesty's Stationery Office, Croom Helm Ltd. Publishers, Heinemann Educational Books, National Economic Development Office, National Institute of Economic and Social Research, Oxford University Press, Times Newspapers Ltd.

List of Symbols

AD	Aggregate Demand	r	Liquidity ratio
AS	Aggregate Supply	S	Savings
BA	Bank Advances	S_F	Savings of firms
C	Consumption	S_H	Savings of households
c	marginal propensity to consume	S_L	Supply of Labour
		T	Taxation
D_L	Demand for Labour	T_F	Taxation of firms
Δ	Change in	T_G	Taxation of goods
G	Government expenditure	T_Y	Taxation of income
G_F	Government purchases from firms	t	Tariff
		W	Money or nominal wage
G_H	Government purchases from households	W/P	Real wage
		X	Exports
H	Hours	Y	National income (output)
I	Investment, investment goods	$	Dollars
		£	Pounds sterling
i	interest rate		
IM	Imports		
IM_F	Imports by firms		
IM_H	Imports by households		
J	Injections		
L	Leakages		
l	Marginal propensity for leakages		
LR	Lending Rates		
M	Stock of money		
MA	Monetary Assets		
M/P	Real money balances		
P	Price level, price		
Q	Quantity		

Glossary of Microeconomic Terms

Average revenue   Total revenue divided by quantity.

Change in demand   If the quantity demanded increases at each price (perhaps because incomes have increased or tastes changed) the demand curve will shift up to the right from D_0 to D_1 in Figure G.2. This will raise the equilibrium price from P_0 to P_1 and the equilibrium quantity from Q_0 to Q_1. What would happen to equilibrium price and quantity if the original demand curve was D_1 and demand fell to D_0?

Change in supply   If the amount people are willing to supply at each price increases the supply curve in Figure G.3 will shift out to the right from S_0 to S_1. This will increase equilibrium quantity from Q_0 to Q_1 and *decrease* equilibrium price from P_0 to P_1. What would happen to equilibrium price and quantity if the original supply curve was S_1 and supply then decreased to S_0?

Demand curve   Shows the relationship between the price of a good and the quantity of that good people will want to demand. A demand curve normally slopes down from left to right as Figure G.1 shows.

Equilibrium price   The only price that can last. The price at which the amount willingly supplied equals the amount willingly demanded. In competitive markets the equilibrium price will be where the supply and demand schedules intersect. This point is labelled in Figure G.1 and shows that in equilibrium Q_0 will be purchased at a price of P_0.

Income elasticity of demand   The percentage change in quantity demanded divided the percentage change in income. If when income rises the quantity demanded rises – the income elasticity of demand is positive, and the demand curve for a product will shift up and to the right. This is the normal case. There are some goods – called inferior goods – that we may buy less of as our income rises. They have an income elasticity of demand which is negative.

Law of diminishing returns If a variable factor (say labour) is added to a fixed factor (say capital) the *marginal physical product* will decline after some point. Think of trying to grow more and more food on a fixed plot of land by adding more and more workers. What would you expect to happen to the extra output per worker as the number of workers increases?

Marginal physical product (MPP) The extra (physical) product produced when an extra unit of a variable factor (say labour) is added to a fixed factor. See Figure G.7.

Marginal revenue The addition to total revenue from selling an extra unit of a product.

Marginal revenue product The extra revenue produced by an extra unit of a variable factor (say labour). It is the *marginal physical product* times *marginal revenue*. In competitive markets where marginal and average revenue are equal it is also equal to marginal physical product times price.

Price elasticity of demand The percentage change in quantity demanded divided by the percentage change in price. If the price elasticity of demand is elastic – i.e. greater than one – then the total expenditure on the product will rise as the price falls. If the price elasticity is equal to one total expenditure will be unchanged when price changes. If price elasticity of demand is inelastic total expenditure on the product will fall as the price falls. Figure G.5 illustrates demand curves of various elasticities.

Price elasticity of supply The percentage change in quantity supplied divided by the percentage change in price. If the amount producers wish to supply does not change when the price changes the elasticity of supply is zero and the supply curve is vertical. If the percentage change in quantity is less than the percentage change in price the supply curve is said to be inelastic. If quantity and price change by the same percentage the supply curve is of unitary elasticity. A straight line supply curve passing through the origin has unitary elasticity. If the percentage change in quantity is greater than the percentage change in price supply is elastic. If a very small increase in price brings forth an indefinitely large increase in quantity demanded the elasticity of supply is infinite and the supply curve is horizontal. Figure G.5 shows supply curves of various elasticities.

Supply curve Shows the relationship the price of a good and quantity that producers are willing to supply of that good. A supply curve normally slopes up from left to right as Figure G.1 shows.

Total physical product (TPP) The total amount of output produced when an extra variable factor (say labour) is added to a fixed factor (say capital). See Figure G.6.

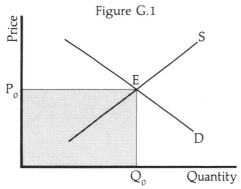

Figure G.1

See *Demand curve, Supply curve, Equilibrium price*

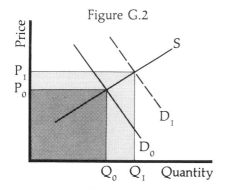

Figure G.2

See *Change in demand*

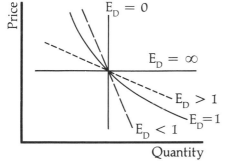

Figure G.3

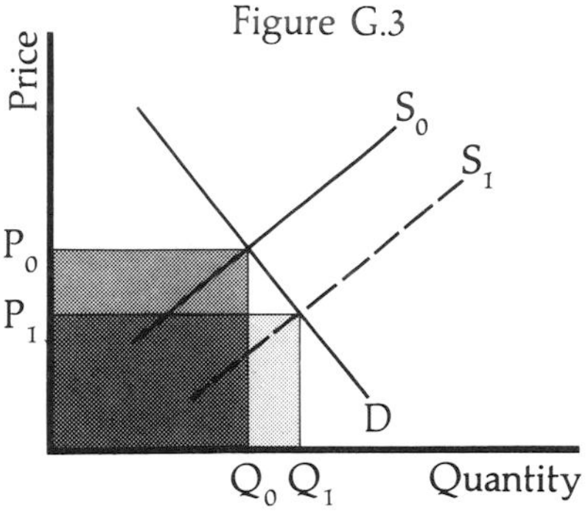

See *Change in supply*

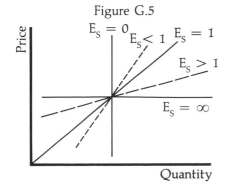

Figure G.4

See *Price elasticity of demand*

Figure G.6

See *Total physical product*

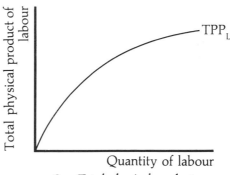

Figure G.5

See *Price elasticity of supply*

Figure G.7

See *Marginal physical product,
Law of diminishing returns*

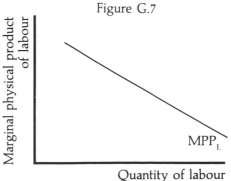

PART I
THE BASIC FRAMEWORK

1

Introduction

This book provides an introduction to inflation and unemployment – two of the main – perhaps THE two main – economic problems facing the industrialized countries of the world. **Inflation** is a sustained increase in the general price level. The official index of the price level[1] in the period 1948 to 1982 is shown in Figure 1.1. **Unemployment** occurs when people are unable to obtain as much work as they would like to at current wage rates. British

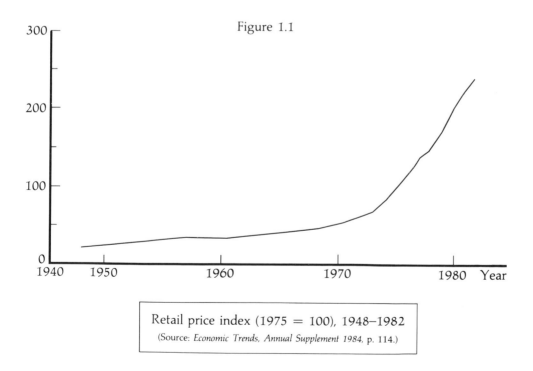

Figure 1.1

Retail price index (1975 = 100), 1948–1982
(Source: *Economic Trends, Annual Supplement 1984*, p. 114.)

---

1. In this introduction the terms 'inflation' and 'the price level' are used interchangeably. This is strictly wrong as is explained in Chapter 5.

rates of unemployed people[2] are shown in Figure 1.2. It can be seen that the rate of increase of prices peaked in the mid-1970s and the rate of unemployment was continuing to rise throughout the period. The book is also concerned with the level of national output and what causes it to change, with investment, the balance of payments, the monetary system and the determination of wages and how changes in these factors may affect output, employment and prices. It also provides a framework for analysing government policy: taxes, government expenditures, the money supply; policy towards investment; wages and the balance of payments; and structural policies designed for example to ensure that labour and capital are well matched to each other.

This book uses aggregate supply and aggregate demand curves as its framework for analysis. The use of aggregate supply and demand curves has two advantages. The first is that they allow us to discuss the determination of prices and output in a unified way. Because output and employment tend to be related this also helps to explain employment and unemployment. Second the techniques of aggregate supply and demand are simple, which is both an advantage in itself and which also makes it possible to consider interesting issues not normally considered in a first-year text.

Figure 1.2   Total unemployed including school leavers, 1949–1983

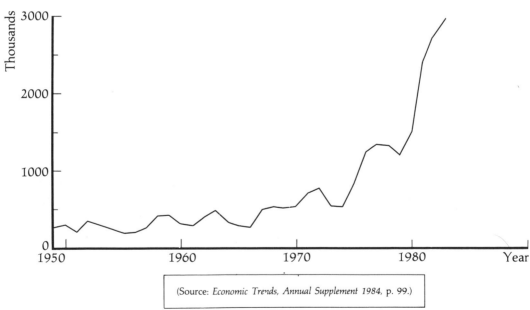

(Source: *Economic Trends, Annual Supplement 1984*, p. 99.)

2.   Unemployment figures – as in Figure 1.2 usually refer to people who are unable to find any work. In Chapter 4 the concept of unemployment is extended to include people who are prevented from working as much as they wish.

The plan of this chapter is as follows. In section A we look briefly at the basic model for determination of the levels of national output and of prices that provide the framework for this book. We then look at circular flow of income in section B. This is useful both because it can help explain how **microeconomics** (the study of small units such as households and firms) and **macroeconomics** (the study of large units such as whole economies) are related to each other, and because the circular flow concept is an important building block for an understanding of macroeconomics. Our particular concern with the circular flow of income is what determines its size. As we will see the size of the circular flow and national output are the same thing, and it is important to be clear about what we mean when we talk about national output. Somewhat confusingly this is most commonly referred to as national income. Section C of this chapter should clear up the terminology where it will be explained that national product, national income and national expenditure are conceptually equivalent.

A THE BASIC MODEL

The purpose of this section is to provide a first glimpse of the basic model that will be used throughout this book. At this stage I simply want to assert that it is useful to look at the economy as a whole as if it behaved rather like a market for a single commodity. The economy is then analysed in terms of supply and demand as in Figure 1.3. Output (quantity) is measured on the horizontal axis: the level of prices is measured on the vertical axis. I have assumed[3] that the supply curve for the economy as a whole – called the **aggregate supply curve** – slopes upwards from left to right. This means that suppliers are only willing to sell increasing levels of output at higher prices. Similarly the **aggregate demand curve** is assumed[4] to slope downwards. This means that more output will be demanded at lower prices.

The intersection of the aggregate supply and demand curve determines both the level of national output and the overall price level. If, as seems reasonable, employment is associated with the level of output – then aggregate supply and demand analysis will go a long way towards determining the amounts of both employment and unemployment.

3. To the Teacher: It is explained in Chapters 4 and 5 that the aggregate supply curve has a positive slope for a variety of reasons including the effects of real money balances, the effects of expectations about price changes on labour supply, and increases in costs as output expands.
4. To the Teacher: It is explained in Chapter 5 that the aggregate demand curve has a negative slope for a variety of reasons including the changing purchasing power of the money wage, the effects of real balances, changes in the distribution of income and changes in the level of exports and imports.

Figure 1.3

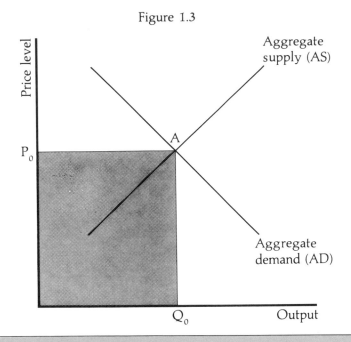

The intersection of the aggregate supply curve and the aggregate demand curve determines the price level and output.

Implications of the model

What are the implications of this basic model for issues such as inflation[5] and unemployment? Suppose the economy is at the intersection of AS and AD in Figure 1.3 which for convenience is labelled A. Suppose further that this happens to represent an undesirably high level of unemployment and an undesirably low level of output. What can we do about it? We may be able to shift the aggregate supply or demand curves to the right. Suppose we were to shift the aggregate demand curve to the right by cutting taxes, or increasing exports, or investment or reducing savings. We can see from Figure 1.4 that this would raise output from Q_0 to Q_1 thus increasing output. It will be argued in later chapters that increasing output will increase employment and reduce unemployment. The increase in output and employment are what is intended but we can see that the effect has also been to increase the price level from P_0 to P_1 which is not desired. Alternatively we might increase output by increasing aggregate supply from AS_0 to AS_1 in Figure 1.5, perhaps by reducing costs or introducing new technology. The

---

5   I am using the terms prices and inflation interchangeably at the moment. This is strictly wrong and the issue is explored in Chapter 5.

increase in aggregate supply would increase output and might also decrease unemployment but would reduce – not increase – the rate of inflation.

Figure 1.4

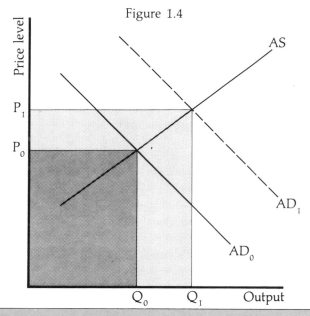

An increase in aggregate demand will raise output and reduce unemployment while raising the price level.

Figure 1.5

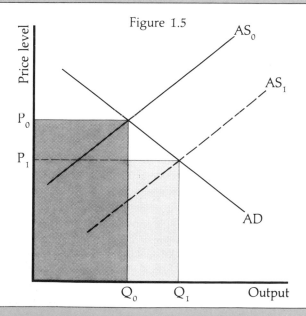

An increase in aggregate supply will raise output and employment while reducing the price level.

Now this very quick glimpse at the model has skated over rather a lot of problems which are the subject matter of this book. However, if you remember the basic framework you will be able to slot the various bits and pieces into place as we come upon them.

Before developing the model it is useful to think about the relationships between individual markets and aggregated markets.

B   THE CIRCULAR FLOW OF INCOME AND RELATIONSHIPS BETWEEN MARKETS

This section is devoted to a discussion of the interrelationships between different parts of an economic system that will help us to understand how individual markets (as studied in microeconomics) are related to the overall economy (as studied in macroeconomics). The relationships between parts of the economy are studied using a circular flow diagram and we will see the size of the circular flow provides three measures of output.

Let us imagine, to start with, a very simple economy with only two sectors: households and firms. This means that in the economy we are considering there is no government, no foreign sector, no financial institutions – only households and firms. It is also assumed that there is no savings and that there are no institutional interferences with the smooth operation of market relationships between firms and households.

Households

Households provide services to firms for which they are paid. For example, members of the household work for firms providing them with the service of their labour for which they receive a wage or salary in return. Some households may also own land which they rent to firms, receiving rent in return for the service provided. Households may also lend money to firms and receive interest, or profits in return. Factor services may be provided directly to firms, as is usually the case with labour services, or may be provided indirectly through firms supplying services (e.g. of accountants) or finance (e.g. banks). Suppose we represent what has been said thus far in Figure 1.6. We have two boxes, one representing the household sector, the other representing the firm sector. If we draw three arrows from the household sector to the firm sector these represent the services of labour, land and capital being supplied to the firms. Coming in the other direction, we have three arrows from the firm sector to the household sector representing the payments of wages, rent, interest and profits. Note that the arrows go in both directions, the arrows from households to firms represent

Figure 1.6

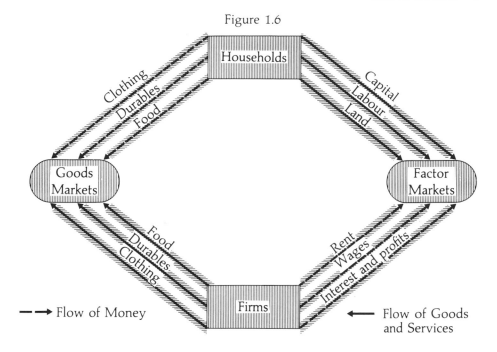

Households supply factor services to the factor markets and demand goods from the goods markets. Firms supply goods to the goods markets and demand factor services from the factor markets. The goods markets determine prices and quantities of goods. The factor markets determine prices and quantities of factors. Household income is determined by their factor endowments and factor prices and this income, together with preferences and the prices of goods, determines the demand for goods. Firms combine factors purchased from the factor market as efficiently as possible to produce goods demanded by the goods markets.

services provided from the households to the firms, the arrows going in the other direction represent payment of money from the firms to the households. Thus, households provide services to firms and receive money payments from the firms in exchange.

Households also purchase goods and services from the firms. Suppose for the purposes of illustration that we assume that households buy three commodities, let us call them food, clothing and durables (e.g. cars, fridges, housing). We can add to our diagram three arrows representing money payments from the households to the firms for these three classes of goods which they purchase. We can also add three arrows from firms to households representing the actual amounts of food, clothing and durables supplied by the firms.

Thus we see that households do two things: they supply services to firms and receive income in return, they also demand goods from the firms and pay for these goods with the money.

Firms

Now let us look at the situation from the point of view of the firms. The firms also do two things. They hire factor services from the households, that is, labour, land and capital and pay for these factor services with rent, wages, interest and profits. On the other hand they provide goods (and services), i.e. food, clothing and durables to the households and receive money in return.

We thus have produced a simplified version of the **circular flow of income**. Note that in fact there are two flows, there is a flow of goods and services going in one direction, that is the actual food, clothing and housing provided from the firms to the households and the services of labour, land and capital provided from the households to the firms; this flow is going in one direction and in the other direction is a flow of money. Money is paid by the firms for factor services and received by the households as their income, and this income is in turn spent by households on purchasing commodities from the firms. It will be remembered that we are at the moment assuming that households spend all of their income, i.e. they do not save.

The ideas underlying the circular flow of income are important and are very useful in understanding many aspects of economics. For example, the three fundamental economic problems have been called 'What?', 'How?' and 'For whom?'. By 'What?' we mean what is to be produced in a society, by 'How?', we mean how shall it be produced, and by 'For whom?' we mean who shall get the goods once they have been produced.

Markets

Let us see how the circular flow analysis can help us to understand how these problems are solved. In Figure 1.6 there are two circles between the two boxes representing the household and firm sectors. One represents the markets for the final goods and services. In the goods markets the households' demands for food, clothing and durables enter from one side and from the other side the firms' supplies of these commodities enter. Thus we have a durables market, a clothing market and a food market, each of which can be represented by a supply and demand curve. In one way or another these supplies and demands will lead to prices and quantities being determined. If, as we have assumed, there are no factors interfering with the free interplay of supply and demand, then prices and quantities will be determined by their interaction. This means that the intersection of the supply and demand curves determines the price of the output and also how much of it should be produced, or in terms of the three fundamental questions 'What is to be produced?' On the other side of the flow we can add another circle for factor markets. From one side we have the firms' demands for labour, land and capital and from the other side the households' supply of these factors, again, labour, land and capital. These markets can also be represented by supply and demand curves with the equilibrium positions showing the amounts of each factor that are supplied and the prices (wages, rent, etc.) that will be paid. Let us look at this market from the point of view of an individual household. That household, let us say, has two working members, each of whom receives a wage. Their total earnings will depend on how much work is done. The amount that each household member would *like* to work will depend on how the household (or the individual member) values the loss of leisure involved in working compared with the extra goods that can be purchased with the income earned. The household supply of labour shows the amounts of labour the household will be willing to supply at various wages. If the household can sell as much labour as it wishes then its labour income will be determined by the wage rate and the amount of labour it wishes to supply at that wage. If that household owns no land which it rents, and no capital which it lends to firms, then the income of that household will be the earnings of the two working members. Thus if we know the amount of factors that a household supplies and the prices of these factors then we know the income of that household. This is of course its income in money terms. If we want to know how much food, clothing and durables this household will purchase we need to know two other pieces of information. One of these is the prices of food, clothing and housing, which we obtain from the commodity markets. Secondly, we need to know the households' preferences or tastes. If we know household income and the prices of commodities that they wish to purchase, then once we know how they wish to spend their money we can determine how much of each commodity the household will purchase, assuming that the household spends all of its income. Coming back to the factor market then, knowing how much of each factor a household owns and knowing the equilibrium price for each factor we can determine the household income; that is to say, it is in this area of the diagram that the question 'For whom?' is decided.

Looking at the position once more from the firms' point of view, the firm is hiring factors of production and is using the services of these factors to produce the goods and services which it supplies to the commodity market. Naturally if the firm wants to maximize its profits it will try to combine these factors in the most efficient possible manner. This is what we mean by the question 'How?'. Depending upon the relative costs of various factors the firm will combine them so as to produce the output required in the cheapest possible way. Firms are owned by households so that if firms make profits the households owning the firms will become better off.

I hope many of you are saying to yourselves, this is what we have done in microeconomics, and indeed you will be right. In microeconomics we look at the workings of individual markets and the workings of firms, although this is not usually done in terms of a circular flow diagram.

Interrelationships between markets

The circular flow of income is one way of looking at interrelationships between markets that focuses on the accounting relationships. It is also worth examining some of the possible economic relationships between markets. To do this I want to examine a hypothetical example of what economists call general equilibrium and a practical example of market interconnections. General equilibrium analysis can be distinguished from what is called **partial equilibrium analysis** which is largely what is done in microeconomics. In partial equilibrium analysis one isolates a particular market and studies it on the assumption that there are not particularly strong links with other markets, whereas in **general equilibrium analysis** one does study the relationships between markets.

General equilibrium

There is a position of 'general' equilibrium when all markets in the economy are in equilibrium – that is when there is no tendency for price or quantity to change in any market. As an example of general equilibriuim analysis let us assume that households decide to purchase less food and more clothing. We could represent this change on diagrams with which you are familiar. If we draw a supply and demand curve for food and a supply and demand curve for clothing we have the equilibrium prices and quantities where the supply and demand curves intersect. If households decide that they want to purchase less food and more clothing this means that the demand curve for food will shift down and to the left whereas the demand curve for clothing will shift up and to the right. In the new equilibrium less food will be produced and more clothing will be produced. In terms of the circular flow diagram is this the end of the story? Clearly, the answer is no. If firms cut back on food production they will need fewer factors necessary to produce food, likewise if they expand clothing production they will need more factors necessary to produce clothing. Suppose we assume that in order to produce food one needs quite a lot of land but not very much labour, and that in order to produce clothing one needs quite a lot of labour but not very much land. As food production is cut back then the food industry will require less labour and less land; however, being land-intensive its reduction in the amount of land needed will be proportionately greater than the reduction in the amount of labour needed. Suppose that the food industry releases three units of land for every unit of labour that it releases. In the clothing industry the reverse situation prevails. Clothing firms will wish to hire more labour and more land; however, being labour-intensive they will want to hire more units of labour than of land. Let us assume that they want to hire three units of labour for every unit of land that they hire – what will happen then if land and labour can be used in both industries?

Taking the position as a whole, the increase in the supply of factors will have been land-intensive while the increase in the demand for factors will be labour-intensive. This means that in the case of land the increase in supply will be greater than the increase in demand, hence the price of land will fall. On the other hand, the increase in the supply of labour will be less than the increase in the demand for labour; therefore, the price of labour will rise. Thus far, we have seen that a change in demand such that households want less food and more clothing will affect not only the equilibrium price and quantity of food and of clothing but also the equilibrium prices and quantities of land and of labour (and of course of capital as well, although we have excluded this from the example). The price of land has fallen and the price of labour has risen. How does this affect household income? Clearly, households that own a lot of land will lose whereas households that own a lot of labour will benefit. Some households will be better off, other households will be worse off. This in turn could affect the demand for food and for clothing once again, and so if we wanted to go into great detail we would need to go around the circle once again; however, the point is that we have an interrelated economic system in which goods markets and factor markets are interrelated.

Interrelated markets

The example above was a hypothetical example of general equilibrium but it is also useful to study an actual example of the interrelationships between different markets. The example focuses on the market for oils[6] used in the manufacture of margarine and shows how an increase in the demand for chickens in the USA led to a reduction in the price of margarine in the UK! Figure 1.7 may help you to follow the argument. In the US the increase in demand for chickens (see Figure 1.7a) led to an increase in output. More chickens meant an increase in the demand for soya bean meal which was a main element in chicken feed. Soya bean meal is produced from soya beans which at the same time produce soya bean oil as a by-product. Thus the increase in the *demand* for soya bean meal and the resulting increase in

6.   This example is based on *Raw Materials and Pricing* by Unilever Ltd, extracts from which appear in C.V. Brown (ed) *Economic Principles Applied* Martin Robertson 1970.

Figure 1.7

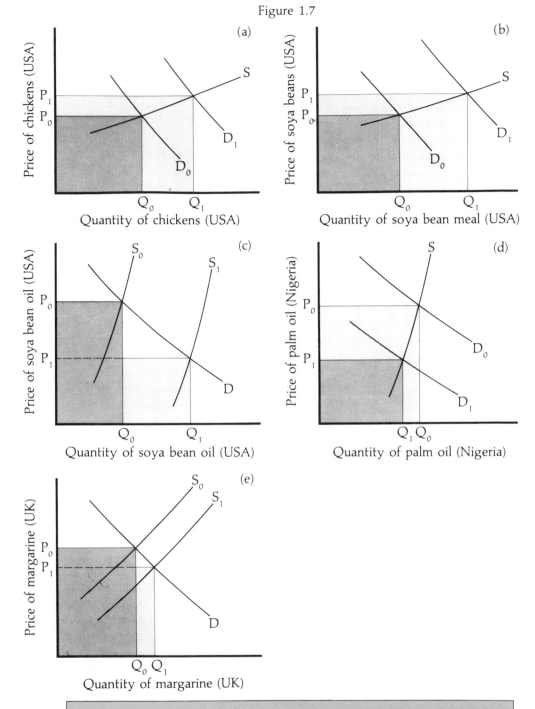

a) An increase in the demand for chickens leads to increased production.
b) The increase in production of chickens leads to an increase in demand
    for soya bean meal for chicken feed.
c) The increased production of soya beans for soya bean meal also
    increases the production of soya bean oil leading to a fall in its price.
d) The lower price of soya bean oil causes it to be substituted for palm oil.
e) The lower price of oils generally increases the supply of margarine.

production (from Q_0 to Q_1 in Figure 1.7b) results in an increase in the *supply* of soya bean oil. With the aid of Figure 1.7c it can be seen that the increase in the quantity of soya oil results in a fall in the price of soya bean oil. Now margarines are commonly made from a blend of oils and when the price of one oil falls margarine manufacturers use more of the oil which has become cheaper and less of others. So when soya bean oil fell in price (from P_0 to P_1 in Figure 1.7d) more soya bean oil was used and the demand for other oils was reduced. One competitor of US soya bean oil was Nigerian palm oil. The fall in the price of soya bean oil led to a fall in the demand for palm oil and this reduced the price of palm oil from P_0 to P_1 in Figure 1.5d. As the supply of palm oil is quite inelastic this fall in price was quite large. So far we have seen that a decision of US consumers to purchase more chickens has been that US soya bean farmers have benefited at the expense of palm oil farmers in Eastern Nigeria, but this is not the end of the story. The fact that soya bean oil became cheaper meant that it was cheaper to produce margarine than it had been before. This helped to hold down the price of margarine in Britain. One could go on talking about repercussions almost endlessly but the point has I think been made – markets are interrelated and in many instances these interrelationships cross national boundaries. What is done in one country affects the well-being of people in other countries and indeed in the example the loss to Nigeria was undoubtedly to at least partially offset the American aid that was being given to Nigeria, making the point that one has to consider not only official aid policies but also the effects of international trade.

The Circular Flow and Economic Aggregates

For much of the rest of this book we will be looking at the circular flow from rather a different point of view: looking at it from the point of view of economic aggregates. We will not lose sight of structural issues. Nevertheless much of the time our concern will be to look not at the composition of the circular flow, not at the individual markets, firms or households but rather at what determines the overall size of the flow. Why should the flow at any particular time be a certain size rather than larger or smaller? It is to these questions that we turn after looking at the question 'What do we mean by national income and how is it measured?' This is important because we are going to be concerned throughout this book with changes in levels of output – or as we will sometimes call it – national income. National income is a measure of the size of the circular flow. It is important because – as we will see – it is related to levels of employment and unemployment, and because we would expect (subject to important exceptions discussed below) to be better off if national income goes up. It is also important to understand the ways in which national income is measured in order to understand how and why it will change.

C   THE CIRCULAR FLOW OF INCOME, NATIONAL INCOME ACCOUNTING, AND ECONOMIC WELFARE

We will be spending quite a bit of time looking at what determines the level of national income and related questions, such as 'Why does national income grow relatively fast, or relatively slowly?' Before doing this, we should consider what we mean by national income. **National income**, or **national output** can be defined as the value of goods and services produced in a country in a year. The detailed study of what goes into national income and how it is measured is called national income accounting. This is an aspect of economics which is specialized, complicated and in my personal view not very interesting. Fortunately, for our purposes, it is not necessary to master a great deal of the detail involved. What we need to know is a few of the basic principles underlying national income accounting.

Basic principles underlying national income accounting

The first of these relates to the question of what we should count. In general, what we count is the final value of productive goods and services. In the circular flow diagram you will remember that there are in fact two flows, a flow of goods and of factor services going in one direction and a flow of money going in the other direction. National income is a measure of the size of this money flow which corresponds to the reverse flow of goods and services. However, there are some money flows in the economy which do not have corresponding flows of goods and services in the opposite direction. Economists call these other money flows **transfer payments**; money is being transferred from one person or group to another without goods or services being given in exchange. An example may help to clarify the distinction. If one purchases a loaf of bread there is a good, namely bread, which is being exchanged for the money. However, the payment of government pensions to old people represents a transfer from the government (and ultimately other taxpayers) to the old age pensioners – the pensioners do not have to do anything, that is, to provide any service in return for their pension. Thus if we say that the national income or product of a country is the value of goods and services produced in that country we do not want to include in the total the value of transfer payments, for as we have seen these do not correspond to any flow of goods or services.

The second principle in national income accounting that we need to understand is that there are three different ways of measuring the value of national output. The three ways can be termed **national income, national product** and **national expenditure** and we will look at each of these methods. All three methods involve measuring the size of the circular flow of income but they measure the flow at different points. Let us take national expenditure first. National expenditure is the total expenditure in an economy in the year on final goods and services. In terms of the simplified model in Figure 1.8, it is the expenditure by households on goods and services. Thus it is measuring the size of the circular flow at the point where the flow leaves households. Now let us look at the national product approach – this is the total value of final goods and services produced. In terms of Figure 1.8 it is the value of goods and services produced. If all goods which are produced are sold, then quite obviously this total must be the same at the previous total for national expenditure. National expenditure and national product will be equal even if everything that is produced is not sold. If part of what is produced is not sold it is treated in the national accounts as investment so that the production of consumption goods plus investment

Figure 1.8

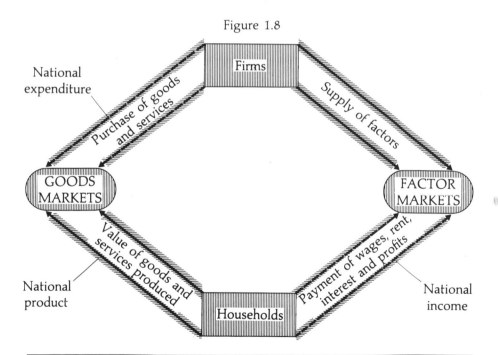

National *income* measures the flow of factor payments from firms. National *expenditure* measures the flow of expenditure from households. National *product* measures the flow of goods and services produced by firms. All these measures of the circular flow are in principle the same.

goods equals national expenditure. Finally, there is the national income approach – this measures the flow of factor payments. In terms of Figure 1.8 it is the value of wages, rent, interest and profits. Once again, this total must be the same as the other two. To see why national product will equal national expenditure in our simple model consider what firms will do with the receipts from selling goods – they will use these receipts to purchase factors from the households. Thus they will pay out wages, rent and interest. It is possible that the sum of these payments will be less than the firm's total receipts, which means that firms have made profits. However firms are owned by households which become better off by the extent of the profits earned by the firm. We thus have three approaches to national income, all of which are measuring the same flow but at different points. Thus they should all in principle give the same answer.

I have said several times that national income, or national product, is the value of **final goods and services** produced and would now like to explain why the word 'final' has been stressed. This is stressed to distinguish final goods and services from intermediate goods and services. Firms buy products from one another and to count the value of these products in addition to the final goods and services would be to double count. Let us take an example. Suppose that a baker produces £2250 worth of bread in a day. This then would represent the day's contribution to national product. However, suppose the baker has purchased £1500 worth of flour from a flour mill and the flour mill has in turn purchased £1000 of wheat. The total value of all three transactions is £4750, i.e. £2250 plus £1500 plus £1000, but adding all three transactions together means that the value of the wheat is being counted three times over, which is clearly incorrect. We can either count the value of the bread only, i.e. £2250; alternatively, we can take what is called the value-added approach. Let us look at the picture from the point of view of the flour mill. The mill sells flour worth £1500 but it has purchased raw materials, i.e. wheat worth £1000; the difference between £1500 and £1000 represents the value added by the flour mill. From the point of view of the baker value added is the price received for the bread, i.e. £2250 less the cost paid for the flour, i.e. £1500; value added is therefore £750. If we now sum value added at all three stages we have value added in wheat £1000, value-added in flour £500, value-added in bread £750, the total value added is £2250, i.e. the same as the cost of the bread. This means that we can look at national product from two points of view. We can either take the total value of final products or alternatively we can take the total of value added at each stage of production and, subject to no mistakes having been made, the two answers should be the same.

UK national income accounts

Thus far we have looked at the three approaches to national income in terms of the circular flow diagram. Before leaving the subject I would, however, like us to look briefly at the actual national income figures for the UK for 1982, which are given in Table 1.1 headed National Income, National Expenditure, and National Product by Industry.

The left-hand portion of the table shows national income. As you can see the basic components are income from employment, that is wages and salaries; income from self-employment; the profits of private companies and the trading surplus of public corporations and other public enterprises plus rent. This gives total domestic income. In terms of the circular flow diagram income from employment and self-employment corresponds to what was there called wages; the gross trading profits of both public and private companies was called profit and of course rent corresponds to rent in the circular flow diagram. For our purposes we need not worry about the meaning of stock appreciation, it in fact refers to the increase in the value of stocks. The residual, the next item, is simply a figure put in, to, so to speak, balance the books and is discussed a bit later. This gives us gross domestic income at **factor cost**. At factor cost simply means that this is the value of the income at the cost of the factors of production that were needed to make it. Gross domestic income is the value of what is produced in the domestic territory of the UK; however, for some purposes it is more interesting to know the value of the income of residents of a country rather than simply of the geographical area. Because Britain has in the past invested a lot overseas, British residents receive income from abroad so that the income of British residents is greater than the income of the geographhical area of the UK. Therefore after adjusting for income from abroad we have the gross national income at factor cost. Part of national income is used to replace capital equipment that is worn out or obsolete and when this is subtracted we are left with net national income at factor cost.

The left-hand portion of the table then looks at national income; that is, it looks at the various factor incomes. In the right-hand part of the table we have national product by industry. This portion of the table shows the contribution of each of the industries to the gross national product.

The third approach is to look at national expenditure and this is done in the centre portion of the table. Here we have expenditure by consumers, the expenditure by public authorities on current goods and services and public and private sector investment expenditure, or as it is officially called 'gross domestic fixed capital formation'. At the moment all we need to know is that we are counting here both consumption expenditure and investment

TABLE 1.1 NATIONAL INCOME, NATIONAL EXPENDITURE AND NATIONAL PRODUCT
(BY INDUSTRY – POUNDS MILLION), 1982

National income (gross national product by category of income)		National expenditure (gross national product by category of expenditure)		Gross national product by industry	
Income from employment	155,133	Consumers' expenditure	167,128	Agriculture, forestry & fishing	5752
Income from self-employment	20,068	General government final consumption	60,082	Energy & water supply	26,037
Gross trading profits of companies	33,344	Gross domestic fixed capital formation	42,172	Manufacturing	56,492
Gross trading surplus of corporation and other public enterprises	9192	Physical increase in stocks and work in progress	−1162	Construction	13,480
Rent	16,166			Distribution, hotels & catering, repairs	29,971
Imputed charge for consumption of non-trading capital	2507	Total domestic expenditure at market prices	268,220	Transport	10,311
		less: indirect taxes	−47,082	Communication	6853
		plus: subsidies	5452	Distributive trades	
Total domestic income	236,410			Insurance, banking & finance, & business services & leasing	29,040

Ownership of dwellings	14,690
Public administration & national defence & compulsory social security	16,724
Education & health services	20,868
Miscellaneous services	14,543
Residual	50
Adjustment for financial services	−12,258
Gross domestic product	232,553
Net property income from abroad	1577
Gross national product at factor cost	234,130

less: stock appreciation	−3907
Residual	50
Gross domestic income at factor cost	232,553
Net property income from abroad	1577
Gross domestic expenditure at factor cost	226,590
plus: exports and property income from abroad	84,119
less: imports and property income paid abroad	−76,579

Gross national expenditure at factor cost	234,130
Gross national income at factor cost	234,130
less: depreciation (capital consumption)	−33,057
Net national income at factor cost	201,073

Source: *National Income and Expenditure*, 1983, Tables 1.2, 1.1, 1.9.

expenditure. There is also a negative item for increase in stocks and work in progress; this refers to goods which have been produced or are in process of being produced but have not yet been sold. This is a negative number because in 1982 stocks were being reduced as part of firms' response to falling demand. In many years this item is positive. You can see that the total of these items is called 'total domestic expenditure at market prices'. If you look at the total, over £268b, and compare this with the figure that we already know to be gross national income of £236b there appears to be a major discrepancy. The primary reason for the difference is that the expenditure figures are at **market prices** whereas the national income figures are at factor cost. Factor cost, you will remember, refers to the actual cost of producing the goods and services, whereas the expenditure figures refer to the amounts of money that people pay for the products. As you are undoubtedly all too painfully aware much of what we pay for cigarettes, alcohol, petrol and many other goods represents in part a tax which is collected by the government. Therefore, if we wish to reconcile the prices that people pay for the products, that is the market prices, with the cost of producing the goods we must make allowances for these taxes on goods. Therefore taxes on goods are subtracted and subsidies, which are the reverse of taxes, are added – this gives us the gross domestic expenditure at factor cost. The other adjustment that we must make concerns transactions with other countries. Part of what people spend is spent on goods which are produced abroad; therefore, if we want to know the value of expenditure in this country we need to subtract the value of imports and also property income paid abroad. We also need to allow for the fact that part of what is produced in this country is paid for by people in other countries. Thus we add in exports and property income received from abroad and what we are left with is gross national expenditure at factor cost. We thus see that the three approaches to national income give us the same answer, as in principle they should. You can see that the three figures for national income, national product and national expenditure are exactly the same but it probably will not surprise you to learn that, when the statisticians actually do the work involved in collecting the figures together, the answer does not turn out to be exactly the same for each approach; the reasons for this are that it is difficult to get many of the figures that are needed and in fact the various approaches do not usually agree exactly. This is the reason for the figure called 'residual' in the left-hand part of the table. The number that is put in there is whatever is necessary to make the totals come out to be the same.

You may well ask how much of the detail involved here you should expect to know about. The answer is we're not concerned with the detail, certainly not with any of the figures that are given, what is the most important thing is that you should understand that in principle the three approaches to national income give the same answer. It would also be useful for you to remember the distinction between payments which represent payments for goods and services on the one hand and transfer payments on the other hand, and to remember the distinction between intermediate goods and final goods, but as I have said, the most important of all is to recognize the equivalence of the three basic approaches to national income, expenditure and product.

National income and welfare

It is both conventional and convenient to assume that if national income goes up we are better off. However it is also potentially misleading. Suppose that we know that in some year national income was 100 and that in some later year it was 500. Does that mean we were 5 times as well off in the later year or even that we were any better off? If between the two years prices had trebled and population doubled, an income of 600 would be required for each person to have the same real income after inflation.

There are a variety of other ways in which income and welfare can move in opposite directions, as the following examples illustrate.

> If people smoke more cigarettes their extra expenditure will cause national income to increase. If they become ill as a result of their smoking additional expenditure on health care will be required increasing national income further. The accounts fail to record both the loss of welfare caused by the illness and the nuisance that smokers cause to non-smokers.

> As national income measures marketed output only it will not record any change in the *output*[7] of do-it-yourself activities. Thus if people grow their own vegetables in their leisure time there may be a fall in national income because fewer vegetables are being purchased and no account is taken of the possibility that the home-grown vegetables are fresher and that the exercise of growing them is beneficial.

> If I insulate my house my fuel bills may fall so that recorded national income falls despite my now being warmer.

> If I change jobs to one nearer my home national income may fall because I spend less on transport.

> If there is a mild winter national income may fall because less is spent on fuel and clothing.

> As people's income rises they usually want to take more leisure – i.e. to work less. The value of the extra leisure is not included in the accounts.

> If more goods are produced there may be more smoking factory chimneys causing extra washing and the extra acid in the air damaging buildings and crops.

7. National accounts do record the purchase of inputs (vegetable seeds, paints) for do-it-yourself.

This list of divergences between national income and welfare could easily be extended, but it is sufficient to make the point that we should not uncritically assume that, if the national accounts show an increase in income per person after allowing for inflation, this means we are better off. We may be. Our welfare may have increased by more than the increase in income, or by less – or we may be worse off. While it is right to stress the ways in which national income and welfare can diverge, it would be wrong to leave the impression that the two are unrelated. It seems very likely for example that the fall in real GNP between 1979 and 1981 was associated with a serious loss of welfare.

CONCEPTS FOR REVIEW

QUESTIONS FOR DISCUSSION

1. What are the effects of (a) an increase in aggregate demand and (b) an increase in aggregate supply, on output and prices?

2. Explain why in principle national income = national product = national expenditure.

3. If we read that the money value of national income has gone up by 10% in the past year can we assume that every person is better off by 10%?

2

Determination of Capacity Output

Within the span of half a lifetime, Britain has descended from the most prosperous major state of Europe to the Western European slum .... If we continue as we have been doing in 1950 – 73 ... by the year 2008 ... Britain will ... have to settle down to be the poorest country in Europe, with the possible exception of Albania.

(Sydney Pollard *The Wasting of the British Economy*, London: Croom Helm, 1982, p.6.)

National output depends upon both the capacity of economy to produce and on the proportion of that capacity that is utilized. In this chapter we look at the determinants both of the level of capacity output and its growth. **Capacity output** is determined by the supplies of factors of production: land, labour and capital.

Measuring the supplies of these factors is difficult because what we are interested in is the number of units of factors measured in terms of some standard efficiency per unit. If every unit of labour and capital were just like every other unit we could simply add up the number of hours of labour supplied and the number of machines in the capital stock. In practice such a task is extremely difficult because some units of labour (e.g. road sweepers) are very different from others (e.g. nationalized industry chairmen) and similar problems arise when trying to measure capital and land. The second difficulty is that the amount of labour actually available for work is likely to depend on the wage rate. It is useful, however, for certain purposes to abstract from these difficulties and to imagine that we can have stocks of factors available. Capacity output is what can be produced from these stocks. Nevertheless it is important to remember that if everyone decided – perhaps because the wage rate had changed – to work longer hours then capacity output would increase.

It would be enlightening to present evidence on rates of growth of capacity output in various countries. There are however two sets of difficulties that mean that in practice it is very much easier to compare rates of growth of actual output per man hour. The first of these difficulties stems from the discussion of the last paragraph. Rates of growth of output may reflect individuals in different countries choosing to supply a larger or smaller amount of work. Thus if country A's actual output grows more rapidly than that of B the reason may simply be that people have increased their hours of work in A while people in B have decreased their hours. The second problem is how to measure capacity. Do we, for example, mean working flat out 24 hours a day 365 days a year?

TABLE 2.1   PHASES OF PRODUCTIVITY GROWTH (GDP PER MAN HOUR)
1870–1976

	Annual average compound growth rates					
	1870–1913	1913–50	1950–76	1950–60	1960–70	1970–76
Australia	0.9	1.4	2.8	2.8	2.4	3.3
Austria	2.1	0.8	5.7	5.9	5.9	5.0
Belgium	1.2	1.5	4.5	3.1	5.0	6.1
Canada	2.0	2.3	2.8	3.1	2.8	2.3
Denmark	1.9	1.7	4.0	3.0	5.1	3.1
Finland	1.8	1.9	5.0	4.1	6.8	3.6
France	1.8	1.7	4.9	4.4	5.3	5.0
Germany	1.9	1.2	5.8	6.8	5.4	4.7
Italy	1.2	1.8	5.3	4.3	6.5	5.0
Japan	1.8	1.4	7.5	5.8	10.1	6.1
Netherlands	1.2	1.5	4.1	3.5	4.7	4.1
Norway	1.6	2.5	4.4	4.1	5.2	3.6
Sweden	2.4	2.9	3.8	3.5	4.8	2.7
Switzerland	1.5	1.9	3.4	3.5	4.0	2.3
UK	1.1	1.5	2.8	2.3	3.3	2.8
USA	2.1	2.5	2.3	2.4	2.5	1.8
Average	1.7	1.8	4.3	3.9	5.0	3.8

Source: Angus Maddison, 'Long-run dynamics of productivity growth', in W. Beckerman (ed.), *Slow Growth in Britain: Causes and Consequences*, Oxford: Clarendon Press, 1979.

Table 2.1 shows average growth rates per hour in a variety of countries in the period 1870-1976. It can be seen that in the post-war period, and especially up to about 1973, the British economy has grown very much faster than in earlier periods. While the British economy was growing rapidly by her own historical standards, other industrialized countries were growing very much more rapidly and as a result Britain's national output has both increased absolutely and decreased relatively. Statistics to back up assertions

Figure 2.1   Gross national product *per Capita,* 15 countries,
1950 and 1978.

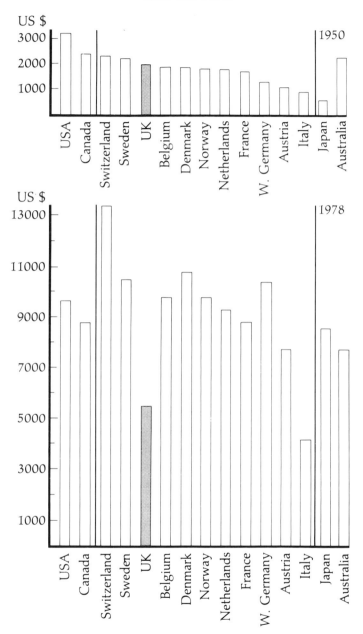

1950: In US $ at 1970 prices; 1978: In US $ at current prices.
Source: OECD, International Surveys; A Maddison, 'Phases of Capitalist Development', *Banca Nazionale del Lavoro Quarterly Review* 121 (1977).
Quoted in Sidney Pollard, *The Wasting of the British Economy,* London: Croom Helm 1982, p. 5.

like this are difficult to interpret partly because, as we have seen, national output figures are not necessarily a very good measure of welfare and partly because additional complications arise when comparing one country with another.[1]

Despite these difficulties comparisons between countries can be instructive. Figure 2.1 shows that in 1950 income per person in Britain was well up amongst the countries shown. By 1978 income per person in Britain was more than $2\frac{1}{2}$ times as high after allowing for inflation, but nevertheless Britain was far behind all the other countries shown except for Italy. These other countries had all grown very much faster.

Part of the explanation of Britain's relatively poor performance – perhaps a major part – can be found in factors determining the growth of capacity output – the subject matter of the present chapter.

A   THE PRODUCTION POSSIBILITY CURVE

A useful graphical way of representing capacity output and the factors that cause it to change is the **production possibility curve** (PPC). On the axes we represent classes of goods we are interested in. Thus if we wanted to look at the defence possibilities we might label the axes guns and butter, but for our purposes it is instructive to label the axes consumption (goods) and investment (goods) as in Figure 2.2. Consumption goods are goods that are consumed in the period in which they are produced (conventionally a year) while investment goods (or their services) are consumed over a longer period. Some investment goods – especially fixed investments in plant and machinery and in items of infrastructure like roads, make it possible to produce more goods in later years. Thus if consumption is reduced this year in order to invest, it is likely that more can be produced in the future.

Given (1) the current stocks of land, labour and capital of a fixed standard of efficiency; (2) a fixed amount of leisure; and (3) fixed technology we can draw a line such as PP in Figure 2.2. This production possibility curve shows possible combinations of production goods (investment) and consumption goods that can be produced with available resources. Any point on or inside the line PP is possible to reach but not points outside it. Society might like to be at a point such as D with high levels of both consumption and investment

---

1.   Suppose that country A is a warm country where most people live near their work and that B is a cold country where most people have to commute fairly long distances. If B has a higher measured national income per person it might be the case that this is due entirely to the extra clothes, heat and travel expenditure. Are the citizens of B then better off?

It might also be the case that price ratios are very different between the countries. Suppose that in A consumer durables are expensive and food cheap while in B the reverse is true. Which prices should we use?

Figure 2.2

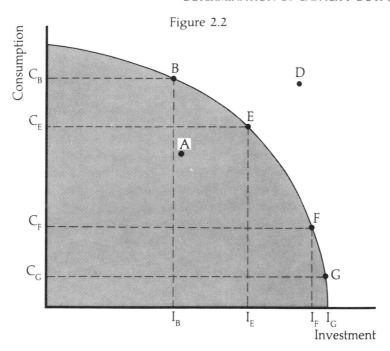

The production possibility curve (PPC) shows combinations of consumption goods and investment goods that could be produced given stocks of factors of known efficiency, technology and fixed leisure. Points like D are impossible to attain, and A is inefficient.

but the resources to permit this are not currently available. The economy could be at a point such as A but point E has more of *both* consumption goods *and* investment goods than A. If the economy is operating efficiently it will be at some point on the line PP – perhaps B or E.

The reader will have noted that PPC has been drawn as a concave line reflecting the assumption of decreasing marginal returns in both industries. If an economy is at E rather than B it will have to give up some consumption $(= C_B - C_E)$ in order to gain extra investment $(= I_E - I_B)$. Note that when resources are concentrated on consumption the sacrifice of $C_E - C_B$ units of consumption brings quite a lot of extra investment $(I_E - I_B)$. However if society is at F the same number of units of consumption $C_F - C_G (= C_B - C_E)$ results in rather less extra investment – only $I_G - I_F$ which is less than $I_E - I_B$.

If there is an increase in (1) land, labour or capital or their efficiency; or (2) technology; or (3) a reduction in leisure; or (4) the efficiency with which the technology is applied, the PPC will shift up and to the right as shown in Figure 2.3.

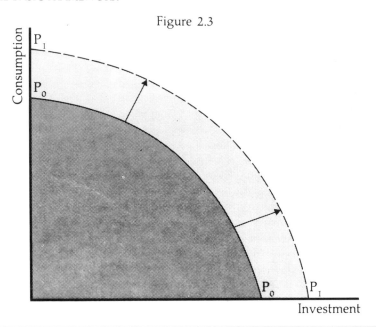

Figure 2.3

Increases in factor stocks, or in technology or reductions in leisure or will make more production possible shifting the PP curve out to the right.

Does it matter whether an economy is at a point like B or one like E? It turns out that it matters quite a lot. It was pointed out above that one of the determinants of capacity output – that is of the PPC – is the stock of capital. The choice between production of consumption goods and the production of investment goods is important, because it is investment which increases the stock of capital. It is useful to distinguish between gross and net investment. Gross investment is the total increase in the capital stock. Part of the investment is used to replace old capital which is worn out or no longer useful. Net investment is the change in the capital stock after allowances have been made for capital replacement.

Suppose that I_B in Figure 2.2 is the amount of investment necessary to replace the existing capital stock. If gross investment were less than this, the capital stock would decline over time as is shown in Figure 2.4. If investment at I_B were just sufficient to maintain the capital stock the PPC would remain the same each year as can be seen from Figure 2.5. Suppose, however, that the economy is at a point such as E where it sacrifices some extra current consumption in order to finance I_E of investment. This increases the capital stock and, as Figure 2.6 shows, the PPC shifts out to the right. This will happen each year so long as positive net investment is taking place that can lead to increased output.

Figure 2.4

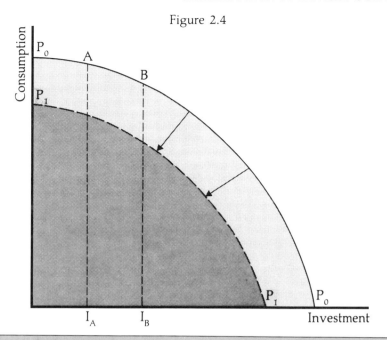

If actual investment at I_A is less than I_B the minimum required to maintain the capital stock, the PPC will shift towards the origin and future production will be lower.

All or almost all modern countries have positive net investment so that their PPCs have shifted out, especially since World War II. However as we will see most of the major economies have had higher net investment than Britain. It is likely that this will have led to their capacity output having grown more than Britain's capacity output. When technical change is rapid high investment carries an added bonus. Countries with high net investment will have a capital stock with a lower average age. If new investment embodies the latest technology – which is often more productive – the younger capital stock will also be more productive.

A final point before looking at the facts. The PPC, it will be remembered, depends *not only* on the amount of factors and on the state of technology *but also* on the efficiency of the factors themselves and on the efficiency with which the factors are combined embodying that technology.

We will see that Britain's record in this respect appears rather worse than her competitors which means that if British efficiency could be increased output could rise with no increase in factors of production and with present technology.

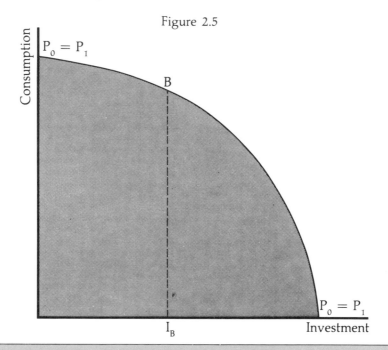

Figure 2.5

If actual investment at I_B is just sufficient to maintain the capital stock, the PP curve will not change.

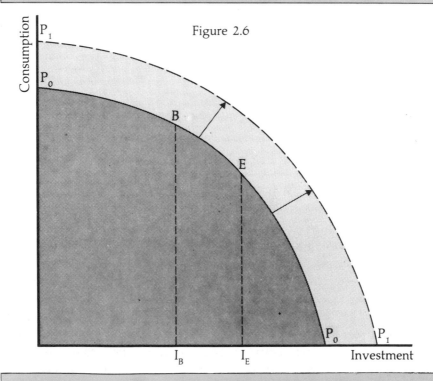

Figure 2.6

If investment is above the level required for capital depreciation the capital stock will grow and the PPC will shift out.

B   CAPACITY OUTPUT IN BRITAIN

It is convenient to begin our examination of the factors determining the growth of capacity output by looking at land, labour and capital – first singly and then in combination.

Land

The total supply of land is nearly fixed. Holland does of course succeed in reclaiming land from the sea from time to time, and elsewhere geological and climatic processes cause bits of land to emerge and other bits to disappear. However it will do no harm for us to proceed on the assumption that the total supply of land is fixed. However land use *is* important and total output may be increased if we change its use from something where productivity is low – e.g. poor farming land to something where productivity is high – perhaps housing or industry.

Labour supplied

Before discussing the significance of labour it is important to distinguish between **the amount of labour supplied and labour supply** The amount of labour supplied refers to the amount of work actually done and labour supply refers to the amount of work people would like to do at current wage rates. I will discuss the amount of labour supplied in this chapter, and labour supply in Chapter 4.

An obvious determinant of the amount of work done is the total population. Figure 2.7 shows the population for the UK from 1961 to 1981. It can be seen that the population rose from about 52 million in 1961 to about 56 million in 1981. It is officially projected that the population will rise to 58 million by 1996.

However it is clear that not all members of the population are available for work. Babies and the very elderly clearly cannot work, but just which age groups should be counted as available for work will depend on social conventions and laws affecting ages of-full time education and retirement, to take only two obvious examples. In the UK the compulsory minimum school leaving age has been raised since the war from 14 to 16 in two stages and in addition a higher proportion of young people have chosen to continue their education beyond the minimum age legally acceptable for leaving school. There are also rules and conventions about retirement. One of the ways in which men and women are treated differently in Britain is that the official retirement age for women is 60 while it is 65 for men. (A strange form of

Figure 2.7   UK population, 1951–81.

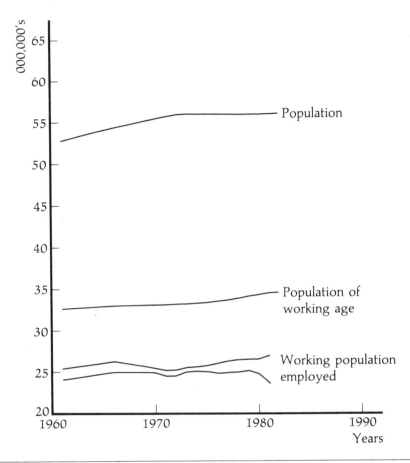

(Source: *Annual Abstract of Statistics,* Various, Table 6.1; Office of Population Census and Surveys. 1970–2010, 1978–2018.)

discrimination because women have a higher life expectancy than men.)

It is useful to define the population between the ages when they are legally supposed to be at school and the official retirement age as **the population of working age**. It is, of course, true that some people who are at school work, as do some who are beyond the official age of retirement. It is also true that many people who are of working age are not available for work. There are many reasons for this, ranging from being in prison to having very severe physical or mental handicaps, but one is of special interest. Some people prefer not to work and have a means of support which makes it possible for them not to work. The most important such group numerically is undoubtedly married women. Until fairly recently there was a convention in some

social groups against women working after they were married and particularly after they had children. However this convention is very rapidly
disappearing amongst younger people. Other groups voluntarily not working include students and small numbers with independent means or state
support.

If we subtract from the *population of working* age those not wishing to work
we are left with the **working population.**[2] *The working population* may be
defined as people who *wish* to work at *current wage rates*. I have stressed *wish*
to work for two reasons: first because as we have seen not every person of
working age will wish to work, and second because some people who would
like to work are unable to get a job. I also stressed at *current wage rates*
because some people might be willing to work only at much higher wage
rates. For example a mother with a young child might be able to earn a low
wage (perhaps because of having little training) and not want to work so that
she could care for her child. If the wage were high enough so she could pay
for a washing machine and send her child to a nursery school she might wish
to work.

Figure 2.7 shows the total population, the population of working age and
the working population for selected years in the period 1961–81. The least
accurate of these figures is the working population. The reason that it is less
accurate than the others is that it is the sum of the **employed population**
(people who actually work) and the **unemployed population**. The unemployed are in principle those who are not at work who would like to work at
current wages, but in practice they are those who are registered as
unemployed. Some people who would like to work will not in practice
register as unemployed, (a) because they do not think it likely they will be
able to get a job and (b) because – in some cases – they are ineligible for
unemployment benefit. It seems likely therefore (1) that the working
population is actually higher than the graph shows and (2) that the margin of
error will have increased as unemployment has increased.

Figure 2.7, which includes both men and women, conceals an important
difference that has emerged between the sexes. It can be seen from Figure 2.8
that the population of working age has grown at similar rates for both sexes.
However the working population of men fell from nearly 17 million in 1970
to just over 16 million in 1980. During the same period the female working
population rose from under 9 million to over 10 million. Thus while the total
working population changed very little, nearly a million men left the labour
force and were replaced by over a million women. This will partly reflect
changing opportunities for women to work in light industries, and in service

---

2.   The working population also includes people outside the age range who are at work.

industries and in part it will reflect the changing social attitude towards work which was mentioned earlier.

As has been noted the working population includes both the employed and the unemployed. Figure 2.8 also shows employment and unemployment by sex. It can   be seen that the fall in male employment has been even greater than the fall in the male work force with the difference, of course,

Figure 2.8   UK population, 1970–80.

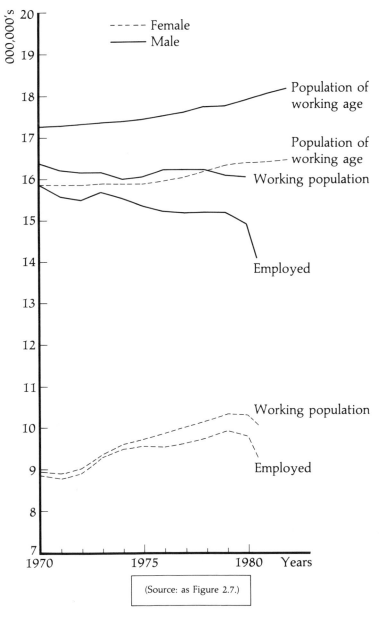

(Source: as Figure 2.7.)

being unemployment. Female employment has risen but less rapidly than the female work force, again reflecting the growth in unemployment.

The total amount of work done depends not only on the number of workers but also on the quantity and quality of work done by each worker. The quality of work is unfortunately virtually impossible to measure across a whole population, but we can look at weeks, days and hours of work. Weeks of work have been falling because of increasing entitlement to paid holidays. In 1961 97% of manual workers were entitled to only 2 weeks paid holiday. By the end of 1981 80% were entitled to holidays of 4 weeks or more. A lot of work is lost because of sickness and invalidity. In 1979/80 females lost 83 million days through sickness and invalidity and males 276 million days, and these levels represented substantial increases over the comparable figures 5 years ealier. Widely varying amounts of time are lost through industrial disputes. In some years as little as 5 million days (as in 1976) while in 1979 nearly 30 million days were lost. Days lost through stoppages are far less than days lost through illness, but stoppages receive far more attention in the press – perhaps justifiably for they cause greater disruption.

The next measure of quantity of work now being done that I want to mention is hours of work. Average weekly hours worked by males in manufacturing fell from just over 46 in 1967 to 44 in 1979 and the figures for full-time females fell from 38.0 to 37.2 over the same period. To sum up it seems reasonable to infer that total hours worked fell by more than the fall in employment shown in Figure 2.7. The reasons for this are (1) longer holidays, (2) more time off sick, (3) shorter hours at work for weeks worked, (4) switch from male to female employment (given that males work longer than full-time women *and* that more women work part time).

Finally I want to discuss labour efficiency and productivity. There are two aspects that are important. First it may be possible to increase output by moving people from jobs where their output is low – perhaps marginal agriculture or a nearly exhausted coal mine – to a job when their output is high. Second the efficiency of the stock of labour may be increased by additional education or training which increases **the stock of human capital**. Some education or retraining may of course be a precondition for moving people into jobs where their productivity could be higher.

The future

What of the future? It would be easy to omit any discussion of the future as too uncertain, but it may be worth a little speculation. Demography gives a bit of a clue. Every year young people enter the labour force and older people reach retirement age. The post-war baby boom peaked in the mid-sixties which means that the peak for people of school leaving age comes in the early 1980s, as can be seen from Table 2.2. If we subtract the number of people reaching retirement age from the number of people of school leaving age we have an approximation of the change in population of working age. The table shows this peaking at 340,000 in 1981 and falling to less than half that number a decade later. This suggests that the population of working age will grow more slowly. If trends towards longer holidays, earlier retirement, more time off for sickness and shorter hours all continue, the total quantity of labour supplied – measured in hours – could well fall. In these circumstances increases in the stock of human capital – by training – and use of labour at the most productive jobs is especially important.

TABLE 2.2

Year	UK population (000s)				Approximate change in population of working age
	Age 16		Age 60	Age 65	
	M	F	F	M	
	(a)	(b)	(c)	(d)	(a) + (b) − (c) − (d)
1961	397	381	323	203	+ 252
1966	387	370	351	258	+ 159
1971	388	373	348	261	+ 152
1976	441	422	317	270	+ 276
1981	493	471	376	248	+ 340
1986	442	417	314	295	+ 250
1991	358	338	299	257	+ 140
1996	360	339	283	246	+ 170

Source: Office of Population Censuses and Surveys. *Population Projections, 1970–2010, 1978–2018.*

We have been looking at statistics on labour supplied. Labour supply – the amount of work people would like to do at current wage rates – may be larger than the labour supplied because some people are not able to work as much as they would like to. Statistics that measure both desired hours and actual hours are not available on a regular basis for individuals who are at work, but a crude measure of the difference between labour supplied and labour supply can be found by looking at the difference between the working population – those who would like to work – and the employed population – those who actually do work. Unemployment is the difference between the employed population and the working population and it can be seen from Figure 2.7 that it has been rising. Unemployment is considered more fully in Chapter 4.

Capital

We now turn to examination of the **stock of capital**. It is useful to distinguish between **fixed capital** – things like factories, machines, roads, schools, housing etc., and circulating or **working capital** – stocks of raw materials, work in progress and finished goods. The capital stock may appear to be much more difficult to measure than land and labour. It is possible to slide over the very real problems of adding up moorland, agricultural land, land for industry, roads, and housing by summarizing the stock of land as so many square miles. Similarly dustmen, lawyers, assembly workers and company chairmen can be crudely amalgamated and we can refer to the stock of people of working age as so many millions of people. Such crude summaries can clearly be misleading – nevertheless there is no equivalent summary for the stock of capital. To list factories, machines, roads, etc. is hardly a summary. We need a common yardstick. It is tempting to think of using money for this yardstick. We use money to add up apples, boats and cigarettes in counting national output.

Why not use money to add up airports, barns and cranes in measuring capital? The question that then arises is how do we price the capital stock. Should we price it at what it cost to produce? This is objective, but is it of much interest to know that a barn cost £100 to build in 1900? Well, why not find out what it would cost to build it now? But suppose the barn is built of stone – no-one would build a stone barn now – it would be too expensive. In any event the barn might have been built for dairy cattle and the land is now used for cereals – or housing. Another approach would be to say we'll forget about what something cost and concentrate on what it is worth. For some things this would be easy to do – our barn probably has a market value – but how much is Heathrow Airport worth on the market? Even if we could find out the market value is this what we really want to know? Suppose we are interested in valuing cranes used to build ships. If there is a recession in world shipbuilding the cranes may be worth very little but if we are interested in the capital capacity should we think about what the cranes would be worth if there was work for the shipyard? But what would be the position if we were to believe that when the shipbuilding recession ends very little of the work would come to British yards? Clearly then measuring the capital stock is far from easy, and in what follows several heroic estimates and incomplete measures are used.[3] Most of these concentrate on changes in the capital stock.

---

3.   Similar problems arise in principle with the measurement of land and labour. How for example do we value an extremely efficient manager who ensures the continuing survival of a company that had become grossly inefficient?

TABLE 2.3   GROSS CAPITAL FORMATION PER HEAD OF POPULATION, 16 COUNTRIES, 1974–1977 ($000)

	1974	1976	1977
Norway	1.9	2.8	3.2
Switzerland	1.9	1.8	2.0
Denmark	1.3	1.6	2.0
Sweden	1.5	1.9	1.9
Austria	1.2	1.4	1.8
Japan	1.4	1.5	1.8
W. Germany	1.4	1.5	1.7
Belgium	1.2	1.4	1.7
France	1.3	1.5	1.6
USA	1.2	1.3	1.5
UK	0.68	0.75	0.79
Ireland	0.53	0.61	0.72
Italy	0.63	0.61	0.69
Spain	0.61	0.67	0.65
Greece	0.46	0.52	0.64
Portugal	0.26	0.39	0.30

Source: Angus Maddison, 'Long run Dynamics of Productivity Growth', *Banca Nazionale del Lavoro Quarterly Review*, no. 128 (1979), p. 19. Quoted in Sidney Pollard, *The Wasting of the British Economy*, London: Croom Helm, 1982, p. 27.

TABLE 2.4   RATE OF GROWTH OF NON-RESIDENTIAL FIXED CAPITAL STOCK PER MAN HOUR (ANNUAL AVERAGE COMPOUND GROWTH RATE; AVERAGE OF GROSS AND NET STOCKS)

	1870–1913	1913–50	1950–76	1950–60	1960–70	1970–76
Canada	n.a.	1.8[d]	4.9	4.5	2.6	2.5
France[e]	n.a.	(1.8)	5.7	3.9	6.5	7.5
Germany	(2.1)	(0.9)	6.4	4.7	7.2	7.2
Italy	2.3[a]	[2.6]	[5.6]	[2.8]	[7.0]	[7.3]
Japan	2.0[b]	[2.9]	8.7[f]	2.7[f]	11.2[f]	8.9[f]
UK	0.6	0.9	4.2	2.8	5.3	4.9
USA	2.7[c]	1.8	3.4	2.6	2.9	2.0
Average	1.9	1.8	5.6	3.4	6.1	5.8

Notes: All figures are adjusted to eliminate the impact of geographic change. Figures in parentheses refer to net stock only, figures in square brackets to gross stock only.
[a] 1882–1913; [b] 1879–1913; [c] 1869/78–1913; [d] 1926–1950; [e] refers to private stock; [f] net stock refers only to the private sector.
Source: Angus Maddison, 'Long-run dynamics of productivity growth', in W. Beckerman (ed.), *Slow Growth in Britain: Causes and Consequences*, Oxford: Clarendon Press, 1979, p. 203.

Table 2.3 shows gross investment per person in 16 countries in the mid-1970s. It can be seen that the UK is well down the list. Part of the capital stock is in housing, which is a final service and as such does not increase production possibilities in the future in the way that factories or machines do, so it is quite common to omit investment in housing when comparing investment. Table 2.4 shows Maddison's estimates of the growth on non-residential capital stock per man hour for the seven biggest economies in the West. The figures are given per man hour as a measure of the amount of capital for a standard unit of labour input. It can be seen that in all the countries the capital stock increased rapidly after World War II. Over the period 1950–76 as a whole the figure for the UK was lower than any of the other countries except for the US. However it can be seen that prior to 1950 the US capital stock increased at least twice as fast as Britain's so even at the end of the period the total capital stock in the US was very much larger than in the UK.

TABLE 2.5   INTERNATIONAL COMPARISON OF ASSETS AND VALUE ADDED PER EMPLOYEE, ONE YEAR (1976)

	Assets per employee (£)	Value added per employee (£)
Motor industry:		
British Leyland	8505	4673
11 Japanese firms	42,020	11,894
Electrical engineering:		
GEC (UK)	9725	5306
Siemens (Germany)	16,479	10,396
Hitachi (Japan)	34,680	9702

Source: F. E. Jones, 'Our Manufacturing Industry – the Missing £100,000 Million', *National Westminster Bank Quarterly Review* (May 1978), pp. 8–17. Quoted in Sidney Pollard, *The Wasting of the British Economy*, London: Croom Helm, 1982, p. 24.

The figures we have looked at so far refer to the economy as a whole. Table 2.5 shows some selected figures for two industries. Once again it can be seen that the capital stock in Britain is very much lower than in the other countries shown.

To summarize: we have seen that for all practical purposes the stock of land is fixed, labour measured in numbers of people of working age is growing very slowly in Britain and labour supply measured in hours is probably falling, and while the stock of capital has grown rapidly by previous

British standards it has grown slowly in comparison with her main competitors. Does this *necessarily* mean that capacity output in Britain per person in Britain is also low? Logically the answer to that question is NO, because it is logically possible that Britain might combine her factors of production more efficiently than other countries.

Capital widening and capital deepening

Before looking at the evidence for productive efficiency it is useful to distinguish between **capital widening** and **capital deepening**. One of the clearest examples of capital widening was the opening of the American West to agriculture. Large areas of land were virtually uninhabited. When farmers moved in, their investment in land clearing, housing and equipment enabled agricultural production to be started. When a plough was purchased it was combined with both fresh land and the newly arrived worker. The capital stock became wider because there were now more ploughs and output increased by the total amount attributable to that plough. In contrast if a farmer in Britain bought a new plough it would almost certainly not be a new farmer on new land. The new plough would probably replace a less efficient or worn out old plough. Perhaps the old plough ploughed two furrows at once while the new plough ploughed three furrows at once. Output would go up but only by one furrow's worth not by three furrows' worth. With capital widening, all the output from the investment is additional output. With capital deepening, output increases by the amount produced by the new machine less the output produced by the old machine The moral is that capital widening raises output more – often much more – than capital deepening.

While vast tracks of empty land are uncommon, when both labour and capital are increasing simultaneously the conditions for capital widening are approximated to. However, it should be remembered that in Britain the population of working age has grown very little, which means a corresponding limitation to the possibilities for capital widening.

There is an important related point. Even if the total labour force is fixed, an effect similar to capital widening can be obtained if people are moved from areas of very low productivity into areas of high productivity. Often in pre-industrialized economies very large proportions of the population are engaged in subsistence agriculture. The marginal product of agricultural workers may be very low or even zero. Thus if people move out of agriculture into industry where capital is available there can be an effect rather like capital widening.

Some countries have had rapid increases in labour available for industry because of natural increase in population (as in Japan) or because of large-scale immigration (as in Western Germany) or because of movements out of low productivity agriculture (as in Japan). Britain had none of these on a large scale. The natural growth of population and of immigration were both low. Most of the movement out of agriculture in Britain occurred before World War II so that little was left after the War.

We have seen then that there is little growth in the population of working age, less growth in the capital stock than elsewhere and that we would expect most of the increase in the capital stock – that is most investment -to be of a capital deepening rather than capital widening type. All of these factors will tend to limit the rate at which capacity output grows.

Productivity

I now want to discuss the efficiency with which land, labour and capital are combined. There are several important aspects to this. First one has to have a work force well matched to the capital stock. Having surplus labour trained in heavy industries is not necessarily well matched to capital stock in electronic or service industries. Second the capital stock has to be used. Sadly – but perhaps understandably – one hears stories of new machines lying idle because the work force and management cannot agree on economic manning levels. Third the capital stock has to be well run by both management and workers if it is to reach its potential.

We have seen that the capital stock per worker is low in the UK so it will come as no surprise to find that output per worker is also low. Figure 2.9 shows estimated manufacturing output per worker in 8 countries from 1973 to 1981. Not only is Britain at the bottom of the league throughout the period but British output is nearly stagnant while in many of the other countries shown it is increasing sharply.

A similar point can be seen from Table 2.5 where it can be seen that value added per employee in Britain is roughly half the German and Japanese firms used for comparative purposes.

While this information provides clear and disturbing evidence of low labour productivity in Britain it does not directly address the area of our immediate concern because as has been said low productivity may be due to a low capital stock alone. If we want evidence on the efficiency with which factors are combined we have to isolate the influence of the capital stock. Pratten has done this in a comparison of labour productivity within international companies. International companies were chosen as the products they produce would be similar in different countries, because all parts of the company were likely to have access to a common pool of knowledge and because company officials could help with an explanation of the differences. Pratten's main findings are summarized in Table 2.6 and it can be seen that he

Figure 2.9　Manufacturing output per employed worker-year 1973–81.

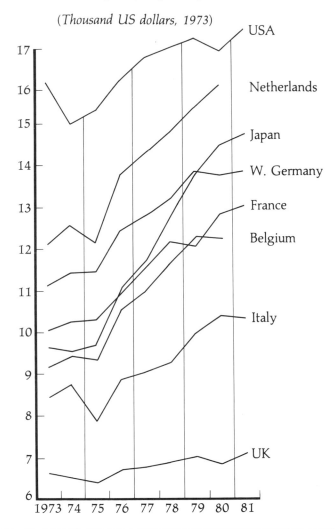

(*Thousand US dollars, 1973*)

USA
Netherlands
Japan
W. Germany
France
Belgium
Italy
UK

1973 74　75　76　77　78　79　80　81

(Source: A. D. Roy, 'Labour productivity in 1980: an international comparison', *National Institute
Economic Review*, Number 101, August 1982, p. 33.)

estimates that productivity in North America (including the USA) is about
50% higher than the UK, while in most of northern Europe it is about 25%
higher with Spain, Brazil, Australia and New Zealand having lower levels.
Pratten's estimates of the causes of these differences are given in Table 2.7. It
can be seen that he estimates that differences in plant and machinery were
relatively small amongst his sample of international companies. As we have
already seen the capital stock per worker is much lower in Britain than in

TABLE 2.6   AVERAGE PERCENTAGE PRODUCTIVITY DIFFERENTIALS (*c.* 1972)

	Number of observations	Unweighted average difference in labour productivity (%)
Compared to the UK:		
North America	50	50
Germany, Belgium, Netherlands and Switzerland	35	27
France	24	15
Sweden and Denmark	11	22
Italy	13	16
Spain	8	−11
Brazil	11	−15
Australia and NZ	9	−15
Compared to Germany:		
USA	18	+14
France	18	− 1
Italy	10	−17
Compared to France:		
USA	11	+18
Italy	10	0

Source: C. F. Pratten, *Labour Productivity Differentials with International Companies*, Cambridge University Press, 1976, p. 5.

these other countries so this is probably not typical of national companies. The largest difference in the UK/North America comparison is differences in rates of output of products and length of production runs. Pratten explains this differential as follows:

> As differences in rates of output of products and production runs cause such differences in labour productivity, the question of why such differences in rates of output occur is clearly an important one. Output of manufacturing industry in the U.S.A. is about five times that of U.K. manufacturing industry. On average, the leading firm in each trade account for a smaller proportion of the output of the trade, but the total number of manufacturers in many trades is not much larger than in the U.K.
> Typically, the output of products by an American manufacturer is four times that of his U.K. equivalent. On average, American companies manufacture at more sites, but the output of products is often concentrated, so the rates of output of products at locations average *perhaps* three times the U.K. rates.

In addition to the economic causes of productivity differentials Pratten estimates behavioural causes which he explains as follows:

> the differential is not simply that more of the U.K. labour force are members of

TABLE 2.7   SUMMARY OF THE CAUSES OF PRODUCTIVITY DIFFERENTIALS[a]

Cause of differential	UK–Germany (%)	UK–France (%)	UK–N. America (%)
Economic causes			
1. Differences in rates of output of products and length of production runs	$5\frac{1}{2}$	$1\frac{1}{2}$	$20\frac{1}{2}$
2. Differences in plant and machinery	5	5	(6)
3. Other 'economic' causes[c]	(2)	(2)	(6)
4. Total	(13)	(9)	(35)
'Behavioural' causes			
5. Incidence of strikes and major restrictive practices	$3\frac{1}{2}$	0	5
6. Other 'behavioural' causes[d]	$(8\frac{1}{2})$	$(5\frac{1}{2})$	(6)
7. Total 'behavioural' causes	(12)	$(5\frac{1}{2})$	(11)
8. Average differential	27	15	50
	Weighted by employment[b]		
9. Total economic causes	(14)	(16)	
10. Total 'behavioural' causes	(19)	(10)	
Average weighted differential	35	28	

Note: The contributions to the productivity differentials are multiplicative not additive.
[a] The figures in parentheses are intended to indicate possible orders of magnitude.
[b] Employment in the UK to which the observations relate.
[c] Other 'economic causes' include differences in product mix, the substitution of labour for materials (or better-quality materials) capacity utilization, and the availability of labour.
[d] Other 'behavioural' causes are effectively differences in manning and efficiency.
Source: C. F. Pratten, *Labour Productivity Differentials with International Companies*, Cambridge University Press, 1976, p. 61.

unions, or that unions in the U.K. are more demanding or politically orientated. It was claimed by many managers that employees in the U.K. were simply less willing to co-operate in achieving high productivity. These differences probably reflect differences of history and tradition. Resistance to the introduction of machinery did not not occur in France and Germany where rapid industrialisation took place a century later than in England, and the harsh traditions of early industrialisation in the North of England were avoided. Industries in Germany, France and the U.S.A. have not had to adjust to as substantial a loss of advantage in overseas markets as that faced by many U.K. firms which had concentrated on Commonwealth markets. Also co-operation with employers by German workers may reflect traditional acceptance of authority.

Summary
Capacity output is determined by the amounts of labour and capital available and the efficiency with which they are combined. In Britain the population of working age is growing slowly and investment is low. This is because Britain had a relatively high proportion of output devoted to current consumption in the 1950s and 1960s and devoted rather less of her resources to net investment. In terms of Figure 2.6 this means she chose a place rather close to B and as a result productive capacity (represented by the production possibility curve) has increased relatively slowly. The productivity of the investment is low because it is of the capital deepening rather than the capital widening sort, because the British market limits the length of production runs and because of behavioural factors. For all of these reasons British productive capacity has grown slowly.

   If we define the short-run to be a period in which capital stock is fixed then – in the short-run – the level of output and employment depends on the proportion of capacity that is employed. That proportion can be explained in terms of aggregate demand and this is done in the next chapter.

CONCEPTS FOR REVIEW

QUESTIONS FOR DISCUSSION

1   Why is it difficult to measure stocks of factors of production?

2   Explain what each of the following would do to a country's productive capacity

a) People decide they wish to work fewer hours.
b) Education and training of the work force is increased.
c) More resources are devoted to net investment.
d) Immigration.
e) People move from low productivity industry to high productivity industry.

3   Account for the relatively slow growth of productive capacity in the British economy since World War II.

4   How does productivity per worker in Britain compare with productivity in other countries? How might the difference be explained?

3

Aggregate Demand and the Determination of Output

The purpose of this chapter is to explain a simple model in which the proportion of capacity output that is actually produced depends on the level of aggregate demand. Aggregate demand refers to the total amount of planned expenditure in an economy. It will be argued in this chapter that planned expenditure will be an increasing function of the level of national income. That means that people will want to spend more when national income is high than they will wish to spend when national income is low. In Chapter 5 it will be argued that aggregate demand is a decreasing function of price. That means that people will want to spend more when prices are low than when they are high. If aggregate demand depends on both the level of income and the price level, and if both the price level and wages have changed a lot since the late 1960s, some justification has to be offered for the decision not to discuss the price level aspects in this chapter. There are three reasons why I think it is justified.

(1) While we now tend to think of both prices and money wages as relentlessly moving upwards the sustained upward movement is in fact a recent phenomenon. Over much of the period for which we have data prices have in fact been falling. An examination of Figures 3.1 and 3.2 shows that there have been short periods – often associated with wars in which prices and wages have risen and fallen very rapidly followed by very long periods when prices have tended to fall slowly. Money wages on the other hand tended to be constant except in war periods, as can be seen from Figure 3.2.

(2) It is particularly important for modern economics that reasonably stable prices and wages characterized the period between the wars when John Maynard Keynes was developing his *General Theory*. Keynes' ideas – or at least a bastard variety of them – were put into practice after World War II and – particularly in the US – prices

49

Figure 3.1   Gross domestic product prices, 1856–1973

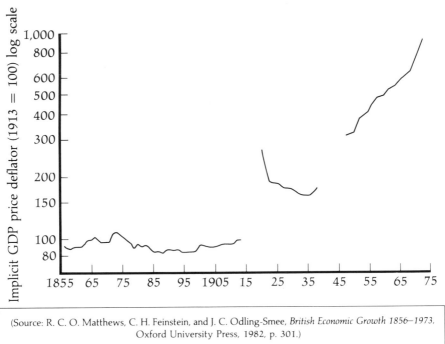

(Source: R. C. O. Matthews, C. H. Feinstein, and J. C. Odling-Smee, *British Economic Growth 1856–1973*, Oxford University Press, 1982, p. 301.)

continued to be very stable until the mid-1960s. (Figures for the UK are given in Table 5.1.) Thus models with constant prices seemed to fit the facts tolerably well and both government policy and academic thinking were in large measure dominated by such models.

(3)   To these two reasons – which amount to saying the model is of historical interest – a third can now be added. It is easier to start with a model which is relatively simple even if no longer very realistic.

It is useful at this stage to make two related distinctions. The first is the distinction between price takers and price makers. **Price taking** firms – such as perfectly competitive firms – accept the ruling market price which in the competitive case is determined by supply and demand. **Price making** firms on the other hand, such as monopolies, set a price and then sell as much as they can at that price. The second distinction is between flexprice models and fixprice models. A **flexprice model** is one in which prices vary in response to supply and demand. If all firms were price takers then flexprice models would be required. A **fixprice model** is one in which prices do not change or, more precisely, where the explanation for price change lies outside the model. If firms are price makers the fixprice model *could* be realistic. Price making firms

Figure 3.2   Changes in Money Wages, UK 1880–1936

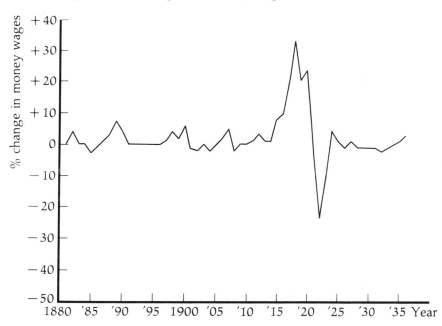

(Source: A. L. Bowley, *Wages and Income since 1860*, Cambridge University Press, 1937, p. 30; in B. R. Mitchell and P. Deane, *Abstract of British Historical Statistics*, Cambridge University Press, 1971.)

may wish to change their prices but it is at least instructive to consider a model in which prices do not change in response to demand changes.

It will be assumed for the rest of this chapter that firms do not change their prices when demand changes. This is *not* consistent with the view that is put forward in Chapter 1 that prices are determined by supply and demand.[1] Nevertheless for the remainder of this chapter we proceed on the assumption that changes in demand will affect output *and* not prices except when the economy is at capacity output. At capacity, output cannot by definition rise and when changes in demand occur they cause prices to change with output constant at the capacity level.

1.   Nor is it in general consistent with a price making model when firms seek to maximize their profits. There are special cases when profit maximizing firms will not wish to change prices when demand changes. For example some intermediate micro texts demonstrate that the profit maximizing price does not change if marginal cost is constant and the elasticity of the new demand curve is the same as the original demand curve at the original price. However if marginal costs are rising profit maximizing firms will normally wish to change their prices. This means that the fixed price assumption is not in general consistent with profit maximization.

A   THE DETERMINATION OF OUTPUT AND EMPLOYMENT
    WITH NO INFLATION

Many of the ideas implicit in the model we are about to examine have been
encountered in the previous two chapters. There is some level of capacity
output determined by the availability of land, labour, capital and technology;
and the efficiency of the factors. It is impossible by definition to produce
more than capacity output. The essence of the model we will explore is that
the proportion of capacity output that is employed is determined by
aggregate demand.

It may help you to see where we are going if we start with an overview of
the model and then look at aggregate demand more closely. In Figure 3.3
output – represented by the symbol Y – is measured on the horizontal axis
and the price level on the vertical axis. The highest output that can be
produced is Y_C and capacity output is represented by the vertical line at Y_C.
Suppose that the level of aggregate demand is AD_0 and that the price level –

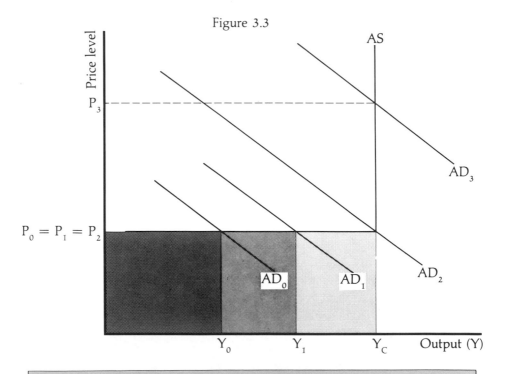

Figure 3.3

In a fixprice model when the economy is below capacity output, AD
determines output and employment and prices do not change. When AD is
above capacity output, increases in AD increase prices, but not output or
employment.

which by assumption is constant and historically determined – is P_0. The actual level of national income will be Y_0. This is below the capacity level of income Y_C so that Y_C-Y_0 of potential output is lost. If, somehow, demand can be increased to AD_1 output will rise to Y_1, but there will, by assumption, be no increase in the price level. Similarly if aggregate demand increased to AD_2 output would rise still further – in this case to Y_C – capacity output. In the fixed price model of this chapter output expands as if along a perfectly elastic (i.e. horizontal) aggregate supply curve at any point to left of Y_C. If aggregate demand were to increase still further to AD_3 it would no longer be possible to raise output because 100% of capacity is already in use. In these circumstances the fixprice assumption is abandoned and the excess demand would lead to higher prices rather than higher output and the price level would rise to P_3. Thus we can see that aggregate demand determines (1) the proportion of capacity output that is utilized when output is below capacity output or (2) the price level when capacity is fully utilized. Reflecting this the AS curve looks like a capital L knocked on its back.

IF land, labour and capital are relatively well matched to each other then when we are at capacity output all factors will be working to capacity. Similarly when output is below capacity there will be surplus capacity of all factors. Sometimes of course the factors are not well matched to each other and we have a problem called structural unemployment, which means that in terms of location or skills the labour force is not well matched to the capital stock. This is a problem that is discussed in Chapter 4 but for the moment it is convenient to assume this problem away. This means that when we reach capacity output we also reach full employment.[2] While output and employment do *not* change perfectly together in practice it is instructive to think of employment rising when output rises, which means of course that employment falls – unemployment rises – when the demand for output falls.

The policy implications of this model are simple and powerful. We can control the level of unemployment by manipulating aggregate demand and provided aggregate demand is kept below AD_2 prices are assumed not to rise. Clearly what we need to understand this better is an explanation of the level of aggregate demand.

B   THE DETERMINATION OF AGGREGATE DEMAND – A FIRST APPROXIMATION

We have seen in the previous section that we require an understanding of aggregate demand to determine output and employment in our simple

---

2.   This is a rather oversimplified view of full employment which is modified in the next chapter.

model. We have already had a preliminary look at AD in Chapter 1 when we examined the circular flow. You will remember that we measured the counterclockwise flow of aggregate demand in Figure 1.6 as either national expenditure where the flow leaves households or, equivalently, as national income when firms make payments for factor services. If the size of the circular flow is a measurement of aggregate demand then if we understand the causes of changes in the circular flow we will also understand the causes of changes in aggregate demand.

Leakages from and injections to the circular flow of income.

Thus far we have been looking at the circular flow of income without considering any factors which could cause the size of the flow to change, or if you like, which could cause AD and hence the level of national income to change. We have been assuming that expenditure in the flow stayed in the flow and that nothing was added to it. In fact this is not the case. Part of the flow is leaking out for various purposes and there are at the same time various injections into the flow, and it is to these leakages and injections that we now turn. The amount of the flow can be said to be in equilibrium if there is no tendency for it to change. *The fundamental proposition about the flow is that it will be in equilibrium when* **desired leakages = desired injections**. Before examining the relationship between desired leakages and desired injections it is useful to look at the categories of leakages and injections beginning with savings and investment.

Categories of leakages and injections

Let us take savings first, We have seen that households receive income in the form of wages, rent, interest and profits; up until now we have assumed that all of households' income is subsequently spent but this is not true, households in fact save part of their income. The amount that they save is at least temporarily and possibly permanently leaked from the circular flow of income. We can therefore put an arrow leaving the circular flow of income in Figure 3.4 at the household sector which is labelled (S_H) for household savings. We thus have our first leakage –household savings. However, firms may save as well. If firms do not distribute all of their profits, the undistributed part represents savings by firms and so we can add another arrow leaving the firm part of the circular flow representing withdrawals for firms' savings (S_F). There is also an injection into the circular flow in the form of investment (I). As most investment is done by firms we may represent this by a single arrow entering the flow at the firm stage.

Leakages and injections also arise from the government sector. Taxation is a leakage from the circular flow. Part of the income of households is taken by the government in the form of personal income taxes and we therefore need

Figure 3.4

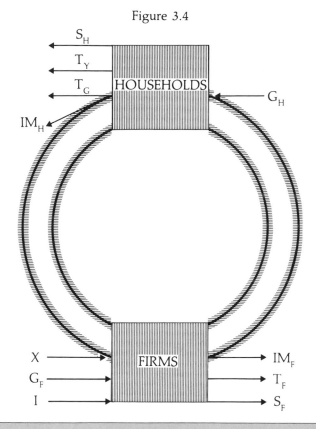

From the circular flow there are leakages for savings from households (S_H) and firms (S_F): Taxes on income (T_Y), on goods (T_G), and on firms (T_F); and imports from households (IM_H) and firms (IM_F). There are injections into the flow for investment (I); Government expenditure to firms (G_F) and to households (G_H): and exports (X).

an arrow from the flow to represent the payment of personal income taxes (T_Y). In addition, we know that part of households' expenditure on goods and services is collected by the government in the form of taxes on goods (T_G), for example, VAT and the excise tax on tobacco. We can represent these taxes on goods and services as a second leakage from the flow. A third leakage for taxes is taxes on firms (T_F) and these can be represented by yet a third arrow. In addition to government withdrawals from the circular flow in the form of various taxes, the government also injects money back into the circular flow. For example, the government purchases goods and services from firms (G_F) and so we need an injection into the flow to represent these government purchases. In addition, the government purchases factor services from households (G_H), for example, in paying the salaries of civil servants and so we need an injection into the flow to represent these government expenditures as well. Thus far we have leakages and injections, for savings and investment and for taxation and government expenditure .

Finally we need to consider leakages and injections relating to international trade. Part of household expenditure is spent on purchasing goods produced in other countries. When someone in this country purchases a Japanese transistor radio, the money, of course, leaves the country and as a result does not flow to a firm in Britain. We can represent this by arrows leaving the flow for imports of final goods from households (IM_H) and raw materials from firms (IM_F). In addition, of course, foreigners buy goods produced by British firms. The expenditure by foreigners on British goods represents an injection into the circular flow and we can add an arrow for exports (X) to represent this. British imports then represent a leakage from the circular flow, whereas British exports represent an injection into the circular flow.

To sum up then, we have three leakages from the circular flow: savings, imports and taxes, and three injections: investment, government expenditure and exports. We can simply refer to the total of savings, imports and taxes as 'total leakages' and the total of investment, government expenditure and exports as 'total injections'. Having looked at the main types of leakages and injections it is now possible to determine the equilibrium position. It has already been stated that this will occur when desired leakages are equal to desired injections. What then will determine desired leakages and injections in a fixprice model?

Desired leakages and injections

Let us start with leakages. It is assumed that **desired leakages** will depend on the level of income – the higher the level of income the higher the level of desired leakages. We take savings first. As people's income rises it is assumed they will wish to save more. This can be represented graphically in the following way. In Figure 3.5(a) we have a graph with the level of income on the horizontal axis and the level of savings on the vertical axis; we can represent this assumption by a line which rises from left to right. Taking taxes next, if we also assume that we have to pay more taxes as our income rises then we have a similar relationship for taxation. The assumption that the amount of taxes we have to pay rises as income rises is, of course, what one would expect with taxes such as income tax. Once again, this assumption can be represented graphically. In Figure 3.5(b) we again put income on the horizontal axis and taxes on the vertical axis and draw in a line to reflect our assumption that taxes rise with income. Turning now to imports, we make a similar assumption. We assume that as income rises people will want to spend more, both on home-produced goods and on goods which are imported. As we are now looking at leakages, we do not need to look for the moment at expenditure on home produced goods as this expenditure remains within the circular flow. However, we do have to look at desired expenditure

Figure 3.5

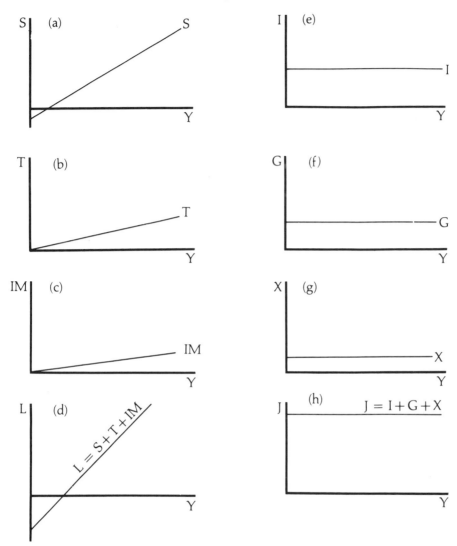

Desired savings (S), taxes (T), and imports (IM) are all assumed to increase as the level of national income rises. As a result total desires leakages also rise with incomes as L = S+T+IM.

Desired investment (I), government expenditure (G), and exports (X) are all assumed to be the same irrespective of the level of income. As a result total desired injections J = I+C+X are also constant.

on goods which are produced abroad, for this expenditure on imports does leave the domestic income flow and once again we are assuming that this type of leakage increases as the level of income increases. Graphically, if we put income on the horizontal axis and desired imports on the vertical axis we can represent this assumption with a line rising from left to right as in Figure 3.5(c).

We have assumed that each of the forms of leakage rises as income increases. If $L = S + IM + T$ and if S and IM and T each increases then of course L must increase as income increases as well, so we can represent this by yet another diagram (Figure 3.5d) with income on the horizontal axis and total desired leakages, i.e. $L = S + IM + T$ on the vertical axis. The line representing total leakages is, of course, steeper than any of the previous three lines, because it represents the sum of all three.

Let us now turn to injections where we make quite a different assumption. We have assumed that leakages increase as income increases. In the case of injections, on the other hand, we assume that the level of **desired injections** remains constant irrespective of the level of income. The desired level of investment is likely to depend on the rate of growth of output, new technology, the price level, the rate of interest, etc. These issues will be examined in later chapters. For simplicity in the present chapter it is assumed that the desired level of investment is the same for each level of income. This is an assumption that we will have to change later on, but for the moment we assume that the level of investment will be the same irrespective of the level of income. Graphically in Figure 3.5(e) we have the level of income on the horizontal axis and on the vertical axis the level of investment, and the line representing desired investment is then a horizontal straight line reflecting our assumption that investment will be the same irrespective of the level of income. We also assume for the time being that government expenditure will be the same irrespective of the level of income, thus with income on the horizontal axis and government expenditure on the vertical axis, we again have a horizontal straight line in Figure 3.5(f). Exports are also assumed to be constant, irrespective of the level of income. Once again, with income on the horizontal axis and exports on the vertical axis in Figure 3.5(g) we have the desired exports represented as a horizontal straight line. This means that total desired injections (J) which are the sum of desired investment plus desired government expenditure plus desired exports will also be constant irrespective of the level of income, and these may be represented graphically by a straight line in Figure 3.5(h) which is the sum of the other three lines and which once again has income on the horizontal axis and in this case total injections (J) on the vertical axis.

Determination of the equilibrium level of income in a fixprice model

Suppose we now draw a new figure, Figure 3.6(a), putting the total desired leakages function and the total desired injections function on the same figure. In this figure we have national income on the horizontal axis and total injections and total leakages on the vertical axis. The desired injections function is represented once again by a horizontal straight line and the desired leakages function by a line which slopes up and to the right. It will now be argued that in the fixprice model the level of national income is determined where desired leakages equal desired injections. To see why the **equilibrium level of national income** is the one where desired leakages equal desired injections it is instructive to consider points where they are not equal. Suppose that the actual level of income happened to be more than equilibrium level which means that desired leakages are higher than desired injections. Desired expenditure on investment, plus desired government expenditure plus desired expenditure, by foreigners, on exports are less than the sum of desired savings, imports and taxes. If the desired level of injections were less than the desired level of withdrawals income would fall. Why would this be so? As desired leakages would be above desired injections some of the plans would be unable to be fulfilled. Suppose it was firms' plans for investment in stocks of goods that were not fulfilled. Firms would find they were unable to sell all they produced. Stocks of unsold goods would start to pile up above the desired level. Actual investment in stock would exceed desired stocks and firms would cut back on production and lay off workers. As a result workers' income would fall. As workers' income fell so would their savings, taxes and spending on imports. As a result income would fall to Y_E. Suppose that the level of income happened to be below the level at which desired leakages and injections were equal. Because desired leakages were below desired injections firms would find they were running short of stocks of goods. This means that their actual level of investment would be below the desired level which remains constant. To attempt to remedy the position firms would hire more workers and increase production. In this case the result is an increase in the level of national income to Y_E. At Y_E desired leakages and injections are equal and there is no tendency for the level of income to change.

The understanding of the relationship we have just been talking about is one of the most fundamental propositions that you are expected to learn in introductory macroeconomics and indeed much of what we do for the rest of this book depends upon an understanding of this fundamental relationship. For this reason it is worth taking some time to ensure that we do fully understand what is involved. It may make an understanding of the basic relationships clear if we look at the same relationships from a different point of view. What we have been saying so far is that the size of the flow, or the aggregate demand for national income, will stay the same when desired leakages from the flow are just balanced by desired injections to the flow. We have, in other words, been looking at subtractions from the flow and additions to the flow. Let us now turn to look at expenditure in the flow itself.

Figure 3.6

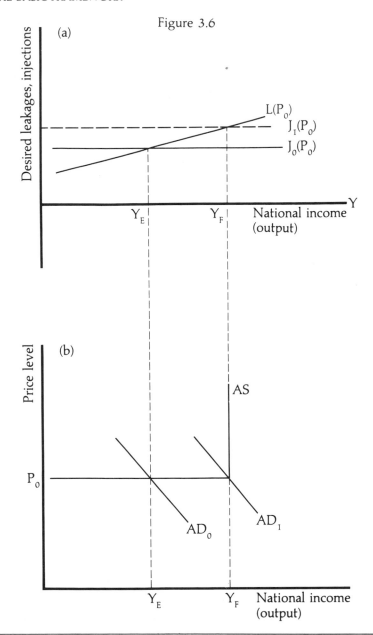

In (a) the equilibrium level of income rises from Y_E to Y_F as a result of an increase in desired injections from $J_{0(P_0)}$ to $J_{1(P_1)}$. This causes the aggregate demand curve in (b) to shift from AD_0 to AD_1. Output rises from Y_E to Y_F but the price level does not change.

We have desired consumption expenditure which rises with income. (The relationship between consumption and income is discussed in detail in Chapter 6.) To this we add injections for investment and government spending and the net injections from the foreign sector – that is exports less imports. Consumption plus investment plus government spending plus net foreign injections represents total expenditure on national income. In symbols this relationship is $E = C + I + G + (X - IM)$. The total expenditure function is shown graphically in Figure 3.7. Because consumption rises with income this line has a positive slope.

A very useful graphical device at this stage is to add to this diagram a 45° line. A 45° line is one that is obviously equi-distant from the two axes,

Figure 3.7

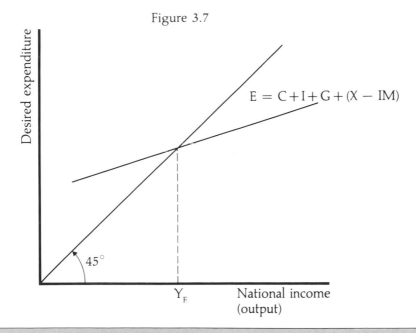

The equilibrium level of income occurs where desired expenditure $E = C + I + G + (X - IM)$ is equal to national income – that is where the desired expenditure function crosses the 45° line. If the economy is to the right of Y_E where desired expenditure is less than income firms will be unable to sell all they produce. They will accumulate stocks of unsold goods and will lay off workers. As a result workers' incomes will fall and they will wish to spend less. This process will stop when desired expenditure equals national income. If the economy is to the left of Y_E desired expenditure will exceed income. Stocks of unsold goods will fall, more workers will be hired and they will spend part of this extra income. The process will stop when desired expenditure and national income are again equal.

therefore, if we are using the same scale for national income on the horizontal axis as for desired expenditure on the vertical axis, a point on the 45° line is one where income and desired expenditure are equal. If income and desired expenditure are equal then there is no tendency for the flow either to expand or contract. If we are to the right of this point where desired expenditure is less than income then the size of the flow will contract because firms would not be able to sell all they produce. Stocks of goods would accumulate so that firms would reduce output and lay off workers so that households' income would fall and they would spend less. If we are to the left where desired expenditure is greater than income the size of the flow will expand because firms will find their stocks of goods are falling and they will increase production and hire more workers who will spend part of this extra income. In other words, where income and desired expenditure are equal is where we have equilibrium.

Reconciliation of withdrawals and injections model with aggregate supply and demand model

The model we have just completed is the standard macroeconomic model used in the great majority of elementary economics texts. It is not useful for explaining changes in the price level, which is one of the major objectives of this text. The framework for doing this is the use of aggregate demand and supply curves. I therefore want to translate what has been said in this fixprice model into aggregate supply and demand terms. This is done with the aid of Figure 3.6. Figure 3.6(a) shows the level of income being determined where desired leakages equal desired injections. On Figure 3.6(a) the leakages and withdrawals functions both show the historically determined price level P_0. This will remind us that in later chapters leakages and injections will depend on the price level. In Figure 3.6(b) the aggregate supply curve has a horizontal segment at the historically determined price level P_0 and a vertical segment at capacity output. The aggregate demand curve which is assumed to have a negative slope passes through the aggregate supply curve at Y_E.

C   CHANGES IN AGGREGATE DEMAND

We have established that when desired leakages (L) are equal to injections (J) there is no tendency for aggregate demand to change in the fixprice model. We have also established that aggregate demand determines the level of national income.

Changes in leakages and injections

If we start from a position where leakages and injections are equal what would happen if any of the leakages (savings, taxes or imports) or injections (investment, government expenditure or exports) were to change? The short answer to this question is that desired leakages and desired injections would no longer be equal and the level of national income as a whole would have to change to restore the equilibrium. As we will see the change in the level of income turns out to be larger than the initial change in leakages or injections that gave rise to it.

Let us examine the process by looking at injections first. Suppose, for example, that people in other countries decide they wish to purchase more of our goods. Our exports rise as a result and because exports are a component of injections, total injections rise. In Figure 3.8 the initial level of injections – including the initial level of exports is given by J_0 and with the leakages function L, this determines national output at Y_0. Because of the increase in exports desired injections rise to J_1 and the equilibrium level of income rises to Y_1. Aside from the fact that this is where the lines happen to cross on the figure, why does the level of income change? With the initial rise in exports there will be an increased demand from home produced goods. Stocks will fall and firms will increase output and take on additional workers. Orders for components will be increased and component companies will also require more labour. As a result factor incomes will rise and you should remember from our discussion of the circular flow in Chapter 1 this should lead to households increasing their expenditure on goods and services. Note that an increase in expenditure from abroad has now led to an increase in domestic demand as well. Firms will also have to order more components and hire additional labour and once again factor incomes will rise. This will lead to a rise in household incomes and once again demand will rise. We now have a perfectly good explanation of why the extra demand for exports has led us to a rise in national income, and in fact we have seen the initial higher demand – in this case from abroad – has brought out still more demand from the home market. You now may want to ask 'Does demand go on rising indefinitely?' The answer to that is 'no' because as incomes rise we have seen that desired leakages will also go up. Some of the money people spend will be on imported goods. Some of the money spent on domestic goods will go in taxes, employees will have to pay more income taxes and people will also wish to save more. This means that the limit to the expansion of income comes when desired leakages are again equal to desired injections. How much income expands depends on the rate of leakages, as we will see in the next section, but first we should notice that a change in the level of desired

Figure 3.8

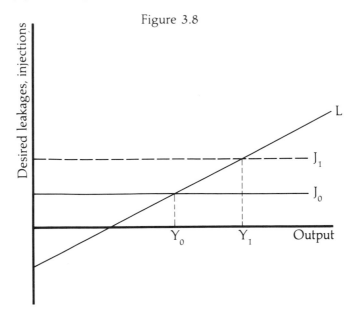

An increase in desired injections from J_0 to J_1 causes the equilibrium level of income to rise from Y_0 to Y_1.

Figure 3.9

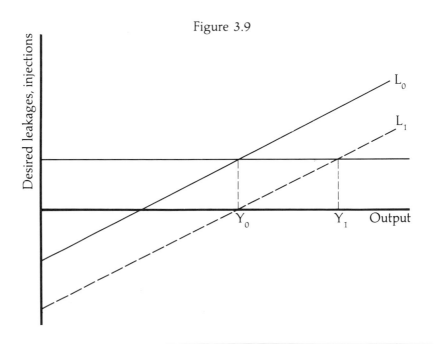

A decrease in desired leakages from L_0 to L_1 causes equilibrium income to rise from Y_0 to Y_1.

leakages will have very similar effects to a change in the level of injections. If the level of leakages is *reduced* it means that more money stays within the flow and the level of income will rise as a result. This is illustrated in Figure 3.9 where leakages *fall* from L_0 to L_1 and it can be seen that income *rises* from Y_0 to Y_1. Why does aggregate demand rise when withdawals fall? Suppose that withdrawals have fallen because of a cut in taxes. If income taxes go down we have more money to spend and if taxes on goods and services go down less of what we spend is siphoned off to the government. The result in both cases is that more is spent buying goods and services from firms. As a consequence firms will increase orders for components and spending on labour and other variable factors. This leads to increased factor income and to still higher national income. Once again expansion in national income will continue so long as desired injections are greater than desired leakages.

Self test

Before proceeding to the next section make sure you work out the effects of *both* increases *and* decreases in the levels of desired leakages and desired injections by completing Table 3.1. I have filled in the 2 cases we have considered and you should fill in the rest.

TABLE 3.1

		National income
Injections		
Investment	rise	
	fall	
Exports	rise	rise
	fall	
Government spending	rise	
	fall	
Withdrawals		
Savings	rise	
	fall	
Imports	rise	
	fall	
Taxes	rise	
	fall	rise

TABLE 3.2

Round	Marginal propensity for leakages	Leakages	Extra expenditure	Total extra expenditure
1			100	100
2	100 × 0.2 =	20 [= 100 × 0.2]	80(= 100 − 20)	180
3	80 × 0.2 =	16 [= 100 × (0.2)^2]	64(= 80 − 16)	244
4	64 × 0.2 =	12.8 [= 100 × (0.2)^3]	51.2(= 64 − 12.8)	295.2
5	51.22 × 0.2 =	10.24 [= 100 × (0.2)^4]	40.96(= 51.2 − 10.24)	336.16
6	40.96 × 0.2 =	8.19 [= 100 × (0.2)^5]	32.77(= 40.96 − 8.19)	368.92
7	32.77 × 0.2 =	6.55 [= 100 × (0.2)^6]	26.22(= 32.77 − 6.55)	395.14
8	26.22 × 0.2 =	5.24 [= 100 × (0.2)^7]	20.98(= 26.22 − 5.24)	416.12
9				
10				
N	0.001 × 0.2 ≃	0	0	
Totals		99.99 ≃ 100		499.99 ≃ 500

The multiplier

We have seen that increases in the level of desired injections or decreases in the levels of desired leakages cause national income to rise, and you should have worked out for yourself that reductions in the level of desired injections or increases in desired linkages will cause income to fall. The more attentive reader will also have noted that the total change in income will be larger than the initial change in leakages or injections. The term **multiplier** is used to refer to the ratio by which the level of income changes to the initial change in leakages or injections. In symbols ΔY represents the change in income, and ΔL and ΔJ the change in withdrawals and injections respectively, so this ratio is $\Delta Y/\Delta L$ or $\Delta Y/\Delta J$. We will see that the size of this ratio is determined by the marginal propensity for leakages. The marginal propensity for leakages is the extra leakages (for savings, taxes and imports) per unit of extra income. We use the symbol l to represent the marginal propensity for leakages. We have noted that the initial or first round effect of the change in spending is to cause a change in factor income which in turn causes further changes in spending which again change factor incomes, thus changing spending still further. These subsequent effects are conveniently termed second round effects despite the fact that more than two rounds are involved. A numerical example may help. Suppose the government decides to raise the total of its expenditure by £100 a year. It can be seen from Table 3.2 that aggregate demand rises by £100 in the first round because there are no leakages. In the second round, however, part of the income goes in taxes and imports and part is saved. Let us assume that the marginal propensity for leakages is one fifth. One fifth of 100 is 20 so 20 leaves the flow and so 80 remains. If leakages are 20% in the next round then one fifth of 80 ($= 16$) leaves the flow and so 64 remains. In each round the addition to income is smaller as are leakages. The Table ends after 8 rounds so to test your understanding of the construction of the table you should fill in rounds 9 and 10 for yourself. Notice that after 8 rounds the total extra expenditure is now over 400 stemming from the initial increase of 100. Notice also that the extra demand is getting smaller in each round. What will the total eventually be? We could go on adding additional rounds to the table but it is simpler to use the formula for summing a geometric series.

The formula for the series $1 + r + r^2 + r^3 + ... + r^n = 1/(1-r)$.
In our example $l = 1 - r$. In other words the multiplier is $1/l$: the inverse of the marginal propensity for leakages.

Alternatively we reach the same result using simple algebra. We know that for equilibrium we must have

$$L = J \tag{1}$$

If we then change J by ΔJ we also know that income must change until the change in J is just matched by a corresponding change in leakages. Thus an extension of the equilibrium condition of (1) is that a change in J (i.e. ΔJ) must be matched by a change in L (i.e. ΔL) so

$$\Delta L = \Delta J \tag{2}$$

We also know that leakages depend on the change in income Y so we can write

$$\Delta L = l\Delta Y \tag{3}$$

Substituting (3) into (2) gives

$$l\Delta Y = \Delta J \tag{4}$$

and dividing both sides by both l and ΔJ gives

$$\frac{\Delta Y}{\Delta J} = \frac{1}{l}$$

which says that the total change in income (ΔY) for a given change in injections (ΔJ) is equal to $1/l$ where is l the marginal propensity for leakages.

If l is large, say half, the multiplier will be $2 = \dfrac{1}{\frac{1}{2}}$ which is quite a small number. A small multiplier means that a change in leakages or injections will cause quite a small change in national output. The reason for the small change in national output is that with a higher marginal propensity for leakages much of the the extra income goes to extra leakages in each round. But if is small, say one fifth, the multiplier will be large – in this case

$5 = \dfrac{1}{\frac{1}{5}}$ because with only 20% being withdrawn demand has to change a lot more before the change in total linkages equals the change in total injections. Diagrammatically if l is low the leakages function will be steep as in L_1 in Figure 3.10. Suppose initially income is 1000 and that injections rise by 100. With $l = \frac{1}{2}$ as on L_1 in Figure 3.10 demand rises to 1200. But if $l = \frac{1}{5}$

as in L_2 demand rises to 1500. It seems likely in practice that the multiplier is quite small – perhaps 2 or even less.

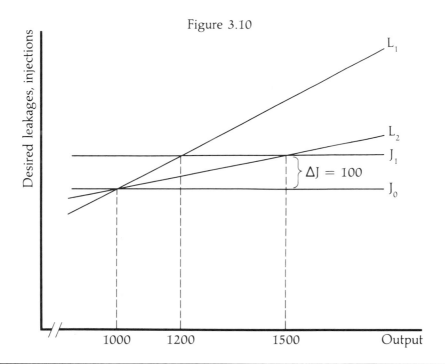

Figure 3.10

> If the MPl is 1/2 as with L_1 a change in J of 100 will raise demand by 200, but if the MPl is 1/5 as with L_2 a change of 100 in J will raise demand by 500.

Policy implications

The policy implications of the model are both simple and powerful. Suppose that we know[3] (1) national output is 1500, (2) the capacity level of output is 1600 and (3) l = one quarter. With output below capacity there will be both lost output and unemployment. To eliminate unemployment what is required is to raise national output from 1500 to 1600. Suppose the government decides to do this by increasing its own expenditure. If you are aware of the argument of the last section you will know that the required increase in government spending will be less than 100 and if you have mastered that argument you will already know that the required extra government spending is 25. The reason only 25 is required is that with $l = \frac{1}{4}$ the

---

3.   The difficulties in actually knowing this are formidable and are discussed in Chapter 11. For the moment it is assumed these difficulties have been overcome.

multiplier is 4 so that the change in aggregate demand will be 4 times the change in injections. Thus the central policy conclusion of this model is that unemployment can be eliminated by either an increase in government spending or by other methods of raising injections or by a cut in taxes or other methods of reducing withdrawals.

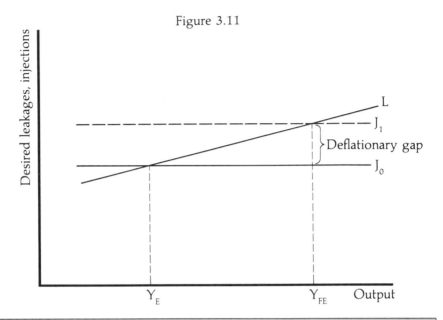

Figure 3.11

The deflationary gap is the deficiency of injections (or the excess of leakages) necessary for the equilibrium level of income to correspond to full employment. It is measured at the full employment level of income.

There is a technical term used by economists to describe this demand deficiency – 25 in the example above. It is called the **deflationary gap**. The deflationary gap is the amount by which injections would need to be raised (or leakages reduced) to make the actual level of demand correspond with the full employment level. The deflationary gap is illustrated in Figure 3.11. With the actual levels of leakages and injections national income is in equilibrium at Y_E. But for full employment – capacity output – aggregate demand would need to be Y_{FE}. This would happen if injections were J_1 rather than J_0. Therefore $J_1 - J_0$ is the deflationary gap.

If the actual level of demand is above the full employment level we then have an inflationary gap such as the one illustrated in Figure 3.12. In this case the equilibrium level of aggregate demand is above the full employment and the **inflationary gap** is the amount by which injections need to be reduced –

Figure 3.12

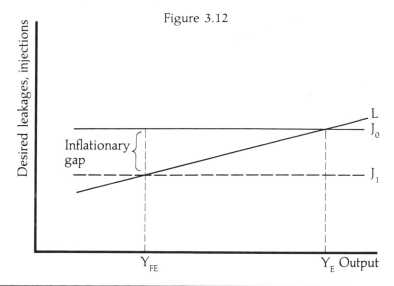

The inflationary gap is the excess of injections (or the deficiency of leakages) required for the equilibrium level of income to be equal to the full employment level of income.

or leakages increased to reduce aggregate demand to the full employment level. It is measured at the full employment level of income.

While the model is a very simple one it formed the basis for much macroeconomic policy for a generation after the Stabilization Budget of 1941 as J. C. R. Dow has explained.

> There is probably no country in the world that has made a fuller use than the United Kingdom of budgetary policy as a means of stabilizing the economy. Since 1941, almost all adjustments to the total level of taxation have been made with the object of reducing an excess in total demand or of repairing a deficiency.[4]

The argument of this section can now be quickly restated in terms of aggregate demand and supply analysis with the aid of Figure 3.6. It will be recalled that with the historically determined price level of P_0, injections J_0 and leakages L_0 determine the equilibrium level of income at Y_E in both parts of Figure 3.6. If desired leakages or desired injections change, the equilibrium level of income also changes. If the full employment level of income were Y_F (capacity output) and if government raised its expenditure to $J_1(P_0)$ in order to close the deflationary gap this would shift the aggregate demand curve in Figure 3.6b to AD_1 confirming that the new equilibrium level of income would be Y_F.

4.   J. C. R. Dow, *The Management of the British Economy 1945-1960*, Cambridge; Cambridge University Press, 1965, p. 178.

D CONFLICTS OF OBJECTIVES

One of the many complications of practical policy making is that there are frequently a plethora of objectives: full employment, low inflation, growth, redistribution in favour of the poor, a favourable balance of payments, etc. Very often these goals may be in conflict, and moving towards one may make another more difficult to obtain. One example of this is the conflict between full employment and a balance between imports and exports that policymakers were very anxious to achieve in the 1950s and 1960s in Britain because they did not want to devalue the currency.[5] This conflict which was responsible for much of the 'stop/go' economic policies of the 1950s and 1960s, can be best explained through a numerical example. Let us suppose that we start with a balance in the balance of payments where imports (IM) and exports (X) are in balance and the marginal propensity to import is 0.25. However let us also assume that the equilibrium level of income is 1500 and that the full employment level is 1600. If the multiplier is 2 the deflationary gap is 50. Suppose the government wants to cure unemployment by increasing government spending by 50. This succeeds in raising demand to 1600 but the increase in demand of 100 has sucked in an extra 25 of imports because the marginal propensity to import is 0.25. The unemployment problem has been temporarily solved but there is now a balance of payments deficit of 25. In the 1950s and 1960s balance of payments deficits often led to 'crises' which were 'solved' by depressing demand to reduce imports. In the process unemployment was increased.

This was the policy referred to in the fifties and sixties as 'stop/go'. When there was a balance of payments crisis aggregate demand was reduced. This created the 'stop'. When the balance of payments was in surplus demand was expanded and there was a 'go'. The problem was particularly severe because of the fixed exchange rate that prevailed at that time. This is a question that is further considered in Part III.

E SUMMARY

If aggregate supply is perfectly elastic up to some capacity output then the levels of national output and employment are determined by aggregate demand. Equilibrium will occur when the total of desired savings (S), taxes (T)

---

5. While there are economic arguments against – and for – devaluation, which are discussed in Part III, at least part of the case against devaluation was that the foreign exchange value of the currency was a kind of national virility symbol. While this has thankfully now largely disappeared one still hears media reports of the pound having had a 'good day' – meaning its exchange value rose.

and imports (IM) is equal to the total of desired investment (I), government (G) spending and exports (X). If desired injections (J = I + G + X) are greater than desired leakages (L = S + T + IM) income rises and if desired L is greater than desired J income falls. If injections or leakages change there will be a change in income which is larger than the initial change in injections or leakages. How much larger depends on the marginal propensity for leakages (l). The ratio of the final change in demand to the initial change in injections or leakages is termed the multiplier and is the reciprocal of l.

Inflationary and deflationary gaps measure the amount by which injections or leakages would have to change to lower or raise income to the level corresponding to full employment. Remember that l is likely to be $\frac{1}{2}$ or more in practice. This means the multiplier is likely to be small in practice. It should also be remembered that the multiplier shows the change in income that will occur in response to a change in leakages or injections if prices are constant – i.e. if the supply curve is perfectly elastic. If the supply curve is not perfectly elastic prices will rise when demand changes and the change in income will be reduced as a result.

CONCEPTS FOR REVIEW

QUESTIONS FOR DISCUSSION

1 Under what circumstances will the circular flow of income be in equilibrium?

2 Explain why national income will change if desired leakages are not equal to desired injections.

3   What is the multiplier?

4   What will happen to (a) output and (b) the price level if aggregate demand increases when the aggregate supply curve is horizontal (elasticity is infinite)?

5   What was the 'stop/go' economic policy of the 1950s and 1960s in the UK and what circumstances gave rise to it?

4

The Labour Market, Unemployment, and Aggregate Supply

In the last chapter we analysed the level not only of output but also of unemployment without mentioning the labour market. Given that the labour market is where the levels of employment and unemployment are determined this is a serious omission[1] made possible only by the unrealistic assumption that prices and wages are both fixed. In this chapter we examine the labour market, the types of unemployment that exist and discuss the relationship between the labour market and aggregate supply.

A   THE LABOUR MARKET IN A FIXPRICE MODEL

When we allow both prices and wages to change things can quickly get complicated. It will help to start by continuing for the moment with the assumption that prices are fixed. We start by looking at the labour market in an economy that consists of a single firm but where that firm nevertheless behaves like a firm in perfect competition. The firm produces a single consumption good using a fixed stock of capital and variable amounts of labour.

You have probably already looked at labour markets for individual firms in your microeconomics, and so hopefully much of what follows will already be familiar to you. We will confine our attention to the short-run when changes in the capital stock are sufficiently small so that they can safely be neglected. It is also assumed that firms wish to maximize their profits.

The demand for labour

The demand for labour depends on the wage rate. If a competitive firm

---

1.   Many elementary and even intermediate microeconomics text books seriously neglect the labour market and as a result put too little emphasis on the importance of supply in the economy.

76

TABLE 4.1 THE DEMAND FOR LABOUR

Hours 1	Total Physical product TPP 2	Marginal Physical product MPP 3	Price (AR) 4	Total revenue product TRP (= MPP × AR) 5	Marginal revenue product MRP 6	Money wage W 7	Total wages TW (= H × W) 8	Profit (= TRP − TW) 9
1	10	9	100	1000	900	300	300	700
2	19	8	100	1900	800	300	600	1300
3	27	7	100	2700	700	300	900	1800
4	34	6	100	3400	600	300	1200	2200
5	40	5	100	4000	500	300	1500	2500
6	45	4	100	4500	400	300	1800	2700
7	49	3	100	4900	300	300	2100	2800
8	52	2	100	5200	200	300	2400	2800
9	54	1	100	5400	100	300	2700	2700
10	55		100	5500		300	3000	2500

wants to maximize its profits you may remember that it will wish to hire labour up to the point where its marginal revenue product is equal to the wage rate. This is the profit maximizing position because the marginal revenue product represents the extra revenue a firm will receive from hiring an extra unit of labour and the wage rate is the extra cost of hiring an extra unit of labour. This can be illustrated by a hypothetical numerical example shown in Table 4.1 and Figure 4.1. The problem is to determine how many labour hours to hire. Columns 1 and 2 of the table show how many units it is possible to produce with various numbers of hours. This is the total physical product of labour. You should remember from your microeconomics that the law of diminishing returns states that as more units of a variable factor (labour) are added to a fixed factor (capital) the extra output will decline after some point and this is reflected in column (3) in the declining marginal

Figure 4.1

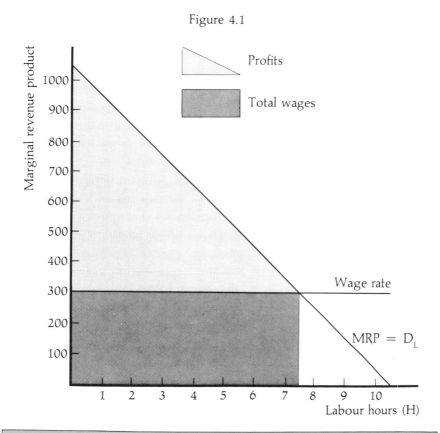

A profit-maximizing firm will hire labour to the point where the marginal revenue product of labour (MRP) is equal to wage rate. For this reason the MRP is called the demand curve for labour. The demand for labour shows the amount of labour people will wish to hire at various wage rates.

physical product of labour.[2] Each unit produced can be sold for the same price which is assumed to be 100. By multiplying the marginal physical product (MPP) by the price we obtain the marginal revenue product (MRP) which shows the amount of extra revenue a firm will earn by hiring an extra hour of labour. If the money wage rate (W) is fixed at 300 we can readily see that the firm will maximize its profits when the MRP = W. For example if the firm were currently hiring 5 units of labour we would want to know if it should hire 6 units of labour. If we increase labour from 5 to 6 units we will add 500 to our revenue but only 300 to our costs so our profits will rise by 200 as can be seen from column (7). If we hire another unit going from 6 to 7 we add 400 to revenue but 300 to cost so that profits rise by 100. Profits are still rising as we hire more labour. Increasing labour to 8 units adds 300 to both revenue and wages so that at 7.5 units profits are maximized and further increases in labour result in a fall in profits.

The marginal revenue product curve from Table 4.1 is plotted in Figure 4.1. Profits are maximized when the wage rate (W = 300) is equal to MRP at 7.5 units. If the wage rate were W = 500 it can be seen that 5.5 units of labour would be hired and if the wage rate was 200 then 8.5 units of labour would be hired. The MRP is thus the demand curve for labour. The total wage bill is hours hired times the wage rate as is shown in the figure. If the only other factor is capital, total profits are the total area under the labour demand curve less wage income.

Labour Supply

Thus far I have concentrated on the demand for labour, and I now want to turn to a discussion of the **Supply of labour**: the amount of work people would like to do at various wage rates. Most people would prefer to do some work to doing none. There may be several reasons for this, such as (1) the social conventions favouring work, (2) enjoyment of the work, (3) enjoyment of social interaction at work, but economists concentrate particularly on (4) if people go to work they will earn money that will enable them to purchase goods and services they would not be able to purchase if they were not at work. In other words people attach more weight – or to use economists' jargon more utility – to the goods and services they can buy with the extra income, than they attach to the leisure they have to forgo to earn that income. Given a free choice people will wish to work to the point where the extra utility from the extra income just balances the loss of utility from the loss of leisure. Now it seems reasonable to imagine that the amount that people will want to work will depend on how much extra goods and services

2. Columns 3, 6, and 7 are stepped down half a space because it provides a better approximation to the change in output to measure it at the midpoint of the interval.

they will be able to buy if they give up an hour of their leisure. In an exchange economy without taxes the amount of goods and services one can buy depends on the wage rate – which for convenience we can assume to be an hourly wage rate.[3] An important question is how a change in the wage rate will affect the the amount of work a person would wish to do. Suppose we consider the case of a person who is able to work any number of hours he wishes to work, and who is paid £2 an hour and chooses to work 40 hours in the week. How would this person react to a cut in his wage to £1 an hour? Would he now wish to work more than 40 hours or less than 40 hours? There are in fact likely to be two forces at work – one making him wish to work more, the other making him wish to work less.

Let us look at what would happen if the person continued to work 40 hours. His total weekly pay would fall from £80 (£2 × 40 hours) to £40 (£1 × 40 hours). This drop in his income would mean he could now purchase fewer goods and services. His real income has thus fallen and it seems reasonable to imagine that the effect of this fall in real income will be to make the person wish to work longer to minimize the fall in his living standards. Economists call this the **income effect**. With a fall in the wage rate the income effect will normally cause people to work more and conversely if the wage rate went up the income effect would normally cause people to work less. However there is another effect. When the wage rate was £2 an hour people were able to gain £2 worth of goods and services by giving up an hour of their leisure. If the wage is only £1 the reward for giving up an hour of leisure is reduced, which means that leisure is now relatively cheaper so people will want more leisure instead of income. Economists call this the **substitution effect**. When the wage falls people will wish to substitute leisure for income – that is they will wish to work less. Conversely if the wage rate rose the substitution effect would cause people to want to work more. To summarize, if the wage rate falls the income effect will normally lead to more work and the substitution effect to less work. Because the income effect and substitution effect work in opposite directions it is impossible to know *a priori* whether a fall in the wage will lead to more work or less work. Figures 4.2a and 4.2b illustrate the two possibilities.

We can thus see that a change in the wage rate of *a worker* may in theory cause that worker to either increase or decrease the number of hours that he wishes to work. Empirical evidence suggests that for men income and substitution effects roughly cancel out leaving the supply curve nearly vertical while for women there is some evidence that hours rise as the wage rises. A non-worker cannot of course reduce hours if the wage rate falls but may wish to start work if the wage rate rises. Overall then the supply curve

---

3.   Other influences on labour supply are discussed in Part D.

Figure 4.2

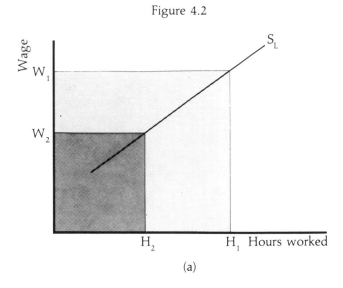

(a)

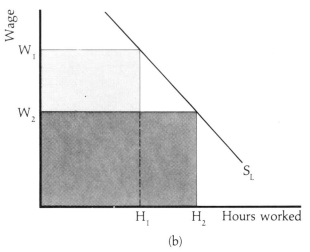

(b)

In (a) a cut in the wage rate reduces desired hours of work because the substitution effect is stronger than the income effect. In (b) a cut in the wage rate increases work because the income effect is stronger than the substitution effect.

of labour hours is probably more like Figure 4.2(a) than Figure 4.2(b) because as wage rates rise women work longer and more people will wish to join the labour force.

B THE LABOUR MARKET IN A FLEXPRICE MODEL

In section A of this chapter we discussed the labour market assuming a constant price level and we now want to look at the implications of changes in the price level. The key to the problem is the relationship between the price level and money wages. In this section it will be assumed that both employers and employees are influenced by the real wage. The **real wage** is the nominal wage divided by an index of the price level. This means for example that, if both prices and wages were to go up by 10%, workers would know they were not better off. (The possibility that workers may think they are better off in these circumstances is called money illusion and is discussed in section D).

   If the price level rises and money wages do not change, firms will wish to hire more labour as the reader should verify by working through the example in Table 4.1 assuming that the price is 150. In this example the real wage falls from $3(=300/100)$ to $2(=300/150)$ and so that amount of labour demanded increases. This example illustrates the principle that the demand for labour is a function of the real wage.

Figure 4.3

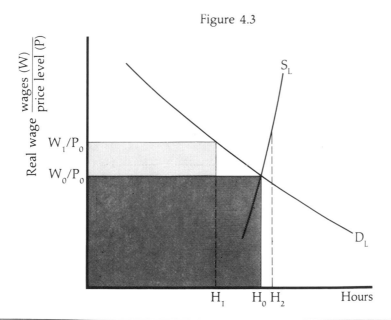

In the 'classical' model the demand for labour (D_L) and the supply of labour (S_L) intersect to determine the real wage and output, thus ensuring full employment. If the money wage were too high at W_1, competitive forces would reduce the money wage to W_0, thus assuring full employment.

Exercise

What would happen if (a) the price fell to 50, (b) the price rose to 150 and the money wage rose to 450 at the same time?

This relationship is illustrated in Figure 4.3 which has the real wage on the vertical axis.

Similar arguments apply to the supply of labour. If when prices are constant the labour supply curve looks like Figure 4.2a then it will also have that shape when labour supply is a function of the real wage (assuming no money illusion). Thus if the money wage went up and the price level did not the real wage would rise and people would wish to work more. But if prices rose and the money wage was constant the real wage would fall and people would wish to work less. The supply curve of labour as a function of the real wage is also shown in Figure 4.3.

This account of the supply of labour has assumed that the only economic influence on the amount of work people want to do is the current real wage rate. Other influences are considered in section D. However before doing this we examine the 'classical' model which assumes in its simplest version that labour supply depends only on the real wage.

C   THE 'CLASSICAL' MODEL

IF, and clearly this is a very big IF, the labour market is perfectly competitive the interaction of supply and demand would fix the wage rate at W_0/P_0 in Figure 4.3 and the amount of employment would be H_0 hours. Full employment is thus at H_0 hours of work. It should be noted that this does not mean that everyone is working 24 hours a day or even that everyone is working at all! Remember that labour supply refers to the amount of work people would like to do at various wage rates. At the current wage rate some people may wish to work overtime, some a standard week of say 40 hours; others may prefer part-time work and some will prefer no work.

If for some reason the money wage rate happened to be above the full employment level at W_1 so that the real wage was W_1/P_0 only H_1 hours of work would be demanded but workers would supply H_2 hours. The result would be unemployment of H_2 less H_1 hours. Experience suggests that this unemployment would consist in part of working people working fewer hours each week than they would like to, and in part of unemployed people who were unable to work at all. If the wage market were competitive the excess supply of labour would drive the money wage rate down to W_0 and full employment would be guaranteed.

It is a matter of debate whether there were economists who believed that the model we have just explored was ever an adequate description of reality but it is common in economics texts to label such models classical models. As we will see most classical economists did not actually believe this was the way the economy works so it is perhaps fairer to put the word 'classical' in quotes. The **'classical model'** is thus one in which there is no unemployment because the wage rate always adjusts in the labour market. If full employment is always assured by the workings of the labour market then this determines the level of output as well as the level of employment given our assumption

Figure 4.4

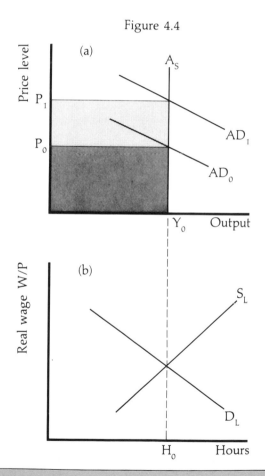

In the 'classical' model the supply and demand for labour determines full employment at H_0 hours and thus also determines the level of output. Aggregate demand influences prices but not output.

that the supply of labour depends only on the real wage rate. As the capital stock is fixed in the short-run, then output is what can be produced with that stock and the labour force working the amount they wish to work. If for some reason people decided they wished to work more the labour supply curve would shift to the right, and the levels of employment and output would both be higher. However for any given supply of labour actual output and capacity output are the same thing. We have now arrived at a position which is a polar opposite from that which we had in the last chapter. You should remember that in that chapter we assumed that output and employment were determined by the level of aggregate demand with no real reference to the labour market and we now have output and employment determined in the labour market without reference to aggregate demand. In a formal sense we now have a perfectly inelastic aggregate supply which diagrammatically is given by a vertical straight line corresponding to full employment. In Figure 4.4 part (b) repeats 4.3 where employment is determined at H_0 hours. In part (a) the same number of hours determines the position of the aggregate supply curve. In this model a change in aggregate demand will change prices but has no effect on employment or output.

It will be noted that Figure 4.4a has output on the horizontal axis and Figure 4.4b has hours on the horizontal axis and it is implied that the relationship between hours and output is constant. While employment and output will move together this is a simplification. The law of diminishing returns means that successive increments of hours will produce successively smaller and smaller increments to output. The relationship between employment and output including diminishing returns is shown in the appendix to this chapter.

We now have one model in which a change in demand affects output but not prices, and another in which a demand change affects prices but not output. This suggests we need to know more about the labour market and aggregate supply.

D   OTHER INFLUENCES ON LABOUR SUPPLY AND ON
      AGGREGATE SUPPLY

In the 'Classical' model the aggregate supply curve is vertical because it has been assumed that labour supply depends only on the real wage rate. If there are other influences on labour supply the aggregate supply curve will not be vertical. In this section the first task is to examine the influences of three other factors on labour supply. It will be shown that each of these factors can shift the labour supply curve to the right and that means that the aggregate supply curve will not be vertical. The classical assumption that money wages adjust to maintain full employment is maintained until the end of the section.

Figure 4.5

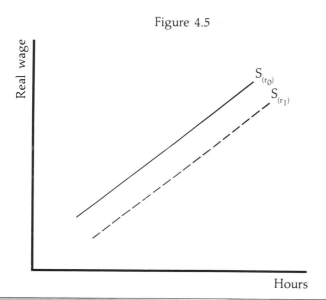

A rise in the rate of interest may increase savings and lead people to increase their labour supply for a given real wage in order to be able to save more.

Interest rate changes

It is convenient to start with interest rates. If interest rates change people may wish to change the amount that they save. It is possible for example that if interest rates rise people will wish to save more. Part of the explanation for this is that as interest rates rise the price of monetary assets falls (see Chapter 8) so that people have to work more in order to restore their previous levels of real wealth. Thus higher interest rates may cause people to alter their desired balance between work and leisure. Specifically if people want to save more they may also wish to work more in order to earn the money to save. Figure 4.5 shows the supply of labour shifting to the right when the interest rate rises from i_0 to i_1.

Changes in real money balances

A second reason for the labour supply to shift is because of changes in real money balances. Money balances are simply people's net holdings of money. **Real money balances** are money balances after taking into account the price

Figure 4.6

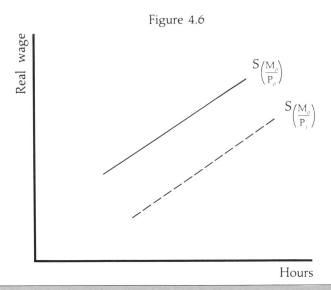

A higher price level will reduce real money balances and people will wish to work harder in order to restore their real money balances towards their original level.

level. This means that real money balances can rise either because nominal money balances rise or because prices have fallen. Of course if prices rise when nominal balances are unchanged then real money balances will fall. How will changes in real money balances affect the supply of labour? If real money balances fall workers will wish to restore them. In order to restore them workers will have to work longer – for any wage rate – so that a *fall* in real money balances will shift the labour supply curve to the right as in Figure 4.6. The Figure shows the initial supply curve S_{M_0}/P_0 shifting to the right to S_{M_0}/P_1 when prices *rise* from P_0 to P_1 because the *rise* in the price level brings about a *fall* in real money balances. The fall in real money balances makes people want to work longer.

Money illusion

Expectations about price changes in the labour market are also important. It seems likely that when prices are stable or only rising very slowly people expect prices to continue to be stable and are unaware – or only partially aware – of the effect of price increases in causing real wages to fall. This is called **money illusion** and refers to a case when people think they are better off when their incomes rise even though prices have risen in the same proportion.

Suppose that the government raises aggregate demand and that this raises

Figure 4.7

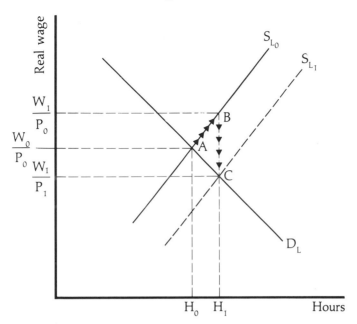

Money illusion causes the labour supply curve to shift downwards. Starting from A an increase in the price level will cause employers to wish to hire more labour and the real wage is lower. Employers will bid up money wages to W_1. As money wages rise by less than prices the real wage is lower. However employees who suffer money illusion believe that the price level will remain at P_0. With a higher money wage they will believe their real wage is higher and will attempt to move out their supply curve S_{L_0} to B. However prices have in fact risen to P_1 so that they end up at C rather than B.

prices. Suppose further that employers increase money wages to attract more workers. If there is money illusion workers will think their real wage has gone up and will supply more labour so that the supply curve shifts to the right. Suppose we start at point A in Figure 4.7 where the money wage is W_0 and the price level P_0 giving a real wage of W_0/P_0. Labour supply is H_0. If aggregate demand increases the price level to P_1 the real wage will fall and the demand for labour will increase. Employers may bid up the money wage to W_1 to attract more employees. If there is money illusion the employees will falsely believe that their real wage has risen to W_1/P_0 and will attempt to move out along S_{L_0} to B. However the price level is now P_1. As a result workers end up at C rather than B, implying a downward shift in the supply curve of labour.

It seems quite likely that in the first couple of decades after World War II when inflation rates were low that there was some money illusion in the labour market. If so this could be one reason why it was possible to combine high output, low unemployment and low inflation in the 1950s and early 1960s.

Exercise

If the expected rate of inflation was *higher* than the actual rate what would happen to the labour supply curve?

Effects on aggregate supply

If the labour supply curve shifts to the right as prices rise for any of these reasons the aggregate supply curve will not be vertical as can be seen with the aid of Figure 4.8. The initial equilibrium in the labour market in the lower part of the figure is at A where the real wage is W_0/P_0. This corresponds to one point – also labelled A on the aggregate supply curve in the upper part of the figure. If when prices are higher at P_1 the labour supply curve shifts to the right, the new position of equilibrium is B where the money wage remains at W_0 but with prices higher at P_1. Once again the corresponding point on the aggregate supply curve is labelled B. The aggregate supply curve has a positive slope because higher prices are causing labour supply to increase. It has been argued that price rises will cause the labour supply curve to shift to the right and the reader is asked to bear in mind that this is an important part of the explanation for the shape of the aggregate supply curve. Nevertheless to avoid making the diagrams unnecessarily complicated the labour supply curve is not shown shifting to the right each time prices rise.[4]

Sticky wages

So far it has been assumed that money wages will adjust to whatever level is required to clear labour markets. In fact money wages may not adjust as required and this provides part of the explanation for structural unemployment and excess wage unemployment (see section F) and demand deficient unemployment (see section G). If money wages are sticky this provides a further reason for the aggregate supply curve to be positively sloped (see appendix).

The explanation of the aggregate supply curve not being vertical does rule out the possibility discussed in Chapter 3 that the aggregate supply curve is

---

4.   This simplification does little harm because it will be assumed that there is sufficient stickiness in money wages to prevent full employment – see section G.

horizontal. The reasons for rejecting a horizontal aggregate supply curve are given in the next chapter. However before leaving the labour market it is necessary to look at unemployment.

Figure 4.8

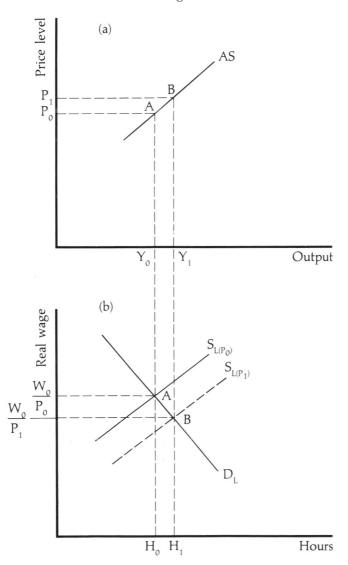

Price increases from P_0 to P_1 will shift the labour curve to the right from $S_{L(P_0)}$ to $S_{L(P_1)}$ in (b) moving the equilibrium position from A to B. The increase in hours of work increases output from Y_0 to Y_1 in (a) and this, together with the higher price level, gives point B on the aggregate supply curve AS.

E   CHARACTERISTICS OF THE UNEMPLOYED

You do not need to be told that unemployment is a serious social problem
causing both financial and social hardship to those who are unemployed.
Unemployment also causes a loss of output to the community as a whole.
You can see from Figure 4.9 that unemployment was very high between the
two World Wars and that there was then a generation of low unemployment
up to the late 1960s.

Figure 4.9   UK Unemployment Percentage Rates, 1880–1968

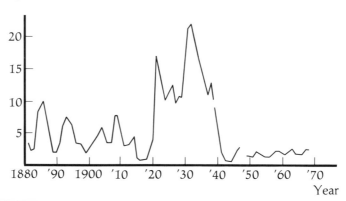

The various data sources are not directly comparable over time, but the differences in no way affect the
general conclusions reached.

Sources: 1881–1913—"British Labour Statistics, 1885–1953", Table 159
          1913–1939—"British Labour Statistics, 1885–1953", Table 160
          1939–1947—"British Labour Statistics, 1885–1953", Table 161
          1950–1968—"British Labour Statistics, 1885–1953", Table 168

Since the late 1960s unemployment has been rising sharply (and with the exception of two temporary dips) steadily, as can be seen from Figure 4.10. It can be seen from Figure 4.11 that as unemployment has risen there has been a particularly large increase in long-term unemployment.

Figure 4.10   Unemployment[1] and vacancies[2]

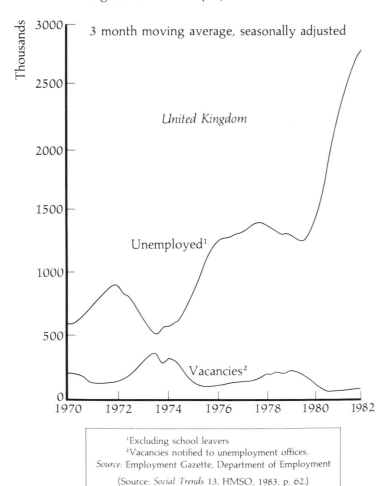

₁Excluding school leavers
₂Vacancies notified to unemployment offices.
Source: Employment Gazette, Department of Employment

(Source: *Social Trends* 13, HMSO, 1983, p. 62.)

Figure 4.11   Unemployment: by duration

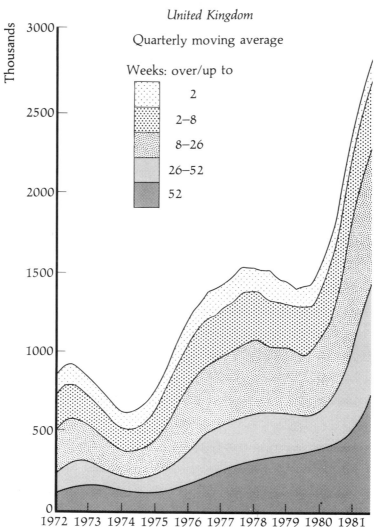

United Kingdom

Quarterly moving average

Weeks: over/up to

2

2–8

8–26

26–52

52

Source: Department of Employment; Department of Manpower Services, Northern Ireland

Source: *Social Trends* 13, HMSO, 1983, p. 61.

The unemployed tend to be males over 55 and people of both sexes under 25 as can be seen from Figure 4.12. Part of the reason for this is that older workers are often encouraged to retire early and also older workers find more difficulty in getting jobs. Unemployment is concentrated amongst young people for three reasons. The first reason for high growth in unemployment in the 1980s is the baby boom in the 1960s (See Table 2.2). Second, in a recession people with jobs tend to sit tight, freezing out those who do not have jobs and especially those who have never had jobs. Third, firms have tended to hire married women returning to the labour market in preference to school leavers.

The increase in unemployment in the 1970's has been very much faster in Britain than in many other countries as can be seen from Figure 4.13.

Figure 4.12   Unemployment: by sex, age, and duration, April 1982, *United Kingdom*

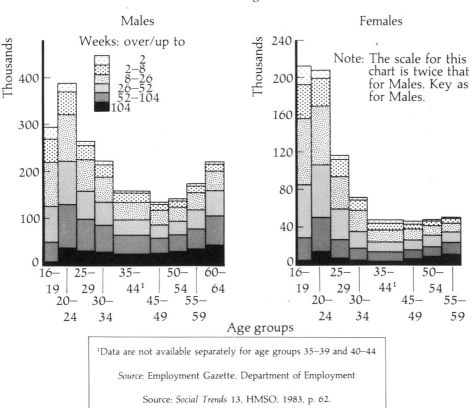

¹Data are not available separately for age groups 35–39 and 40–44

Source: Employment Gazette. Department of Employment

Source: *Social Trends* 13, HMSO, 1983, p. 62.

Figure 4.13   Unemployment rates adjusted to US concepts[1]—
international comparison

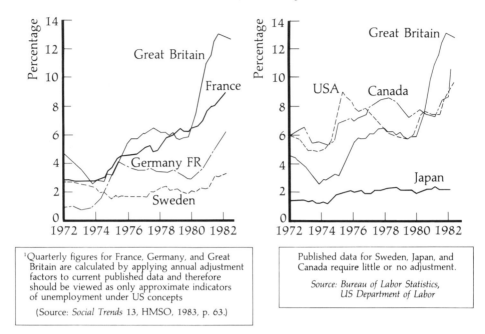

¹Quarterly figures for France, Germany, and Great
Britain are calculated by applying annual adjustment
factors to current published data and therefore
should be viewed as only approximate indicators
of unemployment under US concepts

(Source: *Social Trends* 13, HMSO, 1983, p. 63.)

Published data for Sweden, Japan, and
Canada require little or no adjustment.

*Source: Bureau of Labor Statistics,
US Department of Labor*

F   TYPES OF UNEMPLOYMENT

In the 'classical' model the supply and demand for labour interact to
determine a wage rate that equates supply and demand and ensures that there
is no unemployment. Classical economists (no quotation marks now as I am
no longer trying to misrepresent them) of course recognized that unemployment existed and their explanation of unemployment had much in common
with the modern explanation that follows except that they did not recognize
demand deficient unemployment.

Frictional and seasonal unemployment

People of course change jobs voluntarily for a whole variety of reasons: to
earn a higher wage, to move to a nicer job or one with better prospects or
one in a better part of the country or to move with a spouse who has moved
to a different area. Frequently of course when this happens people find the
new job before leaving the old one – but this does not always happen and
especially if the new job is in a different area it may be impossible. Some of
the unemployed are thus genuinely 'between jobs'. As individuals they may
suffer little, if at all, and society can benefit particularly if people move from a

job where their productivity is low to one where their productivity is high. If by spending more time in job search a better job is found, both the individual and society may benefit.

People who are made redundant at a job will not necessarily take the first job on offer because they may believe that time spent in job search will produce a more satisfactory job. The length of time people will remain voluntarily unemployed is likely to depend on how successful they think the time spent in job search is likely to be and on how pressing the immediate need for income is. For this reason it seems likely that the existence of generous redundancy schemes and unemployment pay may prolong periods of job search and hence raise frictional unemployment. This is not a new view. In 1930 Edwin Cannan wrote of the unemployment insurance scheme introduced in 1911: 'the insurance scheme has reduced the economic pressure which used to make persons grab at every chance of employment' (quoted in M. Casson, *Economics of Unemployment: An Historical Perspective*). Most, but not all, recent evidence suggests that higher unemployment pay prolongs unemployment. Evidence on the extent of frictional unemployment is not easy to get but it can be seen from Figure 4.10 that the number of people unemployed and the number of unfilled vacancies tend to be inversely related and it does seem likely that when unemployment is low and vacancies are high frictional unemployment will be a much higher proportion of the total. Seasonal unemployment is a similar phenomenon. Some industries, such as tourism and toy making have a marked seasonal demand for labour. Individuals who work for these industries may or may not find it convenient to work some months but not others but clearly there is a social benefit in meeting the seasonal demand when it does arise.

Structural unemployment

Structural unemployment occurs when the labour force is not well matched to the capital stock. The mismatch may be in terms of skills or industries or regions or any combination of these.

As new products come on the market other products lose popularity. Technical change alters the skills required to produce the same product. For example books are largely printed by photographic processes which no longer require the setting of metal type. As people's incomes rise they wish to purchase a different pattern of goods. For all of these reasons we would expect the structure of employment to change from time to time. An examination of Table 4.2 shows that between 1961 and 1980 total employment in Britain was fairly constant at around 22 or 23 million but the structure of that employment has changed markedly with all of the main sectors showing a decline except for services where employment increased

TABLE 4.2   EMPLOYEES IN EMPLOYMENT: BY INDUSTRY,* UNITED KINGDOM (THOUSANDS)

	1961	1966	1971	1977	1979	1980	1981 Males	1981 Females	1981 All
Agriculture, forestry, and fishing	710	580	432	388	367	370	270	89	360
Mining and quarrying	727	570	396	350	346	344	316	16	332
Manufacturing									
Food, drink, and tobacco	793	797	770	711	698	681	385	247	632
Chemicals, coal, and petroleum products	499	495	482	472	482	470	320	113	432
Metal manufacture	643	627	557	483	444	401	290	36	326
Engineering and allied industries	3,654	3,778	3,615	3,295	3,269	3,121	2,171	568	2,739
Textiles, leather, and clothing	1,444	1,319	1,124	941	897	813	291	417	707
Rest of manufacturing	1,508	1,571	1,511	1,390	1,386	1,322	873	329	1,202
Total manufacturing	8,540	8,587	8,058	7,292	7,176	6,808	4,330	1,709	6,038
Construction	1,485	1,648	1,262	1,270	1,292	1,265	1,023	109	1,132
Gas, electricity, and water	389	432	377	347	346	347	272	68	340
Services									
Transport and communication	1,678	1,622	1,568	1,468	1,494	1,500	1,164	276	1,440
Distributive trades	2,767	2,920	2,610	2,753	2,826	2,790	1,180	1,455	2,635
Insurance, banking, and finance	684	818	976	1,145	1,233	1,258	577	656	1,233
Professional and scientific services	2,124	2,591	2,989	3,647	3,729	3,717	1,161	2,533	3,695
Miscellaneous services	1,819	2,066	1,946	2,343	2,493	2,519	1,017	1,397	2,414
Public administration	1,311	1,424	1,509	1,615	1,619	1,596	954	625	1,579
Total services	10,382	11,441	11,597	12,970	13,394	13,379	6,053	6,942	12,996
All industries and services	22,233	23,257	22,122	22,619	22,920	22,511	12,264	8,934	21,198

* As at June each year.
Source: Social Trends 13, HMSO, 1983, p. 54.

from 10.4 million (47% of the total) to 13.4 million (59% of the total).

These very considerable changes in employment patterns have not in general been fast enough to prevent structural unemployment. Perhaps the clearest statistical measure of this is the persistence of regional differences in unemployment rates. Table 4.3 shows that Wales, Scotland and Northern Ireland have had persistently higher rates of unemployment than England, and within England the southern regions have fared better than the northern regions.

Why does structural unemployment persist? One explanation is a failure of wage rates to adjust. We can illustrate the argument with Figure 4.14 where for simplicity prices are assumed to be constant. Suppose we group industries into new and old industries. The new industries might be electronics and light engineering and the old industries might be coal, steel and shipbuilding. Suppose further that people are initially split roughly evenly between the two industries. In the new industries the demand for labour is high both because new technology makes productivity (the marginal physical product) high and because high demand makes it possible to charge a high price. Conversely in the old industries the marginal revenue product of labour – the

TABLE 4.3   UNEMPLOYMENT RATES*: BY REGION (PERCENTAGES)

	1971	1976	1977	1978	1979	1980	1981
Standard regions							
North	5.7	7.5	8.3	8.9	8.7	10.9	15.3
Yorkshire and Humberside	3.8	5.5	5.8	6.0	5.7	7.8	12.3
East Midlands	2.9	4.7	5.0	5.0	4.6	6.4	10.2
East Anglia	3.2	4.8	5.3	5.0	4.5	5.7	9.2
South East	2.0	4.2	4.5	4.2	3.7	4.8	8.1
South West	3.3	6.4	6.8	6.4	5.7	6.7	10.0
West Midlands	2.9	5.8	5.8	5.6	5.5	7.8	13.7
North West	3.9	6.9	7.4	7.5	7.1	9.3	13.9
England	3.0	5.4	5.7	5.6	5.2	6.8	10.8
Wales	4.4	7.3	8.0	8.3	7.9	10.3	14.8
Scotland	5.8	7.0	8.1	8.2	8.0	10.0	13.8
Great Britain	3.4	5.6	6.0	6.0	5.6	7.3	11.3
Northern Ireland	7.9	10.0	11.0	11.5	11.3	13.7	18.4
United Kingdom	3.5	5.7	6.2	6.1	5.7	7.4	11.4

* Annual averages, including school leavers.
Source: Social Trends 13, HMSO, 1983, p. 60.

Figure 4.14

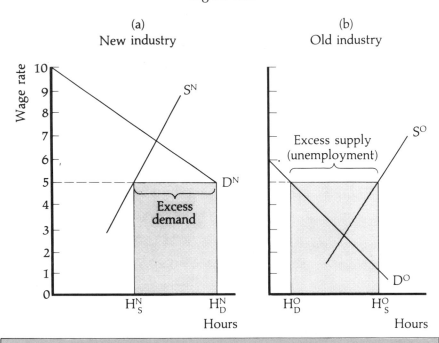

If the wage rate in both old and new industries was 5, there would be structural unemployment with excess demand for labour of $H_D^N - H_S^N$ in the new industry and unemployment (excess supply) of $H_S^O - H_D^O$ in the old industry.

demand for labour – is low both because of low productivity and because of low demand and low prices. In the example in the figure if the wage rate in the new industries were 7 and if the wage in the old industries were 3, supply would equal demand in both and there would be full employment. On the other hand if the wage were 5 in both old and new industries, employment would be H_D^O in the old industries because of demand limitation and H_S^N in the new industries because of supply limitations. There would be an excess demand for labour in the new industries of $H_D^N - H_S^N$ and in the old industries there would be unemployment of $H_S^O - H_D^O$ which means that in the economy as a whole unemployment would be $H_S^O - H_D^O$. Why then don't people leave the old industries and go to work in the new? The new industry may be located in different regions and may require different skills. Moving house and acquiring new skills will incur both monetary costs – for rehousing and retraining, and psychological costs – for being uprooted from friends and relations. People may think these costs are too high relative to the wage rate that is on offer. Suppose the unemployment benefit is 3 – the same as the equilibrium wage in the old industries. Suppose further that people require a differential of 3 to move and retrain. With unemployment benefit of 3 and a wage of 5 in the new industry the change is not worthwhile.

Why then don't wage rates change? In particular why don't the workers in the old industry accept a wage cut? One argument is that unemployment benefit is too high. Referring to the 1911 insurance scheme mentioned above, Clay put it this way in 1929:

> Before the war the consequence [of refusing a wage reduction] would have been unemployment, and unemployment would have involved... early and extreme hardship. It was impossible for the representatives of the wage earners in negotiations to ignore unemployment. Today things are different. (Quoted in M. Casson *op. cit.*)

Most but not all recent evidence supports this view. Another argument is that cuts in money wages are unthinkable.

The arguments against wage cuts in the previous paragraph of course do not apply to wage increases and it is certainly quite easy to imagine that wages in the new industry would be bid up. If the wage in the new industry were bid up to 7 (see Figure 4.14a) that would eliminate the excess demand for labour in the new industries but it would do nothing for unemployment in the old industry (ignoring effects on aggregate demand). However it has been suggested that workers will retrain and move if there is a wage differential of 3. If the unemployment benefit is 3 then people will be willing to leave the old industry when the wage in the new industry reaches 6. The argument is illustrated in Figure 4.15. When the wage in the new industry reaches 6 in Figure 4.15(a) people leave the old industry permanently shifting the supply curve to that industry from S_0^O to S_1^O. This simultaneously shifts the supply curve in the new industry from S_0^N to S_1^N. The new industry is in equilibrium with the wage rate at 6 and employment is in equilibrium at H_E^N hours. In the old industry the wage rate remains at 5 but the shift in the supply curve resulting from workers leaving the industries has reduced unemployment from $H_{S_0}^O - H_D^O$ to $H_{S_1}^O - H_D^O$.

The argument in the preceding paragraphs has ignored effects on real output and on aggregate demand. The movement of unemployed workers out of the old industry does not reduce the output of the old industry. However when these workers become employed in the new industry, output from the new industry will increase, which means that total national output will increase. The total real income of workers in the new industry will increase both because employment has increased from H_0^N to H_1^N and because the wage per worker has increased from 5 to 6. If the workers in the new industry spend part of their income on the goods produced by the old industry that will increase demand in the old industry and reduce unemploy-

Figure 4.15

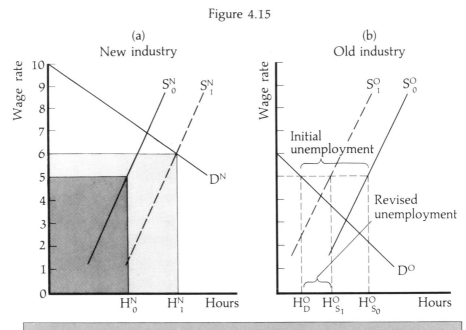

If the wage differential is sufficiently attractive some workers may leave the old industry, eliminating the excess demand for labour in the new industry and reducing unemployment from $H^O_{S_0} - H^O_D$ to $H^O_{S_1} - H^O_{S_0}$.

ment in that industry.[5] Given both the large changes in employment which have taken place (Table 4.2) and the persistence of structural unemployment (Table 4.3) the analysis in these paragraphs is probably quite realistic.

Excess wage unemployment

In the previous section structural unemployment was explained in terms of a wage structure that was too rigid to equate labour supply and demand in different markets. In addition to this argument about wage structures it is frequently suggested that unemployment is caused by the general level of wages being too high: **excess wage unemployment**. The argument runs as follows: If wages are not set by competitive forces general wage rates may be too high: If wages are controlled by trade unionists acting as monopolists they may choose a wage W_1/P_0 in Figure 4.3 and as a result cause unemployment of $(H_2 - H_1)$ 'instead of allowing competition for employment changes to force wages down to the point at which the whole supply of

5. Demand in the new industry could also rise.

Figure 4.16

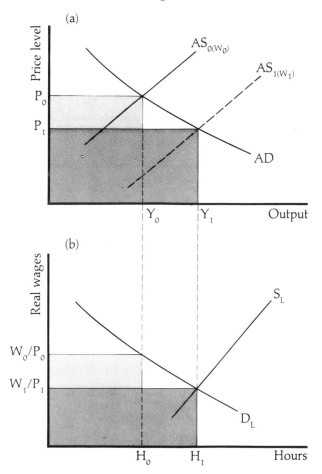

It is argued that a cut in money wages will shift AS to the right and bring about full employment. This neglects the possibility that the AD will shift to the left.

labour is absorbed'. (Henry Clay (1919), quoted in M. Casson *op. cit.*).

The argument can be represented graphically in Figure 4.16. Part (a) contains aggregate supply and demand curves similar to those in Figure 1.1 and part (b) shows the labour market.[6] If the wage is above the level that equates the supply and demand for labour – say at W_0/P_0 in Figure 4.16(b) there will be unemployment and it can be seen from 4.16(a) that aggregate supply and demand will determine output at Y_0 and prices at P_0. Now if money wages fall from W_0 to W_1 the real wage paid by firms will fall and

6.   See appendix for a formal explanation of the relationship between parts (a) and (b) of the Figure.

they will wish to hire more labour. Because their costs have fallen the aggregate supply curve will shift down to the right to AS_1. Output will rise to Y_1. Prices will fall to P_1 and employment will rise to H_1, the full employment level. As we will see it is critical to this argument that the aggregate demand curve does not shift.

But will cuts in money wages actually restore full employment? Keynes spent a whole chapter (19) of his *General Theory* arguing that cuts in money wages would not necessarily restore full employment. He suggested that producers will only hire labour if they expect to be able to sell the goods produced by that labour. That requires an adequate level of aggregate demand. We have seen that the level of aggregate demand depends on the balance between leakages and injections. A fall in wages could shift the leakages function upwards because it will raise the proportion of profits in total income.[7] If profits are all distributed and the marginal propensity for

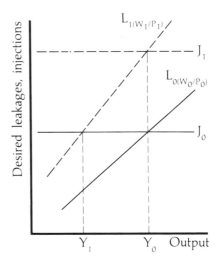

Figure 4.17   Figure 4.18

A cut in the wage from W_0/P_0 to W_1/P_1 would raise the profits to wage income ratio from $(W_0/P_0)AB/O(W_0/P_0)BC$ to $(W_1/P_1)AD/O(W_1/P_1)DE$. If the I from profits exceeds the I from wage income leakages will shift upwards.	A cut in money wages raising the profits to wage income ratio will shift the leakages function upwards, reducing the equilibrium level of income from Y_0 to Y_1. To restore income an increase in injections would be required.

7. Leakages and injections may also be influenced by the levels of real money balances but, for simplicity, that argument is deferred to Part B of Chapter 5.

leakages from profits is higher than from wages the leakages function will shift upwards. The argument is illustrated in Figures 4.17 and 4.18. The wage rate that equates the supply and demand for labour is W_1/P_1 in Figure 4.17 but the actual wage is assumed to be W_0/P_0. Will a cut in money wages from W_0 to W_1 restore full employment? When the wage is W_0/P_0, profits are $(W_0/P_0)AB$ and total wages are $O(W_0/P_0)BC$.

When the wage is W_1/P_1 profits are $(W_1/P_1)/AD$ and wages income is $O(W_1/P_1)DE$. It is clear that the ratio of profits to wages has risen, that is

$$\frac{(W_1/P_1)AD}{O(W_1/P_1)DE} > \frac{(W_0/P_0)AB}{O(W_0/P_0)BC}$$

Now suppose wage earners have a marginal propensity for leakages (l) of 0.3 and profit earners' l is 0.6. The rising share of profits means that the leakages function will shift upwards and the overall l will rise. This can be seen in Figure 4.18. Before the wage cut the leakages function L_0 intersects the injection function J_0 to produce equilibrium income Y_0. The fall in the wage rate shifts the leakages function to L_1 and as a result equilibrium income falls to Y_1. To prevent this fall what is required is an increase in injections from J_0 to J_1. The problem Keynes saw is that there is no mechanism to ensure that this increase in injections will be forthcoming.

Let us pursue the argument assuming that the required increase in injections is *not* forthcoming so that aggregate demand falls. The argument is illustrated in Figure 4.19 which is similar in construction to 4.16. Once again we start from a real wage of W_0/P_0 which is above the full employment level. Money wages are cut to W_1 and the AS curve shifts to AS_1. However, the economy does *not* move to point A – the intersection of AD_0 and AS_1. The reason is that, as we have seen aggregate demand has fallen so that the economy moves to B where AS_1 and AD_1 cross. Note that prices fall more at B than at A. Because prices are lower at B than at A the real wage which is (wages/prices), is higher. Consequently, as can be seen from Part (b), the cut in money wages has only increased employment from H_0 to H_1. This sharp fall in prices means a very large cut in money wages could be necessary to restore full employment. There is even the possibility that the cut in money wages will cause AD to shift down to AD_2, which would mean that the money wage cut would actually increase unemployment.

To summarize, we have seen that a cut in money wages will cure unemployment if the aggregate demand curve is not affected. However the cut in money wage will raise the share of profits and if the l from profits is more than the l from wage income aggregate demand will fall – unless injections increase – and this will blunt the effect of the wage cuts. The

Figure 4.19

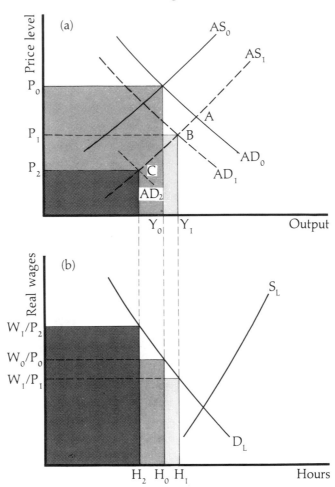

If the cut in money wages shifts the leakages function upwards (see Figure 4.18) the AD curve will shift downwards. This will cause prices to fall sharply which will prevent the real wage from falling far enough to cure unemployment.

difference between the *l* from profits and wage income is critical. If it is nil or small there will be little if any fall in AD, but if the *l* from profits is much less than the *l* from wage income the shift in AD may be large.

We have seen that changes in wages may affect the level of aggregate demand. In the example a cut in money wages reduced aggregate demand because it led to higher profits and higher savings. Similarly an increase in money wages could increase aggregate demand because it could lead to lower profits and lower savings. For the sake of simplicity the effects of wage changes on aggregate demand are ignored in the rest of the text, although the reader will be reminded about the argument in footnotes from time to time.

Demand Deficient Unemployment

The final type of unemployment is unemployment which results from lack of effective demand and this is called **demand deficient unemployment**. This type of unemployment is sometimes termed cyclical unemployment because of variations in aggregate demand due to the state of the trade cycle. We are now in a position to recognize that this is the only type of unemployment that fits the fixprice model of the last chapter.

Cures for unemployment

If unemployment is the frictional type it may be possible to reduce it by more efficient flows of information. Structural unemployment requires policies to encourage flexible wages, and the retraining and relocation of labour. Excess wage unemployment requires wage cuts together with policies to ensure an adequate level of aggregate demand. The remedies for demand deficient unemployment are implicit in the term. We will return to a much more detailed discussion of these issues in Chapters 12 and 13. Before doing this we look more closely at the Keynesian view of the labour market.

G   THE KEYNESIAN VIEW OF THE LABOUR MARKET

The 'classical' view of the labour market is an instructive straw man in which competitive forces cause the money wage to change to whatever level is required to equate the supply and demand for labour and thus ensure full employment. Classical economists in fact recognized the existence of frictional, structural and excess wage unemployment (but failed to recognize that wage cuts can reduce aggregate demand). We thus have a simple and a sophisticated classical view of the labour market. There is also a simple and sophisticated representation of the Keynesian view of the labour market. The simple view – which underlies the model in the last chapter, is that wages – and prices – are completely fixed. We now look at the more sophisticated Keynesian view. It will be remembered – (see Figure 3.2) that when Keynes wrote, money wages were quite stable, and Keynes also recognized that money wages tend to be sticky and especially that actual falls in money wages would be very rare in normal times. In this Keynesian model with sticky wages the level of employment is determined by aggregate demand because of the failure of money wages to adjust. The presence of sticky money wages means that the aggregate supply curve will have a positive slope and its shape will be determined by the shape of the demand curve for labour. The formal derivation of this aggregate supply curve is contained in the appendix to this chapter.

The argument is illustrated with Figure 4.20 which is similar in construction to 4.19. In (a) AS_0 and AD_0 determine output and prices at a level where there is substantial unemployment. Keynes argued as follows. A fall in money wages is unlikely but a fall in real wages may be possible if aggregate demand is stimulated. If by raising injections or reducing leakages we can raise the level of aggregate demand from AD_0 to AD_1 the price level will go up from P_0 to P_1. If the money wage remains at W_0 the real wage will fall from W_0/P_0 to W_0/P_1 and full employment will be restored.

While the Keynesian model can bring about full employment without a *fall*

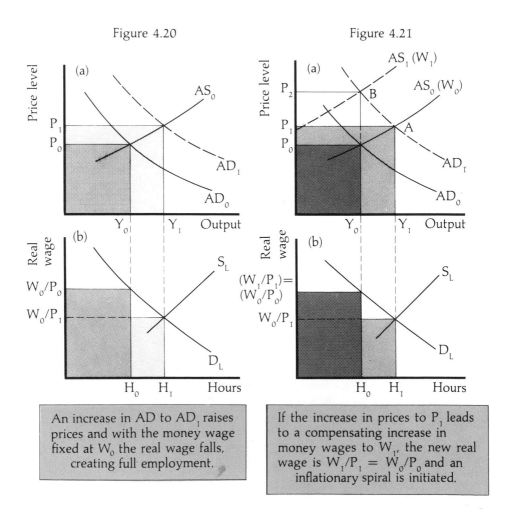

Figure 4.20	Figure 4.21
An increase in AD to AD_1 raises prices and with the money wage fixed at W_0 the real wage falls, creating full employment.	If the increase in prices to P_1 leads to a compensating increase in money wages to W_1, the new real wage is $W_1/P_1 = W_0/P_0$ and an inflationary spiral is initiated.

in money wages it does depend on stable money wages, as can be seen from Figure 4.21. Again we start at the intersection of AS_0 and AD_0 and again aggregate demand is raised from AD_0 to AD_1 raising prices to P_1 and creating full employment. If workers now have an increase in their money wage to compensate for the price rise the real wage becomes W_1/P_1 which is equal to W_0/P_0. The higher money wage (W_1), however, shifts the AS curve to AS_1.[8] The shift in the AS curve raises prices still further to P_2. This rise in prices to P_2 reduces the real wage temporarily and it can be easily seen that a cycle of rising prices and wages is created.

Keynes is best remembered for his emphasis on demand deficient unemployment and it is sometimes forgotten how much emphasis he placed on structural unemployment. In 1937 when – as Figure 4.9 shows – the level of unemployment was still high Keynes wrote:

> It is natural to interject that it is premature to abate our efforts to increase employment so long as the figures of unemployment remain so large. In a sense this must be true. But I believe that we are approaching, or have reached, the point where there is not much advantage in applying a further general stimulus at the centre. So long as surplus resources were widely diffused between industries and localities it was no great matter at what point in the economic structure the impulse of an increased demand was applied. But the evidence grows that – for several reasons into which there is no space to enter here – the economic structure is unfortunately rigid, and that (for example) building activity in the home counties is less effective than one might have hoped in decreasing unemployment in the distressed areas. It follows that the later stages of recovery require a different technique. To remedy the condition of the distressed areas, ad hoc measures are necessary . . . . What is required at once are acts of constructive imagination by our administrators, engineers, and architects, to be followed by financial criticism, sifting, and more detailed designing; so that some large and useful projects, at least, can be launched at a few months' notice.
>
> There can be no justification for a rate of interest which impedes an adequate flow of new projects at a time when the national resources for production are not fully employed. The rate of interest must be reduced to the figure that the new projects can afford. In special cases subsidies may be justified; but in general it is the long-term rate of interest which should come down to the figure which the marginal project can earn. (*The Times*, 1937.)

H   SLACK (LOW LABOUR PRODUCTIVITY)

At the start of this chapter the demand curve for labour was derived from the marginal physical product of labour which in turn was derived from the total

---

8. The reader is reminded that the possible effects of changes in wages on aggregate demand are being ignored.

physical product of labour. The total physical product of labour is the total amount of goods that can be produced with the existing capital stock and with existing technology.

There is however evidence that the amount that is actually produced with the existing capital stock is less than the amount that could be produced. Pratten's work (see Table 2.6) showed that British productivity per worker is generally lower than productivity elsewhere even when the capital stock is the same. If what is actually produced is less than what could be produced the curve relating the actual level of output to input of labour will lie below the TPP and is shown as a dashed line in Figure 4.21. This line may be termed the total actual product curve (TAP). If the TAP shows the actual relationship between labour input and output the actual demand for labour will be the curve that is marginal to the TAP curve and is termed the marginal actual product curve (MAP). It can be seen from part (b) of the figure that the effect of this is to lower full employment hours from their potential level H_p to an actual level of H_a and to reduce the full employment real wage from W_p/P_p to W_a/P_a. Because less output is produced per worker costs of production are higher so that the actual AS curve lies above the potential AS curve. In consequence prices are higher at P_a rather than P_p in part c, and output is lower at Y_a than Y_p. The moral is that inefficient use of labour reduces the real income of workers, reduces output and raises prices.

I   THE AGGREGATE SUPPLY CURVE: SUMMARY

In the fixprice Keynesian model the aggregate supply curve is horizontal. All the other models we have considered allow the prices of goods to be determined by the interaction of aggregate supply and aggregate demand.

The other models of the aggregate supply curve we have considered make different assumptions about the way labour markets work. Models which are termed classical assume that the money wage will always adjust to equate the supply and demand for labour. In the 'classical' model there are no influences on labour supply other than the real wage, and the aggregate supply curve is vertical. In the full classical model interest rate and real balance effects are added and the aggregate supply curve is positively sloped rising from left to right. If there is money illusion in the labour market the aggregate supply curve will be more elastic.

If money wages are sticky employment is determined by the demand for labour and in this more complete Keynesian model the aggregate supply curve has a positive slope determined by the shape of the demand curve for labour.

Figure 4.22

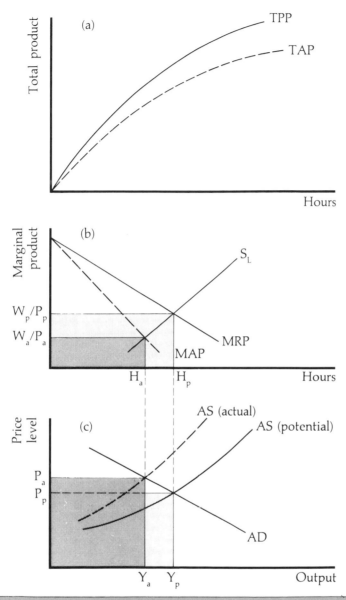

If labour produces less than it could with existing capital and technology, the TAP curve will lie below the TPP curve (part a) and the actual demand for labour will be below the MRP (part b) so that the actual aggregate supply curve lies above the potential supply curve (part c). This reduces employment from H_p to H_a, output from Y_p to Y_a and raises prices from P_p to P_a.

In the rest of this book (except in Chapter 14[9]) the aggregate supply curve will be assumed to be positively sloped for the following reasons: interest rate, real balance, foreign trade and Keynes effects, and sticky money wages. There may also be money illusion operating at certain times.

APPENDIX TO CHAPTER 4: THE RELATIONSHIP BETWEEN EMPLOYMENT AND OUTPUT

The first purpose of this appendix is to spell out the relationship between employment (measured in hours) and output with a fixed money wage. In the

Figure A4.1

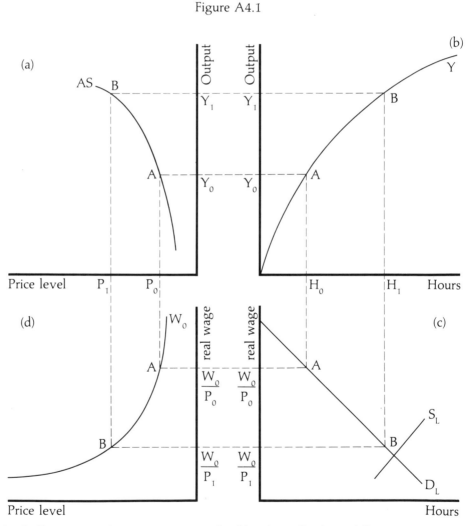

body of the chapter in various figures (such as Figure 4.12) part (a) show output on the horizontal axis and part (b) show hours on the horizontal axis. While it is perhaps intuitively acceptable that output and employment are positively associated a more formal demonstration is given here with the aid of Figure A4.1. Part (a) is like part (a) of the figures in the text except that it is rotated $90°$ so that output is measured on the vertical axis and the price level is measured from right to left on the horizontal axis. Part (b) has output on the vertical axis and employment measured in hours on the horizontal axis. The curve shows the total product of labour. Part (c) shows the labour market and part (d) shows the relationship between the price level and the real wage when the money wage is fixed. Part (d) has the real wage on the vertical axis and the price level on the horizontal axis. The money wage is represented by a rectangular hyperbola. The reason why the money wage can be represented this way is that $W = (W/P) \times P$.

The connection between the various parts of Figure A4.1 can be explained as follows. If we start from a real wage of W_0/P_0 in part (c) we know that this is consistent with employment of H_0 hours, we know from part (b) that Y_0 output can be produced with H_0 hours of work. If the real wage is W_0/P_0 we know from part (d) that if the money wage is W_0 the price level is P_0. Thus P_0 and Y_0 give us one point on the aggregate supply curve in part (a). If the real wage were lower at W_0/P_1 employment would be H_1, output Y_1 (from part (b)), and the price level P_1 (from part (d)) giving another point on the aggregate supply curve. The figure illustrates the point that the relationship between output in part (a) and employment in part (c) is not proportionate as can be seen by inspection (i.e. $Y_1/Y_0 < H_1/H_0$). The reason is that the marginal physical product of labour is decreasing is due to diminishing returns to the variable factor labour when there is a fixed factor-capital.

The second purpose of the appendix is to show the derivation of the aggregate supply curve when the money wage is fixed. The attentive reader will have already grasped the essentials: the points labelled A in the four parts of the figure are all consistent with each other, as are the points labelled B.

CONCEPTS FOR REVIEW

E

QUESTIONS FOR DISCUSSION

1   How will the demand for labour be affected by (a) an increase in money wages, (b) an increase in the price level, (c) an equal percentage increase in money wages and the price level?

2   Under what circumstances will the supply of labour increase with an increase in the nominal wage?

3   Under what circumstances will the aggregate supply curve be vertical – i.e. totally inelastic?

4   If the supply curve is totally inelastic what will be the effect of an increase in aggregate demand on (a) output, (b) the price level.

5   Under what circumstances will the aggregate supply curve be positively sloped?

6   If the aggregate supply curve is positively sloped what will be the effect of an increase in aggregate demand on (a) output, (b) the price level?

7   How could money illusion in the labour market help to explain the low rates of inflation and low rates of unemployment in the first two decades after World War II?

8   What would the effect of a cut in real wages be on output and the price level?

5

Completing the Basic Framework

In this chapter the basic framework is completed with a more detailed examination of the shapes of the aggregate supply and demand curves and by an introduction to inflation. While the basic framework is later refined it is essentially completed in this chapter so an introduction to policy is included that will introduce some issues that are examined in Parts II and III. When supply and demand analysis is used it is assumed that certain things are being held constant. If any of these things which are assumed constant were to change then the supply and/or demand curves will shift. This is true with aggregate supply and demand curves as well as with the supply and demand curves used in microeconomics. Throughout this book the following will be assumed to remain constant when we draw aggregate supply and demand curves:

(1)   the capital stock;
(2)   technology;
(3)   efficiency of use of the capital stock;
(4)   the money wage (except in Chapter 14);
(5)   the functions relating desired injections and leakages *at a given price level*;
(6)   the nominal stock of money (discussed in Part II).

If there are changes in any of these things, the aggregate supply curve and/or the aggregate demand curve will shift.

A   WHY THE AGGREGATE SUPPLY CURVE IS NOT HORIZONTAL

In this section the shape of the aggregate supply curve is further examined. It has been argued in Chapter 4 that the aggregate supply curve will not be totally inelastic. In this section it is argued that the aggregate supply is not perfectly elastic as is assumed in the fixprice model.

Horizontal aggregate supply

In Chapter 3 we introduced the fixprice Keynesian model where we assumed that neither prices nor wages change. You will remember that in that model there is no labour market and the level of output is determined by the aggregate demand curve. Similarly changes in output are brought about exclusively by changes in aggregate demand – see Figure 3.2.

There are three reasons why a horizontal aggregate supply curve is unsatisfactory. First, while the assumption of stable prices and wages may have been reasonably close to reality in the 1930s (see Figures 3.1 and 3.2) and even in the first two decades after World War II, it is certainly not a

TABLE 5.1

	Changes in prices*		Changes in prices*
	%		%
1949	3.0	1967	2.4
1950	2.9	1968	4.8
1951	8.9	1969	5.4
1952	9.4	1970	6.3
1953	3.1	1971	9.4
1954	1.7	1972	7.3
1955	4.6	1973	9.1
1956	5.0	1974	16.0
1957	3.6	1975	24.2
1958	3.1	1976	16.5
1959	0.6	1977	15.9
1960	1.1	1978	8.3
1961	3.3	1979	13.4
1962	4.2	1980	18.0
1963	2.0	1981	11.9
1964	3.2	1982	8.6
1965	4.8	1983	5.3
1966	3.9		

*Percentage change in retail price index over the previous year.

Source: *Economic Trends Annual Supplement*, 1984 edition, pp. 18, 114.

reasonable description of what is happening in the 1970s and 1980s. Table 5.1 and Figure 5.4 show that there was a temporary increase in inflation in 1951 and 1952 associated with the Korean war but with that exception prices rose quite gently until the mid-1960s. From the mid-1960s to the mid-1970s inflation rose in most years, reaching 24.2% in 1975. It then decreased to about 8.3% in 1978 before accelerating to 18.0% in 1980 and then falling to about 5% in 1983.

Second, in addition to its failure to describe reality adequately the model does not reflect Keynes' thinking. Its failure to reflect Keynes' views is not obvious in the standard presentation (as for example in Chapter 3) because the labour market is hidden, but we saw in the last chapter that an increase in aggregate demand is able to expand output and employment only because aggregate demand raises prices and depresses the real wage. The model thus requires rising prices and falling real wages to work. If prices and wages are fixed and the real wage is above the full employment level there is no adequate mechanism to restore full employment in a model with fixed wages and prices.

Third, if the marginal physical product of labour falls as additional labour hours are worked this will increase costs. This is the basis of the argument in the next subsection.

Aggregate supply with positive slope

While models which at least implicitly assume a horizontal segment to the aggregate supply are presented as THE standard Keynesian model in many textbooks this analysis was clearly and explicitly rejected by Keynes himself, who believed that the aggregate supply would be upward sloping. Keynes said

> Thus instead of constant prices in conditions of unemployment ... we have in fact a condition of prices rising gradually as employment increases'. (*General Theory of Employment, Interest and Money* p.296).

This section is devoted to explaining why the aggregate supply curve slopes upwards from left to right.[1] As will be seen it is likely that the elasticity of the aggregate supply curve will fall as output rises. Some of the reasons why the supply curve will not be perfectly elastic (horizontal) are

(1)   As unemployment falls the additional workers hired are likely to be paid the same wage as existing workers but may be less efficient so costs of production will rise.

---

1.   The reasons why the aggregate supply curve is not vertical were given in Chapter 4 Section D.

(2)   As unemployment falls less efficient capital equipment will need to be brought into production and this will increase unit costs further.

(3)   As capacity output is approached output per hour is likely to fall as workers become fatigued as a result of overtime and/or shift working.

(4)   It also seems likely that some industries and/or regions will approach capacity while other sectors still have spare capacity.

Figure 5.1

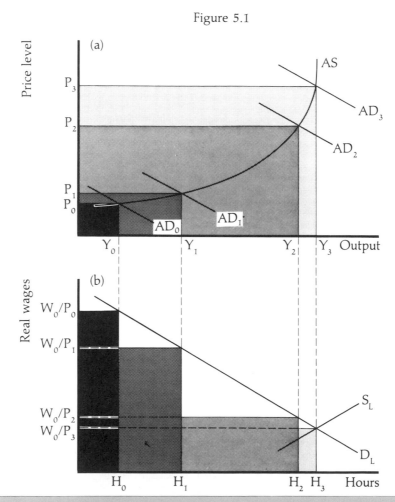

Keynes believed the aggregate supply curve would be shaped like AS in Part (a). When output and employment are low, an expansion of demand causes large increases in output and small increases in prices but with low unemployment a similar increase in AD causes prices to rise more than output.

This means that factors (1) to (3) above will operate sooner in some sectors than in others. As capacity output is approached the aggregate supply curve is likely to become increasingly less elastic as more and more sectors near capacity. This is consistent with Keynes' own view of the shape of the aggregate supply curve which is shown in Figure 5.1. Starting from some low level of aggregate demand such as AD_0 it is possible to expand demand to AD_1 achieving a relatively large increase in output $(=Y_1-Y_0)$ and employment $(=H_1-H_0)$ in exchange for a relatively modest increase in prices $(=P_1-P_0)$. However, as full employment capacity output is approached higher levels of employment can only be 'bought' at increasingly severe penalties in terms of the price level as can be seen from the comparison of AD_2 and AD_3.

B   THE SHAPE OF THE AGGREGATE DEMAND CURVE

The purpose of this section is to give an introductory exposition of why the aggregate demand curve slopes downwards from left to right. If the price level falls spending will rise for five reasons.

Real wage effect

When the price level falls people's money income is worth more. In other words the real wage will rise and this **real wage effect** will lead to an increase in desired levels of consumption of people in employment.

Share of profits effect

As prices fall the share of profits will fall as we saw in Chapter 4 – see Figure 4.17, and if leakages are higher from profits than from wages, leakages will fall. Diagrammatically the **share of profits effect** is illustrated with the aid of Figure 5.2 which is similar in construction to Figure 3.6. In Part (a) the solid lines represent the desired levels of leakages and injections at the initial price level P_0. They determine the equilibrium level of output at Y_0 – given the price level P_0. The point of intersection between L_0 and J_0 which is marked A, corresponds to one point on the aggregate demand curve in the lower part of the figure. It should be noted that both parts of Figure 5.2 have the same horizontal scale for output. The lower part has the price level on the vertical axis while the upper part has leakages and injections on the vertical axis. In the lower part of the figure the point labelled A corresponds to the point labelled A in the upper part of the figure. At the lower level of prices P_1

Figure 5.2

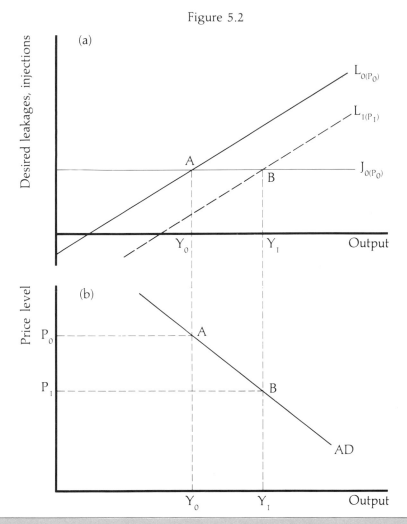

A fall in the price level reduces the share of profits and if leakages are higher from profits than from wages leakages will fall.

people's desired consumption rises so that desired leakages shift down to L_1. The new equality between desired leakages and injections occurs when output is at Y_1. In the upper part of the figure the new equilibrium position is labelled B and this higher level of output Y_1 and lower level of prices P_1 is also marked B in the lower part of the figure. Points A and B thus represent two points on the aggregate demand curve. Other points can be traced out using the same procedure.

Real balance effect

As prices fall the real value of money that people hold will rise. This increase in real balances will make people feel better off. This **real balance effect** means that there will be less need for people to save and so again leakages will fall and again the diagrammatic version of the argument is exactly as before. A fuller explanation of this reason is given in Chapter 6.

Figure 5.3

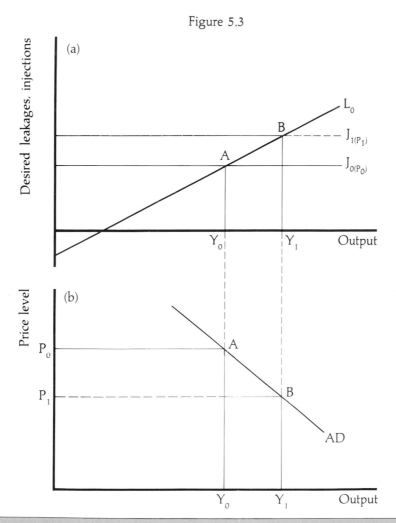

With stable exchange rates a fall in domestic prices from P_0 to P_1 raises exports and hence total injections from $J_{0(P_0)}$ to $J_{1(P_1)}$ raising the level of output to Y_1 in Part (a). The price and output levels are plotted in Part (b).

Foreign trade effects

In an open economy with a fixed exchange rate there will also be **foreign trade effects** on leakages and injections. As prices fall in the home market people will buy domestically produced goods in preference to imported goods if foreign prices are stable. The fall in desired consumption of imported good will again cause the leakages function to shift down unless the exchange rate adjusts. This issue is discussed in Part III.

As prices fall in the home market foreigners will buy our goods in preference to goods produced in their own countries if the exchange rate does not offset the price change (see Part III). The effect is shown in Part (a) of Figure 5.3 where the fall in prices from P_0 to P_1 increases exports so that total injections rise from $J_{0(P_0)}$ to $J_{1(P_1)}$. This increases the equilibrium level of output from Y_0 to Y_1. The original price and output levels give point A and the aggregate demand curve at the new price and output levels give point B.

Keynes effect

A higher price level also reduces the demand for investment goods. This effect, called the Keynes effect, is explained in Chapter 9.

This completes the basic theoretical framework of this book. In the remainder of this chapter the nature of inflation is discussed, and aggregate supply and aggregate demand analysis is used to provide a preliminary analysis of the causes of inflation. Aggregate supply and demand curves are then used to provide a preliminary discussion of problems of economic policy.

C   INFLATION

Inflation is a *sustained* upward movement in the *general* price level. I have italicized two words to emphasize that a once-and-for-all increase in the price level is not the same thing as inflation and because changes in particular prices are not the same as inflation.

If the price level was constant for a number of years and then was, say, to double in a short period of time and then remain constant at this new higher level the general price level would have increased but we would not have inflation. We need then to bear in mind the difference between a change in the price level and inflation. We have seen in earlier chapters that an upwards shift in either aggregate demand or aggregate supply can cause the price level to rise but this will not *necessarily* cause inflation. However in the last chapter we saw how inflation could start. An increase in aggregate demand – a shift in the AD schedule – increased the price level (see Figure 4.21). Wages were then increased to restore real incomes. This caused the AS curve to shift up, which increased prices still further – if wages then increase again to compensate for the prices increase an inflationary process is under way.

It is also important to bear in mind the difference between a change in relative prices and an increase in the price level. If the price of a newspaper rises from 20p to 25p, or by 25%, in a year in which inflation was 10%, then 10% of the 25% increase in the price of the newspaper would be attributable to inflation and 15% to the increase in relative prices.

Measuring inflation

Inflation is most commonly measured by constructing an index of prices paid by consumers. This index is called the **retail price index** (RPI) in Britain. The problem in measuring inflation is what to do if different prices are rising at different rates. Suppose for example that there are three commodities: bread, milk and sugar, and that in a year the price increases are: bread 10%, milk 20%, and sugar 60%. Can we take a simple average of the three price rises and say inflation is 30%? The answer to that question is No, because bread and milk might be a very important part of people's spending with sugar being unimportant. A simple average would thus overstate the rate of inflation by assigning too much importance to the increase in the price of sugar. To find out the correct importance – or weights – of various items of expenditure a large sample of households is interviewed each year in Britain in the Family Expenditure Survey (FES). Weights for the retail price index for a 'typical' family are derived from this survey. While great care is taken in the construction of the retail price index it is nevertheless imperfect for several reasons.

(1) The information is not entirely accurate. For example it is known that the consumption of alcoholic beverages is greatly underestimated in the FES, perhaps because heavy drinkers are less likely to cooperate with the survey process.

(2) The RPI measures inflation faced by a 'typical' household and many households have different consumption patterns. For example non-smokers will be unaffected by an increase in tobacco prices, vegetarians are unaffected by increases in the price of meat, and council house tenants will be unaffected by increases in mortgage interest rates.

(3) The RPI does not include the effects of changes in taxes on living

standards although since 1979 the Government has published a tax and price index (TPI) which does include the effect of tax changes on living standards.

(4)   When some prices rise faster than others this change in relative prices will cause people to change their pattern of consumption. Thus the very rapid increase in oil prices in the 1970s caused many people to switch to other forms of heating. By changing expenditure patterns people reduce the impact that inflation has on them. The RPI thus overstates the importance of inflation. For this reason the weights in the RPI have to be revised from time to time.

Inflation refers to price changes during a particular period and it is now conventional in Britain to refer to the changes in prices over the previous 12 months as the inflation rate. The rate of inflation in Britain is shown in Table 5.1 and is presented graphically in Figures 1.1, 3.1 and 5.4.

Figure 5.4
Rate of inflation (end of year changes in the Retail Prices Index)

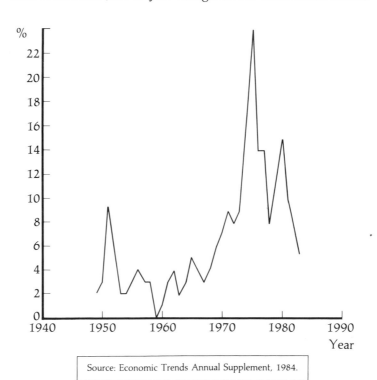

Source: Economic Trends Annual Supplement, 1984.

D   THE COSTS OF INFLATION

This chapter was drafted in Jerusalem in January 1983. When I arrived in Israel I had with me 95 Israeli pounds that my wife had kept after a trip to Israel in 1978. My first purchase was a copy of the *Jerusalem Post*, an English-language newspaper. It cost 22 sheqalim. The rate of inflation in Israel was then running at about 130% a year and between the two visits the currency had been reconstituted with 10 pound = 1 sheqalim. In terms of the old money the paper cost 220 pounds and my eight 10 pound notes and three 5 pound notes were practically useless. It is worth pausing a moment to think about the effects of inflation running at 130%. The *Jerusalem Post* cost me 22 sheqalim (about £0.41 at January 1983 exchange rates). If its price increases at 130% a year it will cost 1416 sheqalim in January 1988 (about £26.22 at January 1983 exchange rates) and 91,139 sheqalim in January 1993 (about £1688).

Although Israel had just fought a war with Lebanon and parts of the Israeli Army still occupied Lebanon the economy then gave the impression to the superficial observer of operating normally. What then are the costs of inflation?

Distributional costs

One of the most important costs of inflation are the **distributional costs**. People who are able to increase their nominal incomes as fast or faster than prices increase, gain at the expense of those that cannot. Sometimes the people who are the greatest losers are already vulnerable groups like the old, but in the UK the state pension and other state benefits are increased annually with inflation. Many private pensions are not indexed and amongst wage earners groups with low bargaining power often lose at the expense of those with high bargaining power. It is possible in principle to reduce this problem by indexing all wages but general indexing is not easy. How for example would the incomes of the self-employed be indexed?

Inflation can cause a redistribution of wealth as well if the prices of some assets rise fully with the general level of prices while others do not. If taxes are not indexed to adjust for inflation some taxes will increase in value – for example the income tax because of the falling real value of allowances, while others, like the taxes on cigarettes and alcohol, will decrease in real terms because some taxes on these goods are expressed as a nominal amount of money per unit.

People who borrow money will find that the real value of their debt falls while those who lend money find the real value of the loan falls. For example in the UK mortgage holders have gained at the expense of those who have saved with building societies. In Israel I met a Professor of Economics whose monthly mortgage payment was 32 sheqalim (a newspaper cost 22 sheqalim). His house was virtually being given to him.

In principle contracts can be indexed but this is not easy to achieve in practice. When inflation is very high even days matter, and at the very least there is the cost of specifying the contract.

Transactions costs

Perhaps most difficult of all to index is money. Money is continually losing its value and if inflation is high it is losing its value rapidly. This means that people have to incur **transactions costs** in order to economize on money balances. In Israel during my visit I noticed long queues at banks. Salaries there are indexed monthly but with inflation running at 10% a month one cannot afford to leave money in the bank. On pay day people – not just sophisticated financiers, but ordinary people – go to the bank and buy shares[2] and index-linked government securities. A week or two later when they need cash they have to go back to sell the securities. These costs are sometimes referred to as 'shoe leather' costs because of the costs of making many trips to the bank wearing out shoes. More important of course is the time involved and the commission one has to pay on the purchase and sale of securities.

Another different type of transactions costs is the process of actually marking up prices, sometimes referred to as the 'menu' costs. In Britain old style petrol pumps would not register a price above £1 a gallon and most garages had to fit new pumps. Coin-operated machines create a special difficulty because of the expense of altering the price and in Israel such machines have virtually disappeared, except for telephones which are operated by tokens which are sold at ever higher prices. While not wishing to overemphasize these costs, they are related to my next point which is the failure of price systems to allocate resources properly.

Allocative costs

In many Israeli supermarkets prices are not marked on many foods because it is too expensive to change them weekly or even more frequently. Instead a code is put on the goods. When the goods are taken to the checkout the attendant punches the code into the cash register which is linked to a

---

2.   The shares are not index linked; the most popular shares were bank shares which rose rapidly in price. Later in 1983 people lost confidence in bank shares. These shares then fell sharply in price.

computer which has the latest prices stored in it against the codes. It becomes very difficult to know the prices that one is paying which means that inflation has **allocative costs**. Prices change so rapidly that they become numbers with little real meaning. A Professor of Economics I met in Israel said he had been told the night before that he would be charged '2500 somethings' an hour by his architect for his house alterations. After the conversation he converted the '2500 somethings' into US$ on the assumption that 'somethings' were in fact sheqalim and found the charge was US$85 an hour which seemed excessive. This made him think perhaps the 'somethings' were the old Israeli pounds. His point was really that although he was paid in sheqalim they were losing value so fast he had to think in terms of a foreign currency. In these circumstances prices become much less efficient allocators of resources.

Uncertainty costs

If the rate at which prices rises was constant at 10% a year or even at 10% a month, it would be easier to adjust than if the rate of inflation varies. If the rate varies it becomes important to be able to predict the rate of inflation. For example businessmen considering an investment might be able to borrow money at 15% when the rate of inflation was 10%. It *appears* that the real rate of interest is 5%—that is the nominal 15% less the 10% inflation. However if he enters a contract on these terms and inflation falls to 6% the real interest has risen to 9%. The reaction to these **uncertainty costs** may be reluctance on the part of borrowers to borrow. Lenders have the opposite worry. If inflation is higher than they expect they lose. To protect themselves against this risk they may insist on *very* high nominal rates of interest. Thus the uncertainty may have a double effect on investment. First it may raise real interest rates – in order to provide a risk premium to lenders who fear that inflation will *rise*. Second it may reduce investment for a given real interest rate because borrowers may fear inflation will *fall*. The resulting investment may reduce the growth of productive capacity and stocks of goods may actually decline. The former will reduce future income growth and the latter can lead to inefficiency if, for example, stocks of spares are indequate.

Political costs

The greatest fear about inflation is that it will accelerate until it becomes hyperinflation and brings high **political costs** perhaps even political collapse. Hyperinflation simply means very rapid inflation which one expert has defined as prices rising by 50% or more *a month* for a period of 18 months or longer. When this happens the strains first on the economy and then on the social and political structure become immense. If the institutions of society cannot withstand these strains it may provide a breeding ground for political extremists as happened in Germany after the First World War.

Costs of moderate inflation

It is clear from the foregoing that high levels of inflation have very high costs associated with them. What about the costs of much more moderate rates of inflation? Even moderate rates of inflation have redistributional costs but if the rate of inflation were, say, 5% a year indexation would be relatively easy. Allocative costs would also be low. Uncertainty costs would probably remain. However if the rate of inflation were held constant at 5% for a number of years uncertainty costs would be likely to diminish. Low rates of inflation would have costs but these costs would probably be quite moderate. Against whatever costs remained one should set the possibility that low rates of inflation may prevent higher levels of output, and lower levels of unemployment. There is however a fundamental problem which is that it is not clear if it is possible to run an economy with a stable low level of inflation. The fear is that unless the rate of inflation is reduced it will continually accelerate.

E   COST-PUSH AND DEMAND-PULL INFLATION

Quite a lot will be said about the causes of inflation later in the book but we already have a model which provides a useful framework for analysis – our aggregate supply and demand curves.

Inflation – a sustained increase in prices – will naturally start with some initial change in the price level. If this process begins with a change on the supply side it is commonly referred to as cost-push inflation. **Cost-push inflation** refers to the initiation of an inflationary process by a shift in the aggregate supply curve. One possibility for this is an increase in money wages brought about by monopoly trade union power. In principle this fits the cost-inflation idea well but in practice it is usually difficult to sort out whether an overall wage increase starts an inflationary process or whether it is a reaction to a process of price increases which has already started. A clearer example of cost inflation is inflation started by an increase in the world market price of certain imported goods. The process of cost inflation can be illustrated in Figure 5.5 taking for illustrative purposes an increase in money wages. Suppose we start from a full employment position when the real wage is W_0/P_0, employment is H_0, output Y_0 and the price level P_0. Money wages are then increased to W_1 causing the AS curve to shift to AS_1.

Figure 5.5

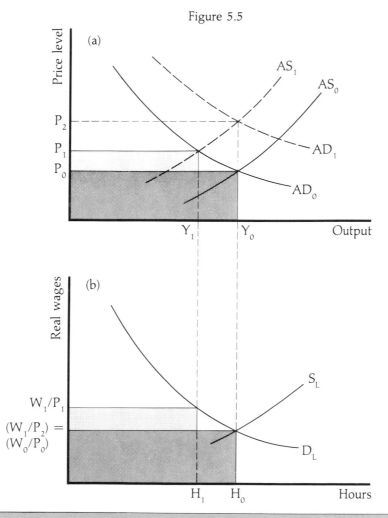

Cost-push inflation refers to an increase in costs that shifts the AS curve from AS_0 to AS_1 increasing prices to P_1. If AD is increased to AD_1 and money wages are again increased to compensate for the higher prices, an inflationary process is started.

This raises the price level to P_1. The increase in prices $(P_1 - P_0)$ will be less than the increase in wages $(W_1 - W_0)$ – in part because wages are only one component of costs. Because prices rise less than wages the new real wage (W_1/P_1) will be higher than the old (W_0/P_1) and employment is reduced to H_1. If the increase in unemployment leads government to expand aggregate demand (by increasing government spending or by cutting taxes) the AD will shift up to the right which will raise output back to Y_1 and prices to P_2. As the diagram is drawn this increase in prices reduces the real wage to $W_1/$

P_2 which is just sufficient to restore full employment. However unions may point to the fall in their real wage from W_1/P_1 to W_1/P_2 and call for a further increase in their money wage causing the AS curve to shift upwards. We have then an inflationary process started from the supply or cost side.

Exercise

Demand Pull Inflation refers to a start in the inflationary process started by a shift in the aggregate demand curve. The reader is asked to work out how demand pull inflation may arise. Start from a position such as that represented by the solid lines in Figure 5.5. Shift the AD curve up to the right and then ask yourself how unions will react to the fall in their real wages.

We have seen that cost-push and demand-pull inflation refer to the way in which an inflationary process starts. In both cases the process once started can continue with an inflationary spiral of increases in costs and prices.

F   INTRODUCTION TO POLICY IMPLICATIONS OF THE BASIC MODEL

A full discussion of policy will follow the extensions to the model to be made later in the book but it is useful to look at the implications of the basic model. It will be remembered from Chapter 1 (see Figures 1.2 and 1.3) that output can be raised and unemployment reduced by either increasing aggregate supply or by increasing aggregate demand. If aggregate demand is increased it will tend to increase prices as well as output, while if aggregate supply is raised it will tend to decrease prices (or reduce price increases) while employment is expanded. It is therefore a mistake to neglect the importance of shifting the aggregate supply curve. We introduce the discussion of policy in the context where it is assumed there is both inflation and unemployment.

Policies to shift the aggregate demand curve

We can shift the aggregate demand curve up to the right by increasing injections or decreasing leakages. Thus increases in investment, government expenditure or exports, or decreases in savings, taxes or imports will increase aggregate demand which as we have already seen (see Figure 1.2) will raise both prices and output. We are now in a position to examine the process by which this happens more carefully with the aid of Figure 5.6. The upper part of the figure shows desired leakages and injections determining output at a given level of prices (see Chapter 3). The middle part of the figure shows aggregate demand and supply determining the levels of output and prices simultaneously. The lower part of the diagram shows the labour market (see Chapter 4). The initial position of equilibrium is shown by the solid lines with the equilibrium points marked A. It can be seen in the bottom part of the figure that the level of employment H_0 is assumed to be well below the full employment level.

Figure 5.6

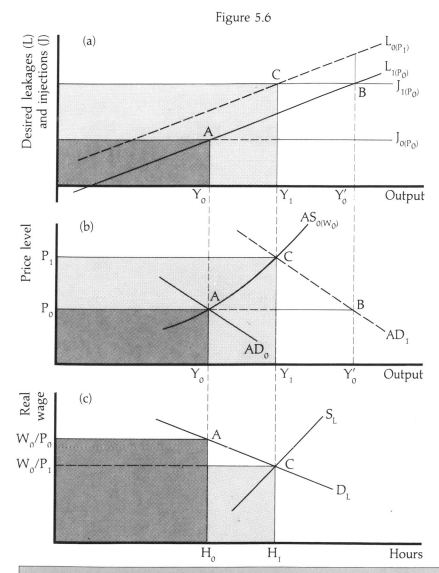

An increase in injections shown in part (a) shifts the aggregate demand curve in part (b) leading to the price level increasing to P_1 and output rising to Y_1. In part (c) higher prices reduce the real wage to W_0/P_1 and employment rises to H_1. This higher price level is also associated (see part (a)) with increased leakages to $L_{0(P_1)}$ because, for example, real balances are lower.

Suppose the government were to decide it wished to eliminate unemployment by increasing the levels of its own expenditure. Knowing how much extra expenditure would in practice be required would be a formidable task in itself, which is not discussed until Part II. For the time being it is simply assumed that government expenditure is increased sufficiently to raise injections to J_1 *at the initial level of prices*. If prices did not change the equilibrium level of output would rise to Y_0^1. The intersection of L_0 and J_1 is labelled B in the upper part of Figure 5.6. This means that the new aggregate demand curve AD_1 passes through the point labelled B in the middle part of the figure. Note that B in the middle part of the figure is associated with a higher level of output Y_0^1 and the original level of prices P_0. The points labelled B are *not* equilibrium points because in the middle part of the figure B does not lie where the AS and AD curves intersect. With the new aggregate demand curve AD_1 the new equilibrium is at the points labelled C. In the middle part of the diagram output and prices are determined at Y_1 and P_1 respectively. With the higher price level P_1 leakages rise to $L_{0(P_1)}$. (You should remember from Part B of this chapter that the increase in leakages associated with a price rise is part of the reason that the aggregate demand curve has a negative slope.) In the labour market shown in the bottom part of the figure the rise in prices to P_1 has reduced the real wage from W_0/P_0 to W_0/P_1 enabling employment to rise from H_0 to H_1.

Policies to shift both the aggregate supply and demand curves

Some of the policies that cause the aggregate demand curve to shift to the right will also cause the aggregate supply curve to shift to the right. A decrease in taxation *might* not only increase aggregate demand but also increase aggregate supply by increasing the supply of labour. There is not a lot of hard evidence that cuts in taxation will increase labour supply but because of the attention this method has received on both sides of the Atlantic it may be worth exploring one way[3] the mechanism could work. The story starts as before with aggregate demand being raised from AD_0 to AD_1. Now, however, the cut in taxes is assumed to increase the supply of labour. People are willing to do more work for the same gross wage so that both the labour supply curve in part (b) and the aggregate supply curve in part (a) shift to the right. Without the change in aggregate supply the economy would have gone from A to B in both Figure 5.7(a) and 5.7(b). With the supply effect it instead goes to C where output is higher and prices lower than at B.

A more soundly based policy to shift both AS and AD curves is an increase in investment. As a component of injections an increase in

3.   Tax cuts will raise the net of tax wage and so could in special circumstances cause a movement along the labour supply curve.

Figure 5.7

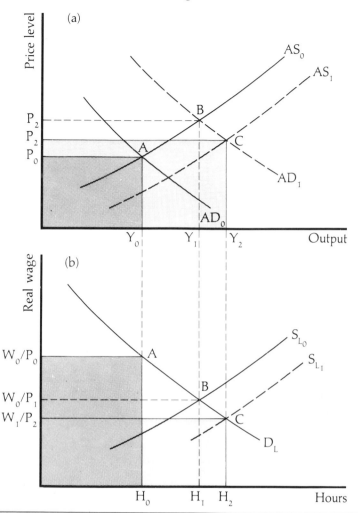

Policies that shift the aggregate demand curve alone will move the economy from A to B. Policies that increase labour supply will shift the aggregate supply curve, and will move the economy to C rather than B. The result is higher output and lower prices. Evidence for this effect is weak.

investment will shift the AD curve. It will probably also (1) raise capacity output, (2) increase the marginal physical product of labour which increases the demand for labour, (3) reduce non-labour costs by, for example, making it possible to use cheaper components e.g. chips rather than transistors or valves. The argument is illustrated in Figure 5.8. The increase in investment raises aggregate demand which shifts the economy from the points labelled

Figure 5.8

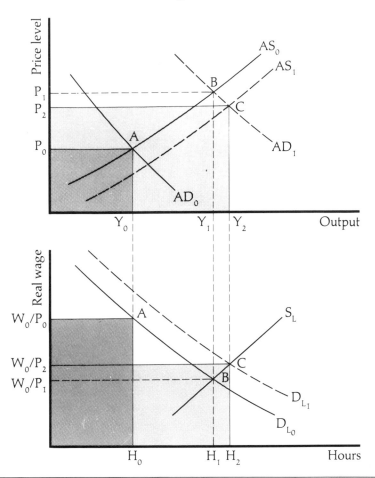

Increases in investment increase both AD and (after a lag) AS. The inclusion of the supply effects means that the economy moves from A to C rather than from A to B. It can be seen that this means higher output, higher real wages and lower prices.

A to those labelled B. In addition however investment also raises aggregate supply – although perhaps only after a lag while new factories are built and/or new machines installed. The effect of the increase in supply is to move the economy to the Cs rather than to the Bs with higher output, higher real income and lower prices. Extra investment will increase the size of the capital stock and this *may* increase the demand for labour shifting the demand for labour to D_{L_I}.

Probably one of the most important reasons for the relatively low growth of productive capacity in postwar Britain has been the neglect of the effects of investment in increasing aggregate supply. It has been easier – for reasons of timing in the budgeting year[4] – and for short-term popularity to concentrate increases in aggregate demand on personal consumption rather than on investment.

Policies to shift the aggregate supply curve

The aggregate supply can be shifted down to the right – or can be prevented from shifting up to the left by policies designed to

(1)   Decrease frictional unemploument – by for example better information about vacancies.

(2)   Decrease structural unemployment by changing relative wages to encourage people to leave old industries in depressed areas for more prosperous industries in expanding areas or by providing facilities and grants for retraining for the skills needed by expanding industries.

(3)   Reduce costs. Costs can be reduced (a) by the more efficient use of resources by, for example, cutting out waste of raw materials, reducing overmanning, ending restrictive practices, and reducing breakdowns of equipment, or (b) by reducing the cost of resources by holding down increases in prices of factors of production.

The most common form of this policy is of course wages or incomes policies. If workers can be persuaded to have a small increase in wages the AS curve will not shift so far up to the left. If the increase in money wages were kept

---

4.   J. C. R. Dow in the standard work on British policy in the immediate postwar period put it as follows:

Keynesian principles of budgeting require that government revenue should be determined not merely in the light of the government's own expenditure, but so as to keep the economy as a whole in balance. The aim may be defined as reducing private expenditure (by raising taxes) when total prospective demand looks like exceeding the capacity of the economy to produce; or stimulating it (by reducing taxes) when it looks like being deficient. . . . The system of forecasting which has been developed to meet this need has therefore to provide forecasts of all the main items in the national accounts . . . the procedure of official forecasting is designed to fit in with the procedure of budget-making. The forecasts are prepared around the turn of the year for the ensuing year . . . investment expenditure, like government expenditure, is treated in the forecasts as being already determined. Consumption is thus the main variable element; taxation the main instrument by which it may be varied.

J. C. R. Dow, *The Management of the British Economy 1945-1960*, Cambridge University Press, 1965, p. 181.

equal to the increase in productivity the AS curve would not shift up at all.

One of the fundamental problems in economic policy is the reconciliation of (2) and (3) above. To reduce structural unemployment we need flexible relative wages. Given that it is very difficult indeed to persuade workers to take a cut in their money wages this means in practice that some workers should have larger increases in money wages than others. Workers in declining industries are unlikely to like losing their place in the wage hierarchy so they also press for high wage increases. The result is both to perpetuate structural unemployment and fuel inflation.

A much fuller discussion of policy is included in Chapters 12, 13 and 17 after we have examined some extensions to the basic model.

CONCEPTS FOR REVIEW

QUESTIONS FOR DISCUSSION

1   Why is the aggregate supply curve unlikely to be perfectly elastic?

2   Why does the aggregate demand curve slope downwards from left to right?

3   What are the likely costs of
    (a) a high rate of inflation
    (b) a constant low rate of inflation?

4   Why is the retail price index an imperfect measure of inflation?

5   Explain how each of the following would affect *the position of* aggregate supply or aggregate demand curves (each event to be considered separately).
     (a) An increase in investment leading to an increase in the capital stock.
     (b) A change in technology which permits more to be produced from the same capital stock.
     (c) An increase in the efficiency with which the capital stock is used.
     (d) An increase in the money wage (consider effects on aggregate supply only).

PART II
EXTENDING THE BASIC FRAMEWORK

6

Consumption and Savings

The purpose of Part II is to extend the model developed in Part I and to examine how it can be used to discuss policy. We examine the determinants of savings (and consumption) and investment; the role of financial institutions in determining the quantity of money and how money influences output and the price level; and examine the problems involved in using government fiscal (tax and expenditure) policy, monetary policy, and labour market policy to control levels of aggregate demand and aggregate supply.

In this chapter the determinants of consumption and savings are examined more closely. In Chapter 3 savings were assumed to increase with income which implies that consumption also increases with income, as is explained in section A. In section B we look at two kinds of evidence about the relationship between consumption and income. This evidence appears at first sight to be contradictory. In section C hypotheses for reconciling the two kinds of evidence are examined and then in section D other influences on consumption are explored.

A SAVINGS AND CONSUMPTION

The relationship between savings and consumption is easiest to see in a model where savings is the only leakage, and investment the only injection. In this model income is the sum of consumption and savings

$$Y = C + S$$

When Y is constant if C goes up, S goes down by the same amount. We can therefore talk interchangeably about the determinants of savings and consumption. In fact economists usually define savings as a residual that is $S = Y - C$. Savings is that part of income that is not spent on current goods.

139

B   CONSUMPTION AND INCOME

One of Keynes' main contributions to economics was to draw attention to the relationship between consumption and income. He wrote:

> The psychology of the community is such that when aggregate real income is increased aggregate consumption is increased, but not by so much as income.
>   J. M. Keynes, *The General Theory of Employment, Interest and Money*, Macmillan, 1936, p27.

This means, of course, that both consumption and savings will increase as income increases. Does the evidence bear out Keynes' view on the psychology of the community? Since the *General Theory* was written a lot of evidence on the relationship between income and consumption has been produced and it does largely bear out Keynes' views. However, there are two rather different ways of looking at the relationship between consumption and income, and these two ways appear at first sight to be inconsistent.

Cross-section consumption functions

One way of looking at the relationship between consumption and income – the consumption function – is called cross-section consumption function and the other is called time series consumption function. A **cross section consumption function** shows the relationship between consumption and income at a particular time. At any one time (say in one year) the total level of income (GNP) in the economy is given. However, there are of course households in the economy with various levels of income. In a cross section consumption function we examine the relationship between consumption and household income at a fixed point in time. Data for cross section consumption functions in the UK are collected in the *Family Expenditure Survey* (which is also used to collect weights for the retail price index – see Chapter 5), and the cross section consumption function for the UK for 1981 is plotted in Figure 6.1. Weekly income is plotted on the horizontal axis and weekly expenditure (consumption) on the vertical axis. The 45° line is a line on which expenditure is equal to income. Points above the 45° line represent expenditure above income and points below the 45° line represent expenditure below income. It can be seen that when weekly income is very low, consumption equals or exceeds total income and that when income is higher expenditure (consumption) is below income. You may want to ask: How is it possible for households to consume more than their income? There are in fact several ways. People can spend money they saved in the past which is sometimes called dissaving. Many people with low incomes are

Figure 6.1

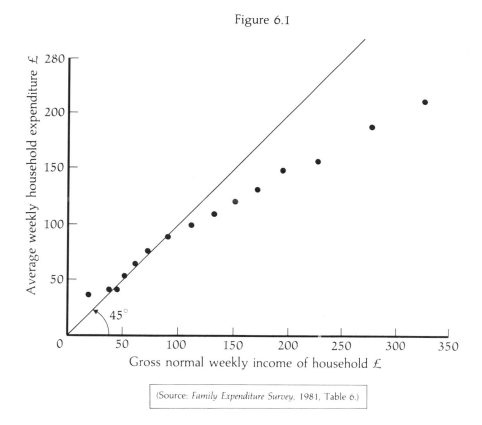

(Source: *Family Expenditure Survey*, 1981, Table 6.)

retired and they may have saved in order to be able to spend more than their pension after retirement. Another way of spending more than one's income is to go into debt. This is common amongst people who are frictionally unemployed, students and others who hope their future income will rise. People who are in long-term poverty may also try to get into debt in many cases but their ability to borrow is likely to be limited.

The marginal propensity to consume

It is clear from Figure 6.1 that as income rises so does consumption. However, it is also important to know how consumption will change if income changes. **The marginal propensity to consume** c is the change in consumption for a small change in income. In symbols $c = \Delta C / \Delta Y$ where ΔC is the change in consumption and ΔY is the change in income. Suppose that initially income is £200 a week and consumption is £180 a week. The **average propensity to consume** which is total consumption divided by total income ($= C/Y$) is 0.9. Suppose that income then rises to £210 a week and that consumption rises to £188. What is the marginal propensity to consume? It is $(188-180)/(210-200) = 8/10$ or 0.8. In this example the marginal propensity to consume is 0.8 which is less than the average propensity to consume (= 0.9).

Figures 6.2 and 6.3 illustrate two possible shapes for cross section consumption functions. In Figure 6.2 the marginal propensity to consume is constant and the consumption function is a straight line. In Figure 6.3 the marginal propensity to consume is falling as income rises; the consumption

Figure 6.2

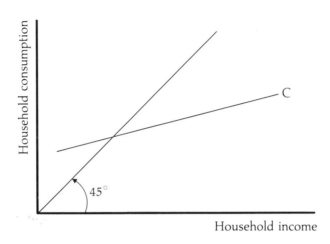

A cross section consumption will be a straight line if the marginal propensity to consume is the same at all levels of income.

Figure 6.3

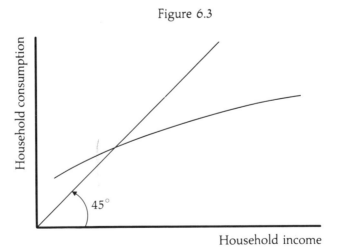

If the marginal propensity to consume falls as income rises the cross section consumption will be a curved line.

function is a curved line. Both of these shapes are consistent with Keynes' view quoted earlier.

Why the shape of the consumption function is important

Why does it matter which shape the short-period consumption function takes? It matters because if the consumption function is like Figure 6.2, a redistribution of income between rich households and poor will not affect total consumption. Thus if we take £10 from a rich household, that household's consumption may fall by say £8. If we give that income to a poor household, that household's income will rise by £10 and if the poor household has the same c, its consumption will rise by 8, leaving total consumption unchanged. Suppose on the other hand that rich households have a lower c than poor households. If we take £10 from a rich household with $c = 0.6$ and give it to a poor household with $c = 0.9$, then total consumption will rise by 3 $(= -6 + 9)$. That is important if we are considering the redistribution of income brought about either through changes in taxes or social security or a change brought about by an alteration of the distribution of income between profits and labour. If profits tend to go to high income households and wage income to low income households and if high income households have a lower c, then a rising share of profits will affect consumption.

Time series consumption function

The other main type of consumption function is the time series consumption function. In a **time series consumption function** the relationship between total consumption and total income is compared at various points of time. Thus in a time series consumption function all households, rich and poor, are grouped together each period. Figure 6.4 shows the relationship between consumption and GNP in post-war Britain. It can be seen that this time series consumption function, unlike the cross section consumption functions in Figures 6.1 to 6.3, lies below the 45° line at all points.

C   RECONCILIATION OF CROSS SECTION AND TIME SERIES CONSUMPTION FUNCTIONS

There appears to be a possible inconsistency between the cross section and time series consumption functions. We might start by supposing we could use the cross section data to predict what would happen over time. Over time as real incomes rise, we might expect that when the poor of period 1

F

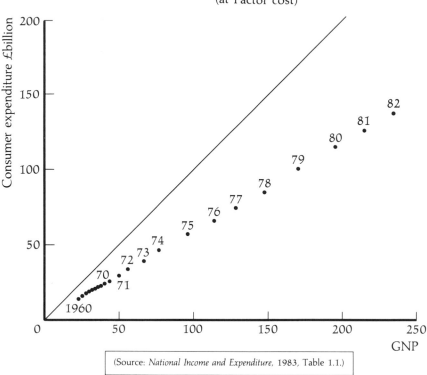

Figure 6.4   Gross national product by category of expenditure
(at Factor cost)

(Source: *National Income and Expenditure*, 1983, Table 1.1.)

become better off in period 2 they would behave like the better-off people behaved in period 1. If one examines the cross section consumption functions, this would imply a very large increase in the savings ratio – much more than the increase in the savings ratio shown in Figure 6.4. Why has that large increase in the savings ratio not occurred? Some of the reasons economists have suggested are discussed below.

Relative income hypothesis

The **relative income hypothesis** suggests that consumption will depend not only on current income but also (a) on one's position in the income distribution – a keeping up with the Joneses argument, and (b) on one's own immediate past income. James Duesenberry, the author of the relative income hypothesis, referred to US budget studies of whites and blacks. At any given level of income the blacks saved more than the whites. As blacks were on average poorer than whites this meant that for any given level of income blacks were higher up the (black) income distribution. Blacks' savings and consumption decisions thus depended on the position in the black income distribution while white consumption depended on the position of an

Figure 6.5

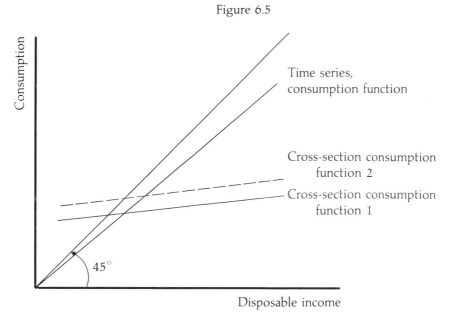

The relative income hypothesis suggests that the time series consumption function is traced out by the cross section consumption function shifting upwards. It shifts upwards because higher incomes increase expectations about consumption and because of the difficulties of reducing consumption when income falls.

individual white in the white income distribution. If everyone in a group gets better off in a way that does not affect the distribution of income the whole cross section consumption function will shift upwards tracing out a time series consumption function as in Figure 6.5.

Duesenberry also noted that the average propensity to consume tended to fall when incomes were rising and to rise when incomes were falling. He hypothesized that consumption was influenced by the previous peak income. If income was above the previous peak households would save to build up their assets. If income fell people would sell assets so as to maintain their consumption near to its previous levels.

Permanent income hypothesis

The permanent income hypothesis is an attempt by Milton Friedman to reconcile the different data by suggesting that consumption is influenced only by permanent income. Permanent income is the income one *expects* to have permanently. One's actual income at any point in time may be either above or below one's permanent income. If one had an unexpected bonus, actual income would be above permanent income, and if one had unexpectedly been put temporarily on short time, actual income would be below permanent income. In the **permanent income hypothesis** it is assumed that transitory elements in income do not influence consumption unless they change a person's view as to what his permanent income will be. Because short period income will contain quite a lot of transitory elements (which do not influence consumption), the short period consumption function will be much flatter than the long period one. Figure 6.6 illustrates this. The relationship between permanent income and consumption is given by the line C_p but the actual consumption function that is measured is C_M. If permanent income is A, consumption is C_{P1} as can be seen by going to A' on C_p and then over to C_{P1} on the vertical axis. However, if transitory income is positive, measured income is B. Going up to the measured consumption function C_M at B' again gives consumption of C_{P1} because the transitory element in income (AB) has no influence on consumption. The reader should satisfy himself that a similar argument applies when transitory income is negative.

Figure 6.6

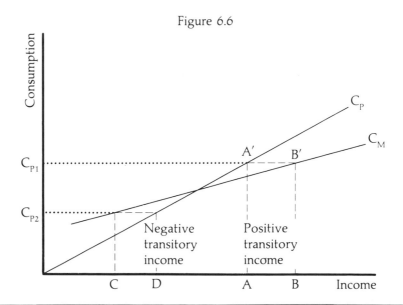

The permanent income hypothesis suggests that consumption is entirely determined by permanent income. Positive (AB) or negative (CD) transitory income affect measured income and consumption. In the long period transitory elements in income will be smaller so that the time series consumption function will be steeper than the cross section consumption function.

Life cycle hypothesis

The **life cycle hypothesis** is an attempt by Franco Modigliani and others to explain consumption in terms of people's position in the life cycle. People's income typically rises during their early working years, then reaches a plateau in middle age before dropping suddenly at retirement. Young people often wish to spend a high proportion of their income to establish their own homes and to provide for young children. Middle-aged people have often completed establishing their homes and their children may have left home. They may therefore wish to save a much larger proportion of their income in order to provide for retirement. As a result the average propensity to consume (= C/Y) of middle aged people will be much lower than the average propensity to consume of the young. Retired people – like the young – will have a high average propensity to consume. Retired people will consume more – for a given income – than the middle-aged, both because their income has fallen and because they can live on the assets they saved in their middle years. These relationships are shown in Figure 6.7. The consumption

Figure 6.7

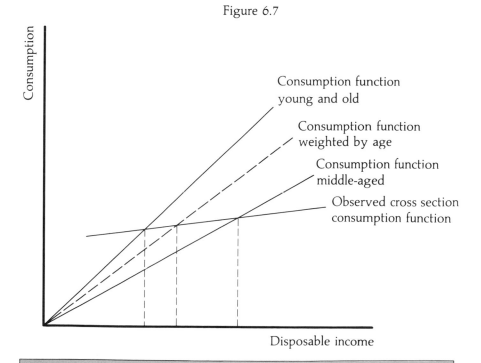

The life cycle hypothesis reconciles cross section and time series data by noting that the middle-aged tend *both* to have higher incomes than the young and the old and to have a lower apc.

functions of the young and old are relatively steep because they have a high apc. The consumption function of the middle aged is much flatter because their apc is lower. The middle aged have higher average incomes. As a result when a sample of households are selected in a cross section study those with high incomes will tend to be the middle aged who consume a lower proportion of their income. Those with low incomes, who tend to be the young and the old will consume a higher proportion of their income.

D   OTHER INFLUENCES ON CONSUMPTION

Income is the most important but not the only influence on consumption. In this section we look at real wealth and the rate of interest as determinants of consumption.

Real wealth and consumption

At one point in time when prices are given, it seems reasonable to imagine that people with high wealth consume more for a given level of income than people with low wealth. Suppose, for example, we have two people who are due to retire in 5 years. Both have an income of £8000 a year. Person A has a non-contributory inflation-proofed pension in addition to the state pension, while B has the state pension alone. It seems likely that A will consume more than B because B is likely to be concerned by the drop in his income in 5 years' time. To protect himself from that drop in income he may wish to save now.

How will this relationship between wealth and consumption be influenced by changes in the price level? We have seen in Chapter 5 that price rises reduce debt which is denominated in money terms so that borrowers (e.g. mortgage holders) have a gain in real wealth while lenders (e.g. building society depositors) have a loss in real wealth. The greater wealth of borrowers of course cancels out the smaller wealth of lenders so that total wealth is unaffected. We can therefore ignore this effect of price changes on consumption.[1]

If the price level goes up, the price of at least some of our assets will go up as well. The prices of some assets may rise faster than inflation. House prices, for example, over much of the post-war period rose faster than inflation in the UK. Prices of other assets may rise rather less than changes in the general price level. One type of asset – net money balances – does not increase in price at all. The result is that increases in prices reduce the real value of net

---

1.   Provided that borrowers and lenders react in the same way to a change in their wealth.

wealth including money balances. The reduction in the real value of net wealth reduces consumption (raises savings). The increase in savings means total leakages are higher and aggregate demand lower. It will be remembered that this **real balance effect** is part of the explanation of the shape of the aggregate demand curve.

Consumption, savings and interest rates

In this section the connection between savings (or consumption) and the rate of interest is examined. Will people wish to save more if the rate of interest is raised? It is clear that interest rates do significantly influence the choice of savings method. If building societies are paying higher interest rates than banks or national savings, people will tend to switch their savings into building societies, but if building society rates are not competitive savers will be attracted to other methods of savings. However, the question I want to explore here is how interest rates may affect the total amount of saving that is done.

   You may remember that when the relationship between wages and labour supply was discussed in Chapter 4 it emerged that the net effect depended on the balance between income and substitution effects. Similarly the relationship between interest rates and savings also depends on the balance between income and substitution effects. The argument is easiest to see if inflation is assumed away. Suppose an individual has £1000 in savings at the start of the year. If the interest rate is 5% he will have £1050 at the end of the year. However, if the interest rate is 10% he will have £1100 at the end of the year. With interest at 10% his net wealth is higher – he is better off – and it has been argued in the section above that if real wealth is higher, spending will be higher – savings less. This is the income effect. As interest rates rise the **income effect** will reduce savings. However if interest rates rise from 5% to 10% the saver will gain more by refraining from immediate consumption. This means there is a **substitution effect** of the higher interest rate that leads to higher saving. In Figure 6.8 savings is plotted on the horizontal axis and the rate of interest on the vertical axis. In part (a) the substitution affect is stronger than the income effect so that increase in the interest rate from i_0 to i_1 raises savings from S_0 to S_1. In contrast to part (b) the income affect is stronger than the substitution effect so that an increase in the interest rate reduces savings from S_0 to S_1.

Real balances, interest rates, savings and labour supply

People's decisions about savings (consumption) involve changing the amount of wealth including real balances that they hold. These decisions will

Figure 6.8

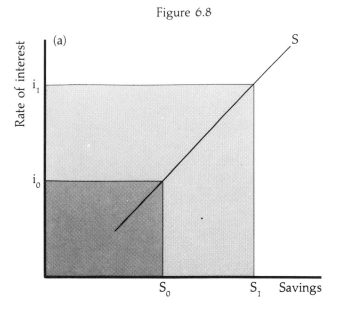

If the substitution effect of higher interest rates outweighs the income effect, raising the interest rate from i_0 to i_1 will raise savings from S_0 to S_1.

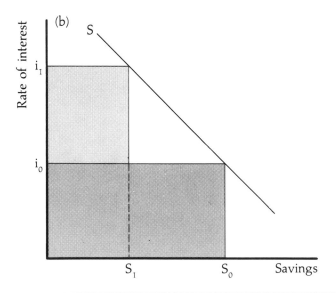

If the income effect of higher interest rates outweighs the substitution effect, raising the interest rate from i_0 to i_1 will reduce savings from S_0 to S_1.

also be related to decisions about labour supply, as we saw in Chapter 4. We may wish to increase work in order to be able to consume more or to be able to save more – or both. Changes in interest rates or in prices can thus change both consumption (savings) decisions and decisions about labour supply.

CONCEPTS FOR REVIEW

	page nos.
average propensity to consume	141
cross section consumption function	140
income effect (on savings)	149
life cycle hypothesis	147
marginal propensity to consume	141
permanent income hypothesis	146
real balance effect	149
relative income hypothesis	144
substitution effect (on savings)	149
time series consumption function	143

QUESTIONS FOR DISCUSSION

1   Is it possible for (a) some households, (b) a whole nation to have consumption that is higher than income?

2   What will happen to total consumption if income is redistributed by taking away income from high income households and giving the same amount of income to low income households?

3   How can one reconcile data from cross section and time series consumption functions?

4   What factors other than income are important in explaining consumption?

5   Will an increase in interest rates cause total savings to rise or fall?

7

Money and the Commercial Banking System

This chapter considers the nature and functions of money and the economic role of commercial banks. As is implied by the word 'commercial' commercial banks are in business to make profits for their shareholders. What separates commercial banks from other commercial firms is that the main liability of banks is money. It is for this reason and because banks can create money, that commercial banks are considered in a book on macro- economics. This chapter looks first at the nature and functions of money and then at banks and their role in the creation of money. In the next chapter we examine the role of central banks – concentrating on how they can influence the stock of money and we are thus in a position to examine the role of money in the economy.

A   MONEY

Before looking at the role of commercial banks we should consider the nature and functions of money. The main functions of money are to act as (1) a medium of exchange, (2) a unit of account, (3) a unit of quotation, (4) a standard of deferred payments and (5) a store of value. We look at these in turn and then consider the question of what we should include in a formal definition of money.

Medium of exchange

Money is used to pay for goods and services. If we have something to sell – perhaps goods or the services of our labour, we are paid in money and we can use this money to purchase other goods and services. If we did not have something to act as a **medium of exchange** we would have to barter, as used to happen in some subsistence economies.

Barter

If a farmer has a surplus of one commodity and wants to exchange this surplus for one or more other commodities it is possible to do this direct exchange by **barter**. Suppose we have a farmer who has an extra cow and wants to buy some cooking pots. He has an immediate problem. Unless he wants a lot of cooking pots he will find that he is getting poor value for his cow. Perhaps instead he will decide to exchange a goat. In the market he has to find someone who (a) has cooking pots for sale and (b) wants a goat. This is termed the **double coincidence of wants** and is a major inefficiency of the barter system. Clearly it is very much more convenient for the farmer to be able to sell his goat to person A and receive for it something that he can use to purchase his cooking pots from person B. This 'something' is then acting as a medium of exchange, that is to say it has become money. Table 7.1 contains a partial list of things that have been used as money.

TABLE 7.1   A PARTIAL LIST OF KINDS OF MONEY

beer	cowry shells	leather	sheep
boar tusks	debts of individuals	nickel	silver
boats	debts of banks	paper	slaves
brass	debts of government	pasteboard	stone
bronze	electrum	pigs	tea
cattle	goats	pitch	tobacco
chickens	gold	playing cards	tortoise shell
chocolate	hoes	porcelain	wampum
cigarettes	horses	porpoise teeth	whale teeth
clay	iron	pots	wine
copper	knives	rice	woodpecker scalps
corn	lead	salt	wool

Source: Based on L. V. Chandler, *The Economics of Money and Banking* New York, Harper and Brothers, 1948, Table 2, p. 49.

Unit of account

Money can be used as a basis for accounting. In the national accounts we use money as a way of adding up diverse products like cows, goats and cooking pots. Firms and households also use money as a **unit of account** in their budgeting decisions.

Unit of quotation

Money also acts as a **unit of quotation**. We can price things in terms of cowry shells or cigarettes or $US or £sterling. If the farmer's goat was worth 100 cowry shells, and a cooking pot was worth 25 cowry shells, then we know that four cooking pots have the same value as one goat. When prices are fixed an enormous amount of time is also saved in buying and selling. I once spent 3 hours buying a carpet from a trader in Nigeria. The original asking price was £48 and I eventually paid £12 only to discover I could have purchased an identical carpet in a store for £10!

It is money's use as a unit of quotation that gives rise to the possibility of money illusion. Money illusion arises when people fail to take the significance of price level changes fully into account. An example of money illusion (discussed in Part I) is people believing they are better off when their money wage goes up when prices go up by the same proportion.

Standard of deferred payment

With money we have a basis not only for making current sales and purchases but also a **standard of deferred payment** that we can use in expressing contracts over time. A dowry can be expressed as so many cows to be delivered on the date of the wedding, a mortgage as £X payable after 20 years, etc.

Store of value

Money may also be able to act as a **store of value**. If money exists the farmer who wanted to sell a cow and to buy a few pots has a way forward. He sells the cow for money – perhaps a number of brass rods of known weight. He then uses a few of the rods to buy his pots and keeps the remainder to make later purchases. In an inflationary period one of the costs is that money becomes less useful – and when inflation is very high money becomes useless as a store of value, because its purchasing power is declining.

Definition of money

Having considered the functions of money we now have to address ourselves to a more formal definition of **money**. Table 7.1 contained a long list of things that have served as money. Why were these things accepted as money? The answer is entirely circular: they were accepted as money because they were accepted as money. People are willing to accept payment in money because they believe that other people are also willing to accept payment in that money.

Some of the things in Table 7.1 such as cows and wine have an intrinsic value. If no one is willing to accept your cow you can always eat it! As money has developed its intrinsic value has become less and less important. When metal was used as money it became common for the sovereign to stamp bits of metal as a guarantee that the metal was of a particular weight. This did not prevent attempts being made to pare off bits of the metal (which is why many coins came to be given a milled edge). Most of the things listed in Table 7.1 suffer from one or more of the following disadvantages: (1) they are hard to divide into small units (e.g. a cow); (2) they are perishable (the living creatures); (3) they are heavy (stone, metal) and difficult and dangerous (because of risk of robbery) to transport. It came to be recognized that many of these disadvantages could be overcome by the use of token money. Instead of carrying around heavy bags of metal (say, gold or silver coins) the bags of metal could be left with a goldsmith who would give a receipt for the metal. Now the original owner of the receipt for the gold or silver might find it inconvenient to exchange the receipt for the precious metal – particularly if he was going on a long journey. Instead of handing over gold or silver when he wanted to make a purchase he would hand over his receipt. This evolved into the currency we use today. The metal used in modern coins is worth less than their face value and of course the intrinsic value of a bank note is practically nothing. The vestigial remains of the idea of warehouse receipts remains in that bank notes have a solemn pledge on them that the central bank – The Bank of England in Britain – 'promise to pay the bearer on demand the sum of one pound'. An American once wrote to the Secretary of the US Treasury demanding $10 in exchange for a $10 bill which said on it that it was 'redeemable in lawful money'. An amusing exchange of letters[1] took place ending with a letter from the Treasury saying that 'lawful money' had not been defined in legislation.

It is fairly obvious that currency – that is notes and coins – should be considered part of the formal definition of money. But of course in a modern society currency never changes hands for many transactions, especially ones of high value. Large transactions are usually settled by the transfer of bank deposits from one person's ownership to another person's ownership. The transfer may take place because a cheque has been written instructing the bank to pay a certain sum to a specified person, or the transfer may use a bank giro or a credit card or bankers' order or direct debit. This suggests that bank deposits should be included in the formal definition of money. Now some bank accounts – called current accounts – can be converted into currency on demand, while for others there may be a waiting period of a few days, weeks or months. Building society deposits have some of the characteristics of bank deposits. In addition there are a whole variety of other assets which have some of the characteristics of money. For this reason there is no entirely

1.   'A dollar is a dollar is a dollar', in L.S. Ritter (ed.), *Money and Economic Activity*, Cambridge Mass: Houghton Mifflin, 1952.

logical dividing line between what is and what is not money. For our purposes we can define **money** as currency plus bank deposits. This is a deliberately slightly vague definition for it does not specify whether all bank deposits are part of the money stock or only some of them. Because of this difficulty in finding a uniquely correct way of defining money the Government publishes several series which differ in the range of deposits included. In looking at Table 7.1 you may have been struck by the terms debts of individuals, banks and governments. An example of a debt of an individual is the goldsmith's receipt for a bag of gold coins. Bank deposits are debts of commercial banks – because the bank has an obligation to repay us the money. Currency is normally the debt of governments.

B   THE COMMERCIAL BANKING SYSTEM

Stylized banking history

Commercial banks as we know them today grew out of the activities of goldsmiths and silversmiths. We have already seen that people found it inconvenient and dangerous to carry around large amounts of precious metals and they would deposit these metals with goldsmiths and silversmiths for safe keeping, receiving a receipt in exchange. Goldsmiths had a strong room for storing their own gold and silver where they also stored their customers' gold and silver. It became apparent that the customers did not mind whether or not they received back the actual coins that had been left for safe keeping. What customers were concerned about was the weight and value of the gold and silver. It also became apparent that not all the people who deposited money with goldsmiths would want it back at the same time. This meant that a lot of the gold and silver would sit in strong rooms serving no useful purpose – except to be there in the extremely unlikely event that all the customers wanted their money back at the same time. The goldsmiths learned that they could safely lend part of the gold left with them for safe keeping. This constituted a significant step in the goldsmith becoming a bank.

Balance sheets of commercial banks

We have seen that commercial banks have dual responsibilities: to their shareholders to make profits and to their customers who have deposited money with them. The money that is deposited with commercial banks is their main liability and the management of the corresponding assets is a large part of what commercial banking is all about. If commercial banks did not have to worry about being able to repay their depositors whenever the

Figure 7.1

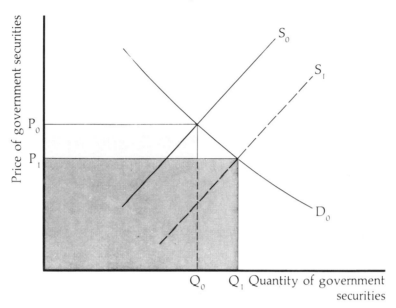

If banks have to sell government securities for cash to meet the needs of its depositors, supply will be increased from S_0 to S_1 and the price will fall from P_0 to P_1. To prevent this loss banks are reluctant to hold government securities unless they are scheduled to be repaid at full value in the near future.

depositors wanted, they would be able to think entirely about making money for their shareholders. This would lead bankers into putting most of their assets into long-term forms such as long-dated government securities or loans to business. The difficulty with an overemphasis on long-term assets is that if an unexpectedly large number of customers wanted to exchange their bank deposits for currency the banks would have difficulty. If a bank wanted to dispose of long-dated government securities in a hurry it could always do so but the price might be very unattractive – particularly if several banks were experiencing difficulty at the same time and all were trying to sell at the same time. During the period that the banks were reducing their stock of securities the flow of securities on to the market would increase. This increase in supply would reduce price as can be seen with the aid of Figure 7.1. With the initial supply and demand for government securities represented by S_0 and D_0 the price is P_0. If banks were faced with a sudden need for currency the supply would increase to S_1 and the price would fall to P_1.

The problem with long-term loans to businesses may be even greater. If firms were suddenly asked to repay long-term loans most would find it

TABLE 7.2   BRITISH RETAIL BANKS SIMPLIFIED BALANCE SHEET as at 16 November 1983

Liabilities	£m	Percentage sterling deposits
Sterling deposits	88,449	100
(of which sight deposits 32418)		(36.7)
Other currency deposits	28,849	32.6
Total deposits	117,298	132.6
Capital and other liabilities	18,613	21.0
Total liabilities	135,911	153.7

Assets	£m	Percentage sterling deposits
Sterling assets		
Notes and coin	1654	1.9
Balances with Bank of England	501	0.6
Market loans:		
Secured money with LDMA	3470	3.9
Other UK monetary sector (including unsecured money with LDMA)	9654	10.9
Other	3959	4.5
Bills: Treasury	293	0.3
Other	2485	2.8
Total advances	62,707	70.9
Banking department lending to central government (net)	451	0.6
Investments:		
British government stocks	5417	6.1
Other	3241	3.7
Other currency assets:		
Market loans	29,028	32.8
Bills	59	0.1
Investments	1459	1.6
Sterling and other currencies:		
Miscellaneous assets	11,533	13.0
Total assets	135,911	153.7

Source: *Bank of England Quarterly Bulletin*, December 1983, Table 3.2—3.4.

extremely embarrassing and many would find it impossible at short notice. This means that an over concentration on long-term securities and advances can mean that the depositor is insufficiently protected. The depositor can be protected by having a much higher proportion of assets in the form of either currency or of assets that can readily be converted into currency. Assets readily convertible into currency with little loss in value are called **liquid assets**. If a very high proportion of assets are held in the form of currency which earns no return – or liquid assets which earn a low return – shareholders would be likely to claim that their interests are being neglected because profitable opportunities were being missed. Too high a concentration on liquid assets would also have important costs for society for it would limit finance available for industry. There is thus the crucial problem of striking the right balance between enough liquid assets to protect depositors' interests and enough high earning assets to protect shareholders' interests and to provide finance for commerce and industry. While this conflict between profitability and liquidity is a real one, shareholders will not always want to press for profitability, for shareholders know that the solvency of the bank is in the interest of shareholders as well as depositors. If liquidity is insufficient depositors may find themselves unable to withdraw their deposits on demand and when this happens people can rapidly lose confidence in

TABLE 7.3   BALANCE SHEET OF THE BANK OF LAGOS, 31 MARCH 1962

Capital and liabilities	£'000	Percentage*	Assets	£'000	Percentage
Capital	99.5	120.1	Cash and balances with		
General reserve			other banks	34.8	42.2
Other reserve			Money at call and		
Profit and loss			short notice		
Deposits and other			Treasury bills		
accounts	82.4	100.0	Investments	0.5	0.6
Liabilities of customers			Loans, advances, etc.	79.6	96.6
for bills, etc.	16.9	20.5	Premises, etc.	20.8	24.0
Other	36.9	44.8	Liabilities for bills, etc.	16.9	20.5
			Formation expenses	5.4	6.6
			Profit and loss	77.7	94.3
Total	235.7	286.0	Total	235.7	286.0

*Of total deposits

Source: C. V. Brown, *The Nigerian Banking System*, George Allen & Unwin, 1966.

banks and one can have bank failures. But failures are rare today – partly because banks have learned to behave prudently and partly because – as we will see in the next chapter – central banks will come to the banks' aid when necessary.

The exact balance between those competing considerations changes from time to time, but Table 7.2 shows how the position looked in the autumn of 1982 for the British retail banks. It can be seen that holdings of note and coin amounted to under 2% of sterling deposits. Other relatively liquid assets included Treasury and other bills (3% of sterling deposits) and market loans (19%). Advances (71%) tend to be particularly illiquid. The other currency assets shown are of varying liquidity.

It can be instructive to compare the balance sheets of the sound British Banks with the balance sheet of a much less sound bank. Table 7.3 shows the balance sheet of the Bank of Lagos for 31 March 1962. While cash items (42%) make it appear liquid the high figure for loans and advances gives the opposite impression, as does the high (26%) proportion of premises and formation expenses. Most worrying of all the profit and loss account appears on the asset side of the balance sheet which means that it is losses not profits which are shown. This means that losses amount to seven-ninths of capital.

The creation of money by commercial banks

In order to protect depositors many countries have laws that require certain assets – usually expressed as a percentage of deposits – to be held in liquid form. In the United States, for example, commercial banks are required to make deposits with the Federal Reserve Bank – as the US central bank is called. In the UK for much of the 1970s banks were required to hold a fixed percentage of deposits in certain specified liquid assets. However since the summer of 1982 a more flexible system has been in operation in which banks have to convince the Bank of England that they are behaving prudently. Exactly what constitutes prudent behaviour will depend on the circumstances of the individual bank. The essence of the system can be captured by assuming that each bank agrees with the Bank of England that it should hold cash plus other liquid assets to a certain specified percentage of deposits. Exposition is simplified by assuming that this ratio applies to all banks. It is convenient to refer to the ratio as the **liquidity ratio**.

We can now describe the process of monetary expansion by commercial banks by making the following assumptions:

(1)   It has been agreed that the prudent ratio of cash plus liquid assets to deposits is 20%.

(2)   We start from a position where banks are operating on that required ratio.

(3)   Banks are assumed to be willing and able to lend out money whenever their actual liquidity ratio is above the required liquidity ratio.

(4)   The new money created is retained within the banking system.

The effects of changing these assumptions will be considered below.

Let us start by assuming that a firm decides to deposit £1m in a bank and ask ourselves how and by how much the banking system can create money. It helps to understand the process if we trace it through using balance sheets. Table 7.4 shows the balance sheet of Bank A before the deposit. It can be seen that cash and liquid assets (£20m) are just 20% of deposits (£100). £1m in cash is now deposited increasing both deposits and cash by £1m. Table 7.5 shows the position after the deposit. Both deposits and liquidity have increased by £1m. The bank is required to keep 20% (£0.2m) of this £1m increase in deposits in cash or liquid assets. Initially, however, it has the full £1m in cash. This means that it has £0.8m in liquid assets in excess of what is required. By assumption the bank will therefore want to increase its advances. The next question is by how much should it increase advances to return the liquidity ratio to 20%?

TABLE 7.4   BANK A, BALANCE SHEET 1

Liabilities	£m	Assets	£m	Excess liquidity £m	Liquidity ratio (%)
Deposits	100	Cash and liquid assets	20		20
		Excess liquidity		nil	
Capital	10	Advances	70		
		Other assets	20		
Total liabilities	110	Total assets	110		

An incorrect argument

You might (wrongly as it turns out) reason as follows. The extra £1m in liquid assets is 20% of £5m. The bank can therefore expand loans and advances until it has increased deposits £5m above the original level, i.e. to £105m. If it followed this fallacious line of reasoning it would agree to lend

TABLE 7.5   BANK A, BALANCE SHEET 2

Liabilities	£m	Assets	£m	Excess liquidity £m	Liquidity ratio (%)
Deposits	101	Cash and liquid assets	21		20.8
		Excess liquidity		0.8	
Capital	10	Advances	70		
		Other assets	2		
Total liabilities	111	Total assets	111		

£4m thus creating a deposit for a customer of £4m.[2] Its balance sheet would look like Table 7.6. Total deposits have increased to £105m and the liquidity ratio is just 20%. What is wrong? The problem is that the person who borrowed the £4m will have done so in order to spend it. He will probably write a cheque for the £4m, perhaps paying for some raw materials. The seller of the raw materials will then take the cheque to his bank. Unless the raw materials seller also banks at Bank A there will be trouble. Suppose the raw materials supplier banks at Bank B. Bank B will not want to hold the cheque but will present it to Bank A for settlement. Bank A will settle the cheque by a transfer of cash or other liquid assets and will at the same time reduce the deposit it had created by the £4m advanced. At the end of this process Bank A's balance sheet will look like Table 7.7. Comparing Tables 7.6 and 7.7 it can be seen that both deposits on the one hand and cash and liquid assets on the other have gone down. Deposits are back to £101m as they were in Table 7.5, but unlike Table 7.5 liquid assets are now only £17m. Bank A is required to hold deposits equal to 20% of deposits or £20.2m (=0.2 × £101m) so that it is £3.2m short of the required liquidity ratio. Clearly Bank A has behaved imprudently.

The correct argument

What would Bank A have been able to do if it was behaving imprudently? To see this we need to go back to Table 7.5 and note that after the deposit of the £1m that Bank A had excess liquidity of £0.8m. Its mistake was to reason that it could lend out more than its excess liquidity.

---

2.   If the lending takes the form of an overdraft rather than a loan the mechanics are slightly different from those described here but the essentials of the argument are not affected.

TABLE 7.6   BANK A, BALANCE SHEET 3X

Liabilities	£m	Assets	£m	Excess liquidity £m	Liquidity ratio (%)
Deposits	105	Cash and liquid assets	21		20
		Excess liquidity		nil	
Capital	10	Advances	7		
		Other assets	20		
Total liabilities	115	Total assets	115		

TABLE 7.7   BANK A, BALANCE SHEET 4X

Liabilities	£m	Assets	£m	Excess liquidity £m	Liquidity ratio (%)
Deposits	101	Cash and liquid assets	17		16.8
		Excess liquidity		− 3.2	
Capital	10	Advances	4		
		Other assets	20		
Total liabilities	101	Total assets	101		

TABLE 7.8   BANK A, BALANCE SHEET 3

Liabilities	£m	Assets	£m	Excess liquidity £m	Liquidity ratio (%)
Deposits	101.8	Cash and liquid assets	1		20.8
		Excess liquidity		0.8	
Capital	10	Advances	70.80		
		Other assets	20		
Total liabilities	111.8	Total assets	111.8		

What is prudent is to lend out its excess liquidity. This means it can lend out £0.8m and its balance sheet will look like Table 7.8. By comparison with

Table 7.5 it can be seen that advances and deposits have both increased by £0.8m. Suppose again the loan is used for the purchase of raw materials and the raw material supplier takes the cheque along to Bank B. After Bank B presents the cheque to Bank A, Bank A's balance sheet will look like Table 7.9.

TABLE 7.9   BANK A, BALANCE SHEET 4

Liabilities	£m	Assets	£m	Excess liquidity £m	Liquidity ratio (%)
Deposits	101	Cash and liquid assets	20.2		20
		Excess liquidity		nil	
Capital	10	Advances	70.8		
		Other assets	20		
Total liabilities	111	Total assets	111		

Bank A's deposits have returned to £101m, its cash and liquid assets have fallen to £20.2 or precisely 20% of its deposits. As far as Bank A is concerned the effect of the move from Table 7.5 to Table 7.9 has been to substitute high- earning advances for low-earning cash and liquid assets. Is this the end of the story? No, because we have to see what happens to Bank B which we assumed is the banker for the supplier of raw materials. Suppose we assume that Bank B, like Bank A, initially has cash and liquid assets equal to just 20% of deposits. Suppose we further assume that Bank B's initial balance sheet looks like Bank A's initial balance sheet shown in Table 7.4. If so its balance sheet after the raw material supplier has deposited his cheque will look like Table 7.10.

TABLE 7.10   BANK B, BALANCE SHEET 1

Liabilities	£m	Assets	£m	Excess liquidity £m	Liquidity ratio (%)
Deposits	100.8	Cash and liquid assets	20.8		20.6
		Excess liquidity		0.64	
Capital	10	Advances	70		
		Other assets	20		
Total liabilities	110.8	Total assets	110.8		

Bank B's cash and liquid assets and its deposits have both increased by £0.8m. Its required cash and liquid assets have increased by £0.16m = 0.2 × £0.8m), meaning it will have excess liquidity of £0.64m. This means it can safely lend out £0.64m making its balance sheet look like Table 7.11. If the £0.64m has been loaned for the purchase of a new machine, and if the supplier of the machine does not bank at Bank B, Bank B's balance sheet will look like Table 7.12 after the cheque has been cleared.

TABLE 7.11   BANK B, BALANCE SHEET 2

Liabilities	£m	Assets	£m	Excess liquidity £m	Liquidity ratio (%)
Deposits	101.44	Cash and liquid assets	20.8		20.6
		Excess liquidity		0.64	
Capital	10	Advances	70.64		
		Other assets	20		
Total liabilities	111.44	Total assets	111.44		

TABLE 7.12   BANK B, BALANCE SHEET 3

Liabilities	£m	Assets	£m	Excess liquidity £m	Liquidity ratio (%)
Deposits	100.8	Cash and liquid assets	20.16		20
		Excess liquidity		nil	
Capital	10	Advances	70.64		
		Other assets	20		
Total liabilities	110.8	Total assets	110.8		

Test your understanding of what has been said by the following. Assume that the seller of the machinery banks at Bank C. Bank C's initial balance sheet also looks like Bank A's initial balance sheet in Table 7.4. Verify for yourself that Bank C will go through the process shown in Tables 7.13, 7.14 and 7.15. Then test your understanding further by working out for yourself that Bank D's balance sheet will look like Table 7.16 at stage 3 if the person receiving

TABLE 7.13   BANK C, BALANCE SHEET 1

Liabilities	£m	Assets	£m	Excess liquidity £m	Liquidity ratio (%)
Deposits	100.64	Cash and liquid assets	20.64		20.5
		Excess liquidity		0.512	
Capital	10	Advances	70		
		Other assets	20		
Total liabilities	110.64	Total assets	110.64		

TABLE 7.14   BANK C, BALANCE SHEET 2

Liabilities	£m	Assets	£m	Excess liquidity £m	Liquidity ratio (%)
Deposits	101.152	Cash and liquid assets	20.64		20.5
		Excess liquidity		0.512	
Capital	10	Advances	70.512		
		Other assets	20		
Total liabilities	111.512	Total assets	111.512		

TABLE 7.15   BANK C, BALANCE SHEET 3

Liabilities	£m	Assets	£m	Excess liquidity £m	Liquidity ratio (%)
Deposits	100.64	Cash and liquid assets	20.128		20
		Excess liquidity		nil	
Capital	10	Advances	70.512		
		Other assets	20		
Total liabilities	110.64	Total assets	110.64		

the advance from Bank C is a customer of Bank D. Table 7.17 summarizes the position for Banks A to D.

It can be seen that, following the initial increase in deposits of £1m, the total change in deposits has reached just under £3m. The process clearly has not come to an end because Bank D's increase in loans and advances will find its way into some other bank – perhaps Bank E or perhaps one of A to D.

TABLE 7.16   BANK D, BALANCE SHEET 3

Liabilities	£m	Assets	£m	Excess liquidity £m	Liquidity ratio (%)
Deposits	100.512	Cash and liquid assets	20.1024		20
		Excess liquidity		nil	
Capital	10	Advances	70.4096		
		Other assets	20		
Total liabilities	100.512	Total assets	100.512		

TABLE 7.17   SUMMARY OF CHANGES IN DEPOSITS

Bank	Initial deposits (£m)	Final deposits (£m)	Change in deposits (£m)
A	100	101.0	1.0
B	100	100.8	0.8
C	100	100.64	0.64
D	100	100.512	0.512
Total change Banks A to D			2.952
Total change whole banking system			approx. 5.0

The bank multiplier and the national income multiplier

What we are witnessing is the sum of an infinite progression which has very strong similarities with the national income multiplier process in a fixprice model. You will remember that in Chapter 3 the multiplier was defined as $1/l$ when l is the marginal propensity for leakages. The **bank multiplier** is $1/r$

where r is liquidity ratio. With the national income multiplier the size of the multiplier is determined by the proportion of leakages. With the banking multiplier the multiplier's size is determined again by the proportion of leakages – in this case into liquid assets.

While there are very clear similarities between the two multipliers they are not identical even in a formal sense. The major difference is that the national income multiplier is a prediction of what *will* happen to national income in a fixprice model in response to an initial stimulus. The bank multiplier in contrast represents *an upper limit* to what *could* happen in response to an initial stimulus. The reasons why the bank multiplier represents an upper limit on what could happen rather than a prediction of what will happen are implicit in the assumptions given at the start of the section on the creation of money by commercial banks. The reasons are:

(1)   Banks will normally wish to hold slightly more cash and liquid assets than they are required to hold to prevent themselves being embarrassed by a deficiency.

(2)   When banks have excess liquidity they will not always increase their advances. They will not increase advances unless there are customers who want to borrow money, and who the banks think are good credit risks.

(3)   Some of the money that banks advance will be held in currency rather than being kept in bank deposits. This creates an additional leakage – into currency – in addition to the leakage into cash and liquid assets. The result of the additional leakage is a smaller multiplier.

You should be able to work out from what has been said that if the cash and liquid asset ratio were 10% rather than 20% the upper limit on the expansion of the money supply would be ten times rather than 5 times the initial change in deposits. This has important implications for central bank control of the money stock, as we will see in the next chapter.

Other functions of commercial banks

This chapter has concentrated on money and the role of commercial banks in the creation of money. While that is the correct emphasis it would be wrong to neglect the other functions of commercial banks. Commercial banks perform a wide variety of services for their customers stemming from the primary function of looking after depositors' money. These services include the transfer of money, management of trusts, and advice on a wide range of financial matters including taxation.

Savings and Investment

One function of special economic significance is the bringing together of savers and investors. If it were not for the existence of financial institutions such as commercial banks this valuable function would be lost. We saw in Chapter 3 that savings is a leakage from the circular flow of income and that investment is an injection into the flow. Savings leave the income flow because households (and firms) want to set money aside in order to be able to make the down-payment on a house or car, or to provide for retirement or contingencies. Firms invest to meet expanding markets or to introduce new products or to reduce costs. The important point is that savings and investment are done by different groups of people for different motives. This divorce of savings and investment decisions is a feature of modern industrialized societies. In agrarian societies savings and investment often go together. For example part of the harvest each year is set aside from current consumption – it is saved in order to provide seed to plant in the spring, i.e. to invest. The problem with savings and investment being directly linked is that people with a surplus available for savings are not necessarily the people who will be best placed to make investments. Banks and other financial institutions thus can provide an important service for society as well as for their customers by bringing together savers and investors.

Conclusion

Banks are important not only because their liabilities constitute the major element of the stock of money, but also because they influence the extent to which the stock of money expands or contracts, and because they bring together savers and investors.

CONCEPTS FOR REVIEW

QUESTIONS FOR DISCUSSION

1   Are Scottish bank notes money? Why? (Note they are not legal tender.)
2   How will high rates of inflation affect the functions of money?
3   How is it possible for banks to create money?
4   What limits banks' ability to create money?
5   Discuss the similarities and differences between the national income multiplier and the bank multiplier.

8

Central Banks and Monetary Control

The purpose of this chapter is to explain the role of central banks, concentrating in particular on the role of central banks in controlling the money supply. The plan of the chapter is as follows: in section A we consider the roles of central banks other than controlling the money supply; in section B we consider the relationship between the yield on bonds and the price of bonds because this is critical to an understanding of the way in which central banks control the stock of money, which is the subject matter of section C.

A FUNCTIONS OF CENTRAL BANKS

The detail of the ways in which central banks work varies from country to country but the following is a fairly typical list of functions.

Currency Issue

Central banks are normally responsible for the **currency issue**. Currency is the main liability of most central banks. Table 8.1 shows a simplified balance sheet for the Bank of England which makes this point. You should note that total currency shown in Table 8.1 is very much less than the total of bank deposits shown in Table 7.2. Bank deposits are the larger component of the money supply by a substantial margin. It can also be seen from Table 8.1 that securities are the main backing for the money supply. At one time currency tended to be backed by gold. It was argued that allowing currency to be backed by government securities was to invite the government to behave irresponsibly and create too much currency (which in turn would lead banks to create too much money – see Chapter 7). How would this be done? Suppose the government decided it wanted an extra £10b to pay civil servants higher salaries or provide for more spending on health or education or roads. The government could go to the Bank of England and say here are

£10b worth of government securities and the Bank of England could say thank you – here are 10 billion crisp new £1 notes. The stock of money would have been increased by £10b at a stroke.

TABLE 8.1   BANK OF ENGLAND—BALANCE SHEET AS AT 16 NOVEMBER 1983

Liabilities	£m	Assets	£m
Issue Department			
Notes in circulation	11,383	Government securities	3585
Notes in Banking		Other securities	7805
Department	7		
Total	11,390		11,390
Banking Department			
Public deposits	37	Government securities	439
Special deposits	–	Advances and other accounts	871
Bankers deposits	699	Premises, equipment and	
Reserves and other accounts	1626	other securities	1060
		Notes and coin	7
Total	2377		2377

Source: *Bank of England Quarterly Bulletin* December 1984, Table 1.

The economic effects of changes in the money supply are considered in later chapters but in the meantime you may want to ask yourself the question 'Given (a) that financing government expenditure by printing money is easy and (b) that the most important alternative – raising taxes – is painful and unpopular why don't governments finance their expenditure by printing money rather than by raising taxes?' As a hint about the answer consider the effect of the two alternatives on the circular flow of income.

While currency is one component of the money supply it is worth making explicit that central banks do not try to control the amount of currency in circulation. If the amount of currency were to be controlled banks might run out of currency, which could cause people to lose confidence in the banks. Thus the central bank may try to control the total stock of money but within that total the amount of currency is determined by demand – that is by people's preferences between holding their money in the form of currency or in the form of bank deposits.

Lender of last resort

We have seen that commercial banks by experience and/or in response to legislation have learned to hold a certain proportion of their assets in the form of currency or other very liquid assets. These are *almost* always sufficient to ensure that banks are able to meet their depositors' demands. It is, however, possible that bad management or a string of bankruptcies during a severe recession could put some banks in a vulnerable position. If people begin to lose confidence in banks they will try to withdraw their money. If an abnormally high proportion of people did this banks will have to convert their liquid assets into currency. It is possible that if people begin to lose confidence in banks generally they will redraw their deposits and reduce banks' liquidity. In consequence a number of banks would be trying to make their assets liquid all at the same time. In this circumstance many people might be trying to sell assets and there could be few buyers (see Figure 7.1). This could weaken banks further and indeed a process rather like this led to the collapse of a number of banks in the United States as recently as the 1930s. In these circumstances modern central banks would provide assistance. In most countries this would be done directly by the central bank buying assets from, or making loans to, the commercial banks. In the United Kingdom there is an intermediary. Commercial banks sell assets to discount houses. This traditionally takes the form of selling a commercial bill. **A commercial bill** is a promise by a company to pay a sum of money on a specified date. For example if company A buys £1m of raw materials from company B it may have 90 days to pay. Company A sends company B a bill – or promissory note – saying it will pay £1m in 90 days. Company B may not want to wait 90 days for its money. If so it takes the bill to its bank who – if both company A and company B have a good credit rating – will buy the bill from company B paying something less than £1m for it. The bill represents a liquid asset for the bank because at the end of 90 days it will be paid £1m. If the bank is short of money before the end of the 90 days it can sell the bill, either directly to the central bank – or in the British case, to a **discount house**. The term *discount* house is used because when the discount house buys the bill it will not pay the full price but will buy the bill at a discount from its nominal price. The discount house can then, if it wishes, rediscount – or sell the bill to the Bank of England. Thus while the story is slightly more complicated in the British case the essence is the same: the central bank is ready when required.

The existence of a **lender of last resort** is a very important safeguard for the whole financial system that may conceivably be put to the test. In the early 1980s a number of developing countries had amassed very large foreign indebtedness, much of it to banks in developed countries. If one of the larger countries defaulted on its debts it could endanger the lending banks. If this were to happen the lender of last resort ought to be able to prevent a collapse. One hopes the test will not be necessary.

Banker to Government

The central bank also usually acts as **banker to government** performing ordinary banking functions for government as well as being responsible for the management of the government borrowing (the implications of the way this is done are discussed in the next section).

B   BOND PRICES AND BOND YIELDS

You cannot fully understand how central banks can attempt to control the stock of money unless you understand the **inverse relationship between bond prices and bond yields**. Bonds are a form of borrowing and the word 'bond' is usually only used when the term of the borrowing exceeds a year. Usually bonds are scheduled to be repaid by a particular date – or range of dates in the future and they also pay interest each year. This rate of interest, which is fixed when the bond is first issued, depends on the circumstances prevailing when the bond was issued. In early 1983 rates of interest on dated British Government Securities outstanding varied from 3% to $15\frac{1}{2}$%. For example Gas 3pc '90/95 is a bond that pays £3.00 per £100 in interest each year and will be redeemed for £100 between 1990 and 1995. Treasury $15\frac{1}{2}$ pc '98 pays £15.50 per £100 in interest and will be redeemed in 1998 for £100. Clearly if both bonds could be purchased for the same price people would prefer an income of £15.50 to an income of £3.00. The result of course is that the price of Gas 3 pc '90/95 will be lower than Treasury $15\frac{1}{2}$ pc '98. On 4 February 1983 the price of Gas 3 pc '90/95 was £61.75 for £100 worth and the price of Treasury $15\frac{1}{2}$ pc '98 was £128.50. Computing yields on bonds with redemption dates is slightly tricky because on the redemption date the government will pay the holder £100. For this reason in calculating the redemption yield in the case of Gas 3 pc '90/95 one has to include both the interest and the capital gain, while in the case of Treasury $15\frac{1}{2}$ pc '98 one has to include both interest and capital loss. The position is complicated further by the difference in tax treatment between income and capital gains. We can avoid these complexities – which do not affect the essentials of the argument by turning our attention to undated securities. **Undated bonds** are bonds where interest is paid each year but where the capital is not redeemed.

The most widely held British Bond is War Loan $3\frac{1}{2}$ pc. War Loan was originally issued to help finance World War I and was formerly known as War Loan $3\frac{1}{2}$ 1952 or after. In the the event the government decided not to redeem it so it is now an undated security. On 4 February 1983 War Loan sold for £32.25 per £100 giving a yield of 11.08% (= 3.50/32.25). At the same time another undated stock, Consols $2\frac{1}{2}$ pc, sold for £22.75 giving a yield of 11.10%.

You should note:

(1)   The price of both undated securities was very much below the nominal value of £100. As we will see this is because yields generally were very much above the $2\frac{1}{2}$–$3\frac{1}{2}$% range.

(2)   The price of both undated securities was also well below Gas 3 pc '90/95. The price of the latter was higher partly because holders of Gas 3 pc '90/95 will also have a capital gain to look forward to as the price rises to £100 by the redemption date.

(3)   The prices of War Loan $3\frac{1}{2}$ pc and Consols $2\frac{1}{2}$ pc had adjusted to give an almost identical yield.[1]

   The most important thing to understand from those examples is why bond prices and yields vary inversely. Suppose we consider the case of a £100 undated bond paying interest at 5%. The owner of the bond will receive an income of £5 a year so long as he owns the bond. Leaving aside the costs of buying and selling bonds how much would you be willing to pay for a 5% bond if the only alternative was a bank deposit account that paid 10%? Clearly the answer must be less than £100 because if you put £100 in the bank you would receive £10 in interest, while if you paid £100 for the bond you would receive only £5 in interest. This suggests that, to put the bond and the bank deposit on an equal footing, you should pay £50 for the bond. If you paid £50 for the bond it would then yield 10% (= 5/50) which is the same as the bank deposit. You should be able to extend the argument to explain to yourself the expected prices for the bond shown in Table 8.2

1.   There are a number of technical reasons why the pattern of yields is more complicated than has been allowed for. Other factors include when the interest is to be paid (the price rises gradually before interest is paid then drops back), whether tax is deducted at source for everyone, for British residents only or for no one.

TABLE 8.2   EXPECTED PRICES ON AN UNDATED £100 BOND
WITH A 5% NOMINAL RATE OF INTEREST IN RELATIONSHIP TO
ALTERNATIVE INTEREST RATES[a]

Alternative interest rates (%)	Expected bond price (£)
2.5	200
5	100
10	50
15	$33\frac{1}{3}$
20	25

[a]Assuming bond prices are not expected to change.

C   CENTRAL BANK CONTROL OF COMMERCIAL BANKS

Central banks usually have responsibility for controlling at least some of the activities of commercial banks. The legal powers of the central banks vary from country to country, as do the ways in which these powers are interpreted. Some of the powers are designed to encourage good banking practice amongst the commercial banks – for example by ensuring adequate amounts of capital. Our interest, however, is focused particularly on ways in which the central bank *may* **control the stock of money.** I want to assume for the time being that the central bank wishes to control the stock of money. As we will see it may not always wish to do so. It will be remembered from Chapter 7 that prudence and/or legislation requires commercial banks to keep part of their assets either in cash or in forms that can be readily converted into cash with little capital loss. The principal methods of controlling the money stocks involve operating on this cash or liquidity base. The most important ways of doing this are (1) changing the required ratio of cash and/or liquid assets to deposits; (2) directly controlling banks' ability to lend; and (3) influencing the amount of liquidity banks hold. As we will see it is the direct influencing of commercial bank liquidity through what we call open market operations that is the most important. It is however useful to consider them in the order given above.

Changing liquidity ratios

Perhaps the most obvious way of changing banks' ability to lend is through **changing liquidity ratios** that commercial banks are required to keep.

TABLE 8.3   ALL COMMERCIAL BANKS, BALANCE SHEET 1

Liabilities	£b	Assets	£b	£b	Liquidity ratio (%)
Deposits	100	Cash and liquid assets	20		20
		Excess liquidity		0	
Capital	10	Advances	70		
		Other assets	20		
Total liabilities	110	Total assets	110		

TABLE 8.4   ALL COMMERCIAL BANKS, BALANCE SHEET 2

Liabilities	£b	Assets	£b	£b	Liquidity ratio (%)
Deposits	100	Cash and liquid assets	20		20
		Excess liquidity		10	
Capital	10	Advances	70		
		Other assets	20		
Total liabilities	110	Total assets	110		

TABLE 8.5   ALL COMMERCIAL BANKS, BALANCE SHEET 3

Liabilities	£b	Assets	£b	£b	Liquidity ratio (%)
Deposits	200	Cash and liquid assets	20		10
		Excess liquidity		0	
Capital	10	Advances	170		
		Other assets	20		
Total liabilities	210	Total assets	210		

Suppose that Table 8.3 represents the combined position of all commercial banks when both the required and the actual liquidity ratio is 20%. If the central bank wished to encourage commercial banks to lend it could reduce the required liquidity ratio to 10%. It can be seen from Table 8.4 that commercial banks would be required to hold only £10b in cash and liquid assets while their actual holdings were still £20b. As a result the banks would now have excess liquidity of £10b, which means that the commercial banking system as a whole could now expand deposits from £100b to £200b (see Table 8.5). For reasons given at the end of Chapter 7 it should be clear this expansion represents an upper limit to what could happen and not a prediction of what would happen.

If, starting from the position outlined in Table 8.3, the central bank wanted to reduce the money supply rather than to increase it, it could raise the liquidity ratio above 20%. Banks would be required to convert other assets or advances into liquid assets. This would be an extremely painful process. Other assets (see Table 7.2) include things like government bonds which could fall sharply in value if banks had to sell them in large numbers (see Figure 7.1). Calling advances from bank customers would at best be exceptionally unpopular and could easily lead to financial embarrassment including bankruptcy amongst the banks' customers. It is for this reason that changes in liquidity ratios are not widely used despite the fact that they could undoubtedly cause the money stock to change substantially.

Special deposits

The mechanics by which the above process takes place varies from country to country. Some countries specify liquid asset ratios and give the central bank the power to vary these ratios. In the United States banks have to hold deposits at The Federal Reserve Bank (The Fed.) and The Fed. can vary the required ratio. In Britain the liquidity ratio is determined on the basis of what is considered prudent and the ratio is not varied for purposes of monetary control. However a similar effect to varying the liquidity ratio is used from time to time when the commercial banks are required to hold certain **special deposits** at the Bank of England. These special deposits are required to be held in addition to the cash and liquid assets that have to be held against deposits as a regular feature of the system. Requiring the banks to hold – or to increase their holdings of special deposits thus reduces their ability to lend. Conversely releasing special deposits can encourage banks to lend.

Direct controls

The ability of commercial banks to create money can be limited by **direct**

controls by the central bank. The central bank may impose controls on total lending or on lending for particular purposes by, for example, controlling lending for personal consumption. These controls may be mandatory with sanctions against banks that break them, or they may be in the nature of advice only. There are several kinds of difficulty with these kinds of controls. (1) If they are not mandatory they may be ineffective. (2) They may have little effect because of an ability to substitute. For example if the central bank were to restrict advances for purposes other than exports then firms could use internal funds (retained profits) for domestic projects and could borrow for exports. (3) Severe restrictions on total advances can harm both banks and their customers.

Open market operations

Because of the difficulties with other methods of control the most important way in which central banks try to influence the money supply in most countries is through its management of the national debt. In part this is a question of whether the debt should be increased or reduced but I want to concentrate on debt management designed to influence the process of monetary creation by the commercial banks.

The basic idea is simple. If the central bank can influence the cash and liquid asset holdings of commercial banks this will then influence the total money supply. If the central bank wants the money supply to expand it will wish to increase commercial banks' cash and liquid assets. This will create excess liquidity which will make it possible for banks to grant additional advances, thus increasing the money stock. If the central bank wishes the money stock to contract – or to grow more slowly – it will wish to reduce commercial banks' holdings of cash and liquid assets. If, when this happens, commercial banks have excess liquidity this excess liquidity will be reduced or removed, which will prevent the banks from expanding loans.

The main way that this is done is through **open market operations**. Open market operations refer to buying or selling government securities on the stock market (the 'open' market). Suppose the central bank wished to encourage banks to expand the money supply. It will purchase government securities. The sellers of the securities will be paid by cheque, which they will typically deposit at their bank. The commercial banks will have increases in both deposits and liquid assets, which will make it possible for them to institute a multiple expansion of the money supply. Conversely if the central bank wishes to contract the money supply it will sell government securities. Buyers of these securities will pay for the securities – usually by cheque – and in this case deposits and liquid assets will fall by the same amount, which will reduce the liquidity ratio. The reduction in liquidity will make expansion of loans more difficult – if there was excess liquidity – or may make some reduction in lending necessary – if there was no excess liquidity. In either case the total change in the money supply can be greater than the amount of securities bought or sold.

TABLE 8.6   ALL COMMERCIAL BANKS, BALANCE SHEET 4

Liabilities	£b	Assets	£b	£b	Liquidity ratio (%)
Deposits	105	Cash and liquid assets	25		23.8
		Excess liquidity		4	
Capital	10	Advances	70		
		Other assets	20		
Total liabilities	115	Total assets	115		

It is instructive to see how open market operations affect bank balance sheets. Suppose we start from the position shown in Table 8.3 and that the central bank purchases £5b in securities on the open market. After the purchase the balance sheets of the commercial banks look like Table 8.6 because the sellers of the securities will in all probability present their cheques to their banks increasing both deposits and liquid assets. Banks now have excess liquidity of £4b (= 0.8 × £5b). What is the upper limit to bank deposits now?

TABLE 8.7   ALL COMMERCIAL BANKS, BALANCE SHEET 5

Liabilities	£b	Assets	£b	£b	Liquidity ratio (%)
Deposits	95	Cash and liquid assets	15		15.8
		Excess liquidity		−4	
Capital	10	Advances	70		
		Other assets	20		
Total liabilities	95	Total assets	95		

Figure 8.1

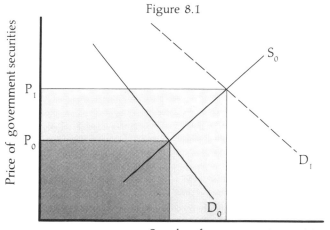

The effect of open market purchases of government securities is to raise the price of securities and to lower the yield.

Figure 8.2

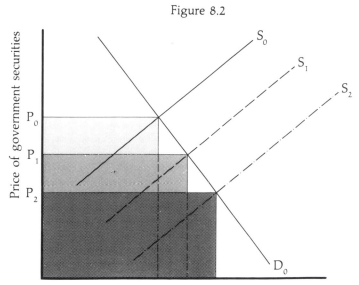

The effect of open market sales of government securities is to expand the supply (to S_1) and to lower the price to (P_1) and to raise the yield. If banks become short of liquid assets they may have to sell their own government securities, increasing the supply on offer further (to S_2) and reducing the price to P_2.

What if the central bank wished to reduce the stock of money? Again suppose Table 8.3 is used as the starting point and that the central bank now sells £5b in securities. The buyers pay for their securities by writing cheques. When these cheques are cleared both deposits and liquid assets are reduced. After the sale the position looks like Table 8.7 (see page 180) where there is now a deficiency of liquid assets, and the commercial banks will have to go through the painful process of reducing advances or other assets. To avoid embarrassing their customers by calling in advances the probability is that banks will try to sell some of their less liquid investments.

We saw in the previous section that bond prices and yields are inversely related to each other. What we now need to do is to look at the implications of open market operations for bond prices and yields. Suppose the central bank wishes to expand the money stock so that it is purchasing more government securities each day while the process continues. This will, of course, raise the price of these securities, as can be seen from Figure 8.1 which has the quantity of securities offered for sale each period on the horizontal axis and the price on the vertical axis. Given the existing supply of securities (S_0) and demand for securities (D_0) there is an initial price level (P_0). The central bank's open market purchase shifts the demand curve to D_1 raising the price to P_1. The increase in the security price reduces the yield on the security. Conversely open market sales increase the supply of securities (from S_0 to S_1 in Figure 8.2) reducing their price from (P_0 to P_1). If (see previous paragraph) banks become short of liquid assets and have to sell their own securities this will increase the supply further to (S_2) decreasing the price further (to P_2). What will happen to the yield on these securities as the price falls?

We have seen

(1)   that the main method of control of the money supply is open market operations;
(2)   that open market operations affect security prices;
(3)   that security prices and yields (interest rates) are inversely related.

On the basis of these facts we can establish a proposition which can be stated in two equivalent ways.

Either the authorities can control EITHER the stock of money OR the rate of interest, but not both.
Or   the authorities can control EITHER the stock of money OR the price of government securities but not both.

I will argue in the next chapter that the second form of this proposition is the more useful. You are however undoubtedly more used to thinking about interest rates than security prices. Governments have to choose between control of interest rates and control of the stock of money. There are times when governments think control of the stock of money is very important (as for example in the early years of Mrs Thatcher's government) and there are other times when control of bond prices (interest rates) is seen as more important.

CONCEPTS FOR REVIEW

QUESTIONS FOR DISCUSSION

1   Why have bank failures been rare in industrialized countries in the post-war period?
2   Why has the price of War Loan been so far below par in the 1970s and early 1980s? Under what circumstances would you expect the price to rise to 100?
3   Look up the prices of government securities in a newspaper and account for the major price variations that you find.
4   Explain the most important ways that central banks can decrease the supply of money. Why is the most reliance placed on open market operations?
5   Why is it impossible for a central bank to control *both* bond prices and the stock of money?

9

Investment

Investment is that part of the gross national product which is not consumed in the year that it is produced. This includes production of factories, machines, roads, schools, hospitals, houses, and manufacturers', wholesalers' and retailers' stocks of raw materials, semi-processed goods and finished goods. In principle investment also includes the acquisition of consumer durables such as cars and washing machines but for practical convenience consumer durables are normally included in comsumption. We have seen (in Chapter 2) that part of **gross investment** or total investment, is used to replace parts of the capital stock that are worn out or obsolete. The balance, **net investment**, represents an addition to the capital stock.

Investment is particularly important in macroeconomics because it is a component of aggregate demand and because it influences aggregate supply through its effect on capacity output and on costs of production. You will remember from Chapter 2 that a major reason why Britain has grown so much more slowly than its competitors since the Second World War is that investment has been lower in Britain.

This chapter has been put between the chapters on the role of commercial banks and central banks in the monetary creation process (Chapters 7 and 8) and the chapter that discusses the role of money in the economy (Chapter 11), because as we will see investment has a critical role in the way in which money affects the economy.

A THE STOCK OF CAPITAL AND THE FLOW OF INVESTMENT

Capital is a stock concept. It is the total amount of factories, machines, roads, houses etc. in existence at a point of time. Investment is a flow concept. It is the amount of new factories, machines etc. produced in a year. Part of gross investment is used to replace part of the capital stock which is worn out or no longer useful. This part of investment is termed **depreciation**. The other part of investment is called net investment and represents additions to the stock of capital. The relationships[1] between investment and the capital stock are shown below.

Planned[2] net investment	=	Desired capital stock for next period – less the actual stock of capital.
Planned gross investment	=	Planned net investment plus replacement investment
Replacement investment	=	Depreciation
Actual Capital Stock	=	Last period's desired capital stock plus last period's unplanned investment.

We can deduce from this that

Planned gross investment	=	Net investment for this period as planned last period less last period's unplanned investment plus replacement investment.

B   THE INDUCEMENT TO INVEST I: – NO INFLATION

The purpose of this section is to explain investment decisions taken by commercial enterprises. The argument is simplified by initially assuming that prices are fixed. The analysis is most directly relevant to companies outside the public sector where it is convenient to assume that the objective is profit maximization. Much of the analysis is also applicable to nationalized industries, but it is not directly applicable to public sector investment in

1.   Assuming it is possible to adjust the size of the capital stock quickly.

2.   The distinction between planned and unplanned investment arises directly from the definition of investment in the first sentence of this chapter. Investment is defined as a residual – that part of production that is not consumed. Most investment is planned. People plan to install machines, build houses, office blocks, port facilities, etc. Some investment however is not planned. Of special importance is investment in stocks of raw materials, semi-manufactured goods and manufactured goods. Some investment in stocks is of course planned. Manufacturers will plan to hold raw materials that they need to process and they will also need to hold stocks of the products that they have to sell in order to meet their customers' needs, as will wholesalers and retailers. Suppose, however, that sales unexpectedly slump. The result is an unexpected, i.e. an unplanned, investment in stocks. Conversely, if sales were unexpectedly buoyant, stocks would fall and there would be unplanned investment which would be negative in this case. Disinvestment would have taken place. You should remember from Chapter 3 that this is an important part of the process of changing the level of national income if desired leakages and injections are not equal to each other.

schools, roads, etc., where there is not a marketable product and where non-commercial decisions may be paramount.

The essential point is that the demand for investment goods is derived from the demand for the stock of capital. What then influences the desired stock of capital? There are a number of influences on the desired capital stock including (1) potential sales of the products that can be produced by the capital; (2) the production costs of these goods; (3) the price of the capital equipment[3] and (4) the availability and cost of finance.

The inducement to invest – that is the motive for investment decisions – can be explained either in terms of the effects of interest rates on investment or in terms of the effects of bond prices (monetary assets) on investment. We saw in the last chapter that interest rates (bond yields) and bond prices are inversely related to each other, so in one sense it makes no difference whether the explanation is in terms of interest rates or of bond prices. If the argument is stated in terms of interest rates it can be restated in terms of bond prices and vice-versa. The convention in economics is to state the argument in terms of interest rates. I believe that convention is not helpful and that it makes the explanation of investment decisions unnecessarily complicated because one has to continually think about the inverse relationship between bond prices and yields. In this chapter I will explain the connection in terms of bond prices. The main reason why the explanation is easier if we use bond prices is that it enables the explanation to be made more easily in terms of supply and demand curves.

The market for investment goods

It is convenient to begin the discussion of the investment goods market by assuming that there is no inflation and that the market behaves like a competitive market with both the quantity and the price of investment goods being determined by supply and demand. The market is represented in Figure 9.1 with the quantity of investment goods on the horizontal axis and the

3.   There are in fact two prices of capital goods that we need to consider – the price of the existing stock of capital goods and the price of new capital goods (investment goods). Given that the capital stock is very large relative to the level of investment in any one year it might be expected that the price of investment goods would be set by the price of the existing capital stock. This would be the correct view if capital goods were all the same and if markets were competitive. The view taken here is that new and second-hand capital goods markets are separate. The demand for new capital goods will of course be influenced by the prices of the existing stock but new and second-hand capital goods are not perfect substitutes. This is because of (1) lack of information about the availability and the condition of second-hand capital stock; (2) the costs of dismantling, transporting and reassembling capital – which can of course be prohibitive if, for example, roads or permanent buildings are built in what turn out to be the wrong locations; (3) in practice old capital stock often embodies an out-of-date technology. In the text we concentrate on the price of investment goods.

Figure 9.1

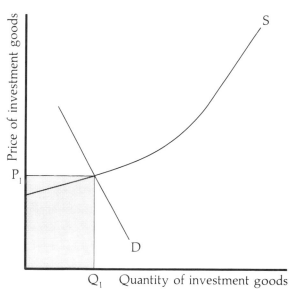

The supply curve of investment goods is upward-sloping and is quite elastic at low levels of output but becomes less elastic as the capacity of the industries producing investment goods is approached. The demand for real assets is downward-sloping, reflecting the fact that investment will be more profitable if the price of investment goods is low. The position of the curve depends upon prospects for profits, the price of monetary assets and the availability of finance. The level of investment is determined by the intersection of the demand and supply curve.

price on the vertical axis. The supply curve is assumed to be quite elastic when the firms supplying investment goods are working well below capacity and to become much less elastic as their capacity is approached.

The demand for investment goods

It is being assumed that the primary motive for investment is the prospect of future profitability. When a businessman considers the purchase of a real asset, he will have to compare the cost of that asset with the contribution it can make to his profitability. Suppose the businessman is considering the purchase of a mini-computer for £10,000 to be used to control his stocks of components. By keeping an accurate record of his stocks he hopes both to avoid running out of components and to avoid the expense of holding excessive stocks. The mini-computer salesman has estimated the savings at £3000 a year, but the businessman thinks it might be safer to assume £1500 a year after paying for a service contract on the computer. He estimates the computer will last 10 years and his experience of the rate of development of computer technology suggests to him that the value of the computer in 10 years will be negligible. He thinks it likely then that spending £10,000 now will generate savings of £1500 a year for 10 years. Is this a sensible investment? The most common way of answering that question is to use the pay-back approach. In the pay-back approach you calculate the number of years it is likely to take to recoup the sum invested. In this example it would be $6\frac{2}{3}$ years ($= £10,000/1500$).

The pay-back method has the very considerable merit of simplicity. Alternative investments with different pay-back are evaluated and the shortest selected. The firm may instead select some maximum pay-back period that it will accept for projects. If the rule were 7 or more, the computer would pass the test. If it were 6 or less, it would not. Against the advantage of simplicity there are two disadvantages. The first disadvantage is that the pay-back method takes no account of what happens after the pay-back period. If there were two investments each costing £10,000, each producing savings of £1500 a year, but where one would produce the savings for 7 years and the other would produce the savings for 20 years, they would both have a pay-back period of $6\frac{2}{3}$ years despite the fact that it is fairly obvious that the 20-year investment is preferable. The second disadvantage of the pay-back method is that it does not take into account the timing of receipts and payments. In our example £10,000 is being spent today in order to reduce costs by £1500 a year for 10 years. How do we compare £1500 in year 10 with £1500 now? It should be fairly obvious that £1500 today is worth more than £1500 in a year's time and that £1500 in a year's time is worth more than £1500 in 2 years' time, etc. The reason for this is that if we have £1500 now we can purchase some monetary asset (e.g. by purchasing a bond or opening a savings account) that will pay us interest each year. This means that the present price of £1500 will be below the price of a promise to pay £1500 in a year's time. Similarly the present price of a promise to pay £1500 in 2 years' time will be less than the present price of a promise to pay £1500 in 1 year's time. If we know all of these prices we can then calculate the price of a monetary asset producing this pattern of returns. We then compare the price of this monetary asset with the price of the investment good. If the investment good costs more than the monetary asset then it will be more profitable to buy the monetary asset. On the other hand if the investment good is less expensive than the monetary asset it will be the better buy. In terms of our example if the monetary asset cost more than £10,000, the computer would be the better buy; if the monetary asset cost less than £10,000, the monetary asset would be preferable.

The argument in the previous paragraph can be restated in terms of interest rates and this is what is conventionally done. We saw in the last chapter that interest rates and bond prices are inversely related. The route suggested in the last paragraph is to purchase investment goods when the price of monetary assets is high and to buy monetary assets when the price of monetary assets is low. One can reach the same conclusion by a more circuitous route by calculating first the rate of return on the purchase of the   computer and second the rate of return on the monetary assets. The rule then becomes to buy the investment good if it has the higher rate of return and to buy the monetary asset if it has the higher rate of return.

Working in terms of asset prices rather than yields is much simpler and it has the added advantage of focusing more attention on the prices of the investment goods. The interest rate approach can easily lead students to lose sight of the importance of the price of investment goods. In the approach advocated here prices of investment goods enter the argument directly. This is shown in Figure 9.1 where the demand curve for investment goods is drawn with a downward slope.

To summarize: the desired change in the capital stock, that is demand for investment goods, depends on

(1) the price of investment goods
(2) profitability prospects
(3) the price of monetary assets
(4) the availability of finance.

The demand curve for investment goods – as for example in Figure 9.1 – shows (1) directly and will shift if any of (2), (3) or (4) change. We will now explore how changes in (2) to (4) will affect the demand curve for investment goods.

B   CHANGES IN THE DEMAND FOR INVESTMENT GOODS

Profitability prospects

The assessment of the returns from an investment is not an exact science. Firms do not *know* how much a cost-savings investment will *actually* reduce costs. They do not *know* when they plan expansion by how much sales will actually rise. They do not *know* how successful they will be if they introduce a new product or a new model or if they enter a new market. In all of these cases there is risk and uncertainty. While studying the technical character-istics of new machines and the size of new markets can narrow the extent of uncertainty, businessmen will normally have to take investment decisions not on hard facts but on hunches, gut feelings or 'animal spirits'. Changes in these necessarily subjective views about the future can be brought about by changes in factual information – for example if current sales rise businessmen may think it more likely that future sales will rise; changes in stock markets or exchange markets, or in published forecasts, or in foreign economies, or indeed many other factors may cause potential investors to become more optimistic about the future, shifting the demand curve for investment goods up and to the right, or they may become less optimistic, shifting the demand curve down to the left.

The price of monetary assets

We saw in the last chapter that the price of monetary assets depends upon the supply of monetary assets available and on the demand for monetary assets, and this relationship is repeated in part (a) of Figure 9.2 where the initial supply of monetary assets (S_0) and the demand for monetary assets (D_0) determines the price (at PMA_0). Part (c) shows the market for investment goods (as in Figure 9.1). The initial supply (S_0) and demand curves (D_0) determine the price of investment goods (PI_0) and the quantity of investment goods. Let us suppose that the solid lines just described represent both markets being simultaneously in equilibrium. Let us imagine further that authorities undertake open market purchases increasing the demand for securities from D_0 to D_1 in part (a) of Figure 9.2, and raising the price from (PMA_0 to PMA_1). If potential investors were previously indifferent between the purchase of monetary assets and investment goods the rise in the price of monetary assets will make people wish to purchase more investment goods and fewer monetary assets, which means that in part (c) the demand curve for investment goods will shift up to the right, raising both the price of investment goods (from PI_0 to PI_1) and the quantity of investment goods (from QI_0 to QI_1). Part (b) of Figure 9.2 shows the relationship between the price of *monetary* assets and the quantity of investment goods. Note that the vertical axes of parts (a) and (b) both measure the price of monetary assets, and that the horizontal axes of parts (b) and (c) both measure the quantity of investment goods. The reader can see that the points labelled A on the three parts all correspond to the initial positions before the open market purchases and the points labelled B all correspond to the position after the open market purchases. The line in part (b) connecting points A and B thus shows the relationship between the *price* of *monetary* assets and the *quantity* of investment goods. It is called the **marginal efficiency of investment** schedule and it shows how the amount of investment is affected by the price of monetary assets.

Figure 9.2

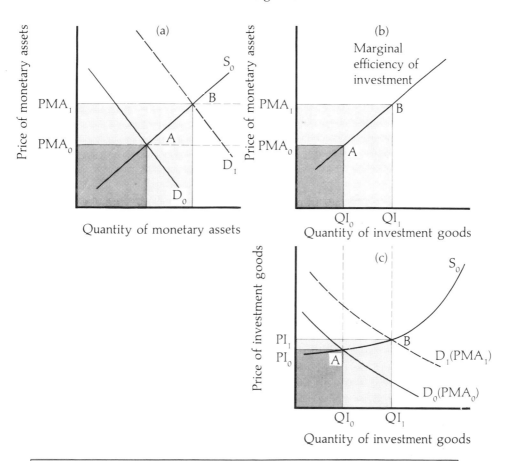

This figure shows how open market operations affect investment. Open market purchases increase the demand for monetary assets from D_0 to D_1 in (a) raising the price of monetary assets from PMA_0 to PMA_1. The increase in price of monetary assets makes it more attractive to purchase investment goods. This increases the demand for investment goods in (c) raising sales from QI_0 to QI_1. (b) shows the relationship between the price of monetary assets and the quantity of investment goods demanded.

The availability of finance

Firms can finance their investment from (a) issuing new shares, (b) retained profits, and (c) borrowing; (a) is not very important; (b) is important and largely a function of past profitability. However (c) is given most attention here as it must be directly affected by monetary policy. The exposition is illustrated with the aid of Figure 9.3 which examines the market for bank

Figure 9.3

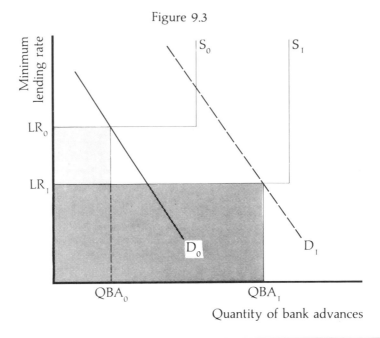

Figure 9.3 shows the effects of open market operations on the market for bank advances. Open market purchases ease conditions in the market for monetary assets which leads banks to reduce their lending rates from LR_0 to LR_1. Banks' liquid assets ratio increases expanding their lending capacity from S_0 to S_1. Open market purchases also increase investment (see Figure 9.2) which increases the demand for bank advances from D_0 to D_1. The consequence is an increase in the quantity of bank advances from QBA_0 to QBA_1.

advances. The amount of bank advances demanded each period will depend on the terms on which they are available, which for simplicity can be taken to be the banks' lending rate as well, of course, as the demand for investment goods. (If firms want to invest more, they will probably want to borrow more from banks.) The supply curve of banks advances has two segments. The vertical segment is determined first by the amount of cash and liquid assets, second by the legal or customary liquidity ratio between deposits and the liquid assets which was discussed in Chapter 8 and third by the rate at which banks are willing to use up any excess liquidity. Up to this maximum banks are assumed to be willing to supply any amount of advances that meet their requirements for creditworthiness at the banks' lending rate. The lending rate is determined by the circumstances in the market for monetary assets. When the price of monetary assets rises, the lending rate on bank advances will fall.[4] It is assumed initially that the amount of liquid assets and the liquidity ratio combine to set an upper limit on bank advances of S_0. Up to this level the supply of banks advances is perfectly elastic at the base lending rate so that the supply curve is the ⌐⌐ -shaped line S_0.

Suppose that the authorities now undertake open market purchases.[5] This will have several effects on the market for banks' advances. We begin with the effects on the supply of bank advances. We have seen in Figure 9.2(a) that this will raise the price of monetary assets and we saw in the last paragraph that this will lower the banks' lending rate (from LR_0 to LR_1 in Figure 9.3). In addition the open market purchases will increase banks' deposits and liquid assets by equal amounts, thus increasing their excess liquidity (see chapter 8). The effect of this will be to increase banks' capacity to lend, shifting the vertical segment of the supply curve to the right until the excess liquidity is exhausted. In the previous subsection it was pointed out that open market purchases will raise the price of monetary assets and as a result increase the demand for investment goods (from $D_0(PMA_0)$ to $D_1(PMA_1)$ in Figure 9.2(c)). The increase in the demand for investment goods will also increase the demand for banks' advances (from D_0 to D_1 in Figure 9.3). The effect of open market purchases is thus to

(1) reduce the banks' lending rate
(2) increase the capacity of banks to lend
(3) raise the demand for investment goods
(4) raise the demand for banks' advances,

so that at the end of the process there should be both more bank lending[6] and more investment.

D   THE INDUCEMENT TO INVEST:II – WITH PRICE CHANGES

The purpose of this section is to show that the inducement to invest will be reduced when the general price level is raised. This is one of the reasons why

---

4.   The conventional way of stating the proposition is to say that when interest rates in the money market fall the lending rate will fall. The reader should realize that the two approaches are equivalent.
5.   The reader should test his understanding of this section by working through the implications of open market sales.
6.   The increase in bank lending comes about both because the demand curve has shifted (from D_0 to D_1 in Figure 9.3) and because the lending rate has fallen (from LR_0 to LR_1).

the aggregate demand curve is downward-sloping.[7] This section is concerned with the effects of the actual price level on investment. The effects of uncertainty about the rate of inflation on investment were considered in Chapter 5.

The argument of this section is as follows:

(1)   High prices reduce the real value of net wealth, including the real value of the money stock (M/P).

(2)   The fall in the real value of the money stock reduces the demand for monetary assets which lowers the price of monetary assets.

(3)   The fall in the price of monetary assets reduces the demand for real assets. As a result investment – the quantity of investment goods purchased – falls.

(4)   The fall in investment reduces total injections and hence the equilibrium level of income.

7.   Other reasons are given in Chapter 5. It might be expected that a higher price level would increase the demand for investment goods by increasing the expectation of higher profits. However the higher price level will also reduce the supply of investment goods. The argument is illustrated in the accompanying figure. At the original price level QI_0 is invested. If the general price rises to P_1 the demand for investment goods rises to Q_1^D and the supply of investment goods falls to Q_1^S. This creates excess demand in the investment goods market raising the price of investment goods to P_{I_1} so that the real price of investment goods returns to its original level.

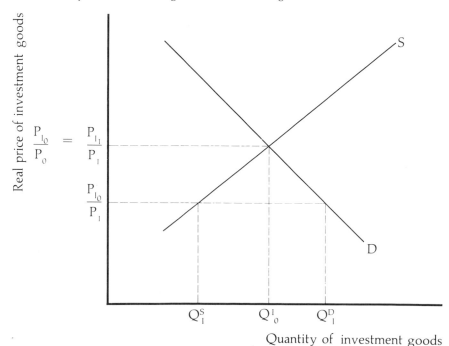

Figure 9.4

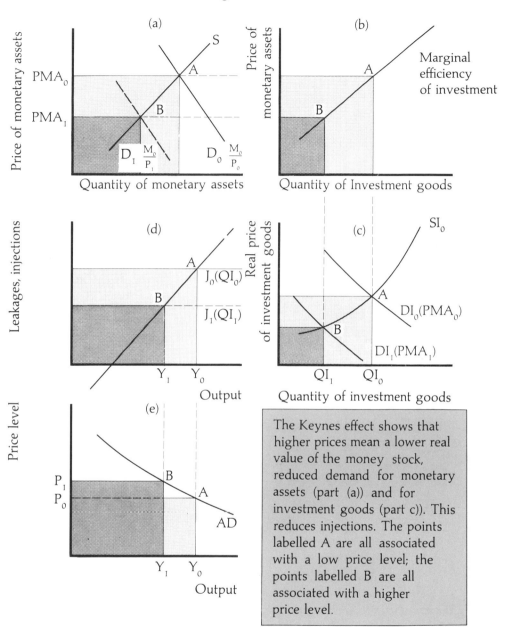

The Keynes effect shows that higher prices mean a lower real value of the money stock, reduced demand for monetary assets (part (a)) and for investment goods (part c)). This reduces injections. The points labelled A are all associated with a low price level; the points labelled B are all associated with a higher price level.

The argument can be illustrated with the aid of Figure 9.4. Parts (a), (b) and (c) have the same layout as Figure 9.2. Parts (d) and (e) are similar to Figure 5.3. At the initial price level (P_0) the purchasing power of the stock of money (M_0) is M_0/P_0. This gives rise to an initial demand for monetary assets in part (a) and with the initial price of monetary assets (PMA_0) there is an associated demand for investment goods in part (c). The initial demand and supply curve of investment goods determines the level of investment (QI_0). The initial level of investment is a component of the initial desired level of injections (J_0) in part (d) that with the desired leakages functions (L_0) determines the equilibrium level of output Y_0 at the initial price level. The initial price level (P_0) and level of real income (Y_0) determine a point on the aggregate demand curve. These initial points are all labelled A in the figure.

Suppose we now examine the implications of some higher price level (P_1). With the same nominal money stock (M_0) the real money stock will fall to M_0/P_1 which will lower the demand for monetary assets in part (a) of the figure. This will reduce the price of monetary assets from PMA_0 to PMA_1. In part (c) this causes investment to fall from QI_0 to QI_1. The fall in investment reduces injections in part (d) from J_0 to J_1 which reduces the equilibrium level of output from Y_0 to Y_1. We can thus see in part (e) that the higher price level (P_1) is associated with a lower level of aggregate demand (Y_1). The points labelled B refer to the position with the higher price level. This effect of higher prices in reducing investment and aggregate demand is called the **Keynes effect**.

E   THE ACCELERATOR

It will be remembered from section A of this chapter that positive planned net investment occurs when the desired capital stock exceeds the actual capital stock. This is particularly likely to happen when output is rising which is why fluctuations in industries producing capital goods tend to be larger than in industries producing consumer goods. When there is a change in the level of activity in consumer goods industries, the level of activity in capital goods industries tends to change by a larger amount. The term **accelerator** is used to describe this accelerated change of activity in the capital goods industry. If output in a consumption good industry is constant, and if the industry is working fairly close to capacity levels, it will have to undertake investment to replace equipment that wears out. This creates a steady demand for investment goods. If the level of output in the consumption good industry were to fall, the industry might not need to replace all of its machines as they wore out and its net investment might fall sharply for a period of time. On the other hand if the consumer good industry wanted to increase output and was already operating at or near full capacity it might need to increase its investment sharply.

The argument is illustrated with a numerical example in Table 9.1. It is assumed in this example

(1)   that £3 of capital stock is required to produce £1 of output;
(2)   that the capital stock lasts 10 years after which it is worthless and has to be replaced;
(3)   that the one tenth of the present capital stock has been purchased in each of the last 10 years;
(4)   that new capital stock can be acquired and installed without delay when needed.

TABLE 9.1

Year	Output	Desired capital stock	Actual capital stock	Replacement investment needed	Net investment needed	Gross investment needed
	(£m)	(£m)	(£m)	(£m)	(£m)	(£m)
	(1)	(2)	(3)	(4)	(5)	(6)
1	100	300	300	30	–	30
2	100	300	300	30	–	30
3	110	330	300	30	30	60
4	120	360	330	30	30	60
5	125	375	360	30	15	45
6	110	330	375	–	–	–
7	110	330	345	15	–	15

In year 1 the capital stock is £300m and output is £100m which means that the actual capital stock (column 3) and the desired capital stock (column 2) are equal to each other. One-tenth of the capital stock (£30m) will wear out and must be replaced (column 4). But no net investment is needed so that gross investment is also £30m (column 6). If output is unchanged in year 2, there will be no change in investment. Suppose however that in year 3 output increases by 10% to £110m. This means that the industry will now need a capital stock of £330m. As before it will need replacement investment of £30m but it will now require net investment of £30m, bringing gross investment to £60m. The result of a 10% increase in the output of the consumption goods industry from £100 to £110 has been a 100% increase in the output of capital goods industry from £30m to £60m. In year 4 if the output of the consumption goods industry increases from £110m to £120m, the desired capital stock will increase to £360m, and gross investment of £60m will again be required – half for replacement and half for expansion of the capital stock. Note, however, that while the output of the consumption goods industry has continued to expand, the output of the capital goods industry has remained constant. If in year 5 output increases still further to £125m it can be seen that the output of the capital goods industry will actually fall. Once again £30m will be needed for replacement but now only £15m will be needed for net investment, so that gross investment falls from £60m to £45m. In year 6 output falls to £110m. While this is still above the initial level, the reader should verify that no investment is required because the industry can afford to discard part of its capital stock without replacing it. In year 7 output remains at £110m, the desired capital stock is £330m and the actual capital stock is £345m. This means the industry can discard £15m of the £30m capital stock that has worn out but it needs to replace the other £15m.

The numerical example in the table is very useful in illustrating the acceleration principle but it gives a more precise impression than the reality that underlies it. In practice the ratio of capital to output can be varied by, for example, working overtime or by starting a second shift. The life of the capital stock is not rigidly fixed and can, for example, often be extended by additional expenditure in maintenance. Delivery periods are variable. When the capital goods industries are not working to capacity, delivery will be much quicker than when they are at capacity.

Stock cycles

Fluctuations in investment of stocks of raw materials, semi-manufactured goods and manufactured goods are similar to fluctuations of investment in fixed assets. Suppose that manufacturers, wholesalers and retailers all desire to hold a level of stocks equal to some proportion of their sales. If sales are constant, ordering for stock will be constant. If sales rise, ordering for stock will rise more than proportionally. If sales fall, ordering for stock may diminish sharply as firms try to reduce stock levels to be consistent with the lower level of sales. Destocking was a significant contributory factor in the fall in output in the UK in 1980 and 1981.

CONCEPTS FOR REVIEW

QUESTIONS FOR DISCUSSION

1 What effect will open market operations have on
   (a) the price of monetary assets
   (b) bank advances
   (c) the level of investment
   (d) the level of output
2. What are the advantages and and disadvantages of the pay-back
   approach to the appraisal of investment projects?
3 Why do fluctuations of output in investment goods industries tend to be
   larger than fluctuations in output in consumption goods industries?
4. What is the Keynes effect and how does it work?

10

Forecasting

We all have an interest in forecasting both the weather and economic policy. Forecasts can be official or unofficial; they can be elaborate or based on hunch or hearsay. A weather forecast can be made by information collected by satellites being used in elaborate models, or by glancing at the sky, or asking grandfather if his big toe aches. Similarly economic forecasts can be official or unofficial, elaborate or simple, they can be based on modern theory or outdated theory or no theory at all. Forecasts can also be right or wrong. Weather forecasters and economic forecasters have at least two things in common: they are not always right and they try to learn from their mistakes in order to improve their forecasts.

Economic policy obviously *attempts* to improve the economic performance of the economy. Policy changes can only affect the *future* performance of the economy. This is an awkward fact because it means that sensible policy changes are possible only if we have a pretty clear idea of how the economy would behave if present policy continued. We cannot *know* how the economy will behave in the future with certainty because policy makers cannot pull out of their desk drawers neatly labelled aggregate supply and demand curves for next year. Next year's aggregate supply and demand curves cannot be known but they can in principle be forecast.[1]

One of the reasons why forecasting is difficult is that it is necessary both to forecast *what* will happen *and* to forecast *when* it will happen. The right policy at the wrong time and the wrong policy amount to much the same thing. This point is illustrated in Figure 10.1. This figure has capacity output

---

1. In practice much more effort has been put into forecasting aggregate demand than in forecasting aggregate supply. In the UK, HM Treasury has an elaborate econometric model with several hundred equations that is used to forecast aggregate demand and there are a number of private models that are, in a very broad sense, similar. In my view economic policy might have been better if much more effort had been devoted to forecasting aggregate supply. The text does not belabour this point and is therefore perhaps a better description of how forecasting ought to be done than how it is done.

and various measures of demand on the vertical axis and time on the horizontal axis. For convenience it is assumed that capacity output grows at a steady rate and this is illustrated by the broken line in the figure. The assumed time path of aggregate demand in the absence of any policy changes is shown by the solid line which for convenience shows a regular cyclical pattern around the growth of capacity output. When demand is above capacity output there is an inflationary gap in terms of the model of Chapter 3 and when demand is below capacity output there is a deflationary gap. A perfectly conceived policy would just offset the inflationary and deflationary gaps and would involve altering the level of demand by the amount shown by the dotted line so that the sum of pre-policy demand (the solid line) and policy-induced changes (the dotted line) would sum to capacity output (the broken line). Suppose that the policy represented by the dotted line were implemented but that instead of it being perfectly timed the timing was completely out of phase. In that event the actual course of aggregate demand would be represented by the dashed line. It can easily be seen that the dashed line has much larger inflationary and deflationary gaps than there would have been if no policy changes had been implemented.

Figure 10.1

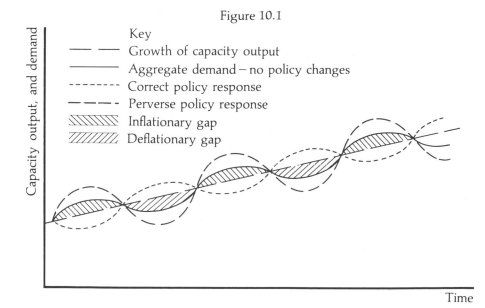

The figure illustrates the point that variations in aggregate demand shown by the solid line might be offset by policy changes represented by the dotted line. If the timing of these changes was wrong the policy changes could make matters worse, as shown by the dashed line.

The plan of this chapter is as follows: in section A there is a discussion of the shifts in aggregate supply and aggregate demand that can occur even when policy is not changed; in section B there is a discussion of the importance of lags, section C contains a discussion of a recent British forecast prepared by HM Treasury and section D discusses private sector forecasting.

A   SHIFTS IN AGGREGATE SUPPLY AND AGGREGATE DEMAND

Even if there are no changes in economic policy it seems very likely that there will be changes in both aggregate supply and aggregate demand and these are considered in turn.

Changes in aggregate supply

Each year there are likely to be some forces shifting the aggregate supply curve out to the right and others shifting aggregate supply up and to the left.

Increases in aggregate supply

The following will increase aggregate supply thus shifting the aggregate supply curve from AS_0 to AS_1 in Figure 10.2(a):

(1)   Net investment that increases capacity output.
(2)   Investment that reduces cost/increases productivity.
(3)   Investment in things or in people that reduces structural unemployment.
(4)   An increase in labour supply (labour supply curve shifting to the right).
(5)   Cost reductions including more efficient use of labour (reduction in slack).

Decreases in aggregate supply

The following will decrease aggregate supply thus shifting the aggregate supply curve up to the left in Figure 10.2(a)
(1)   Increases in structural unemployment.
(2)   Decreases in labour supply.
(3)   Increases in wage rates and other labour costs.
(4)   Increases in non-wage costs.

Net effects on aggregate supply

We have seen that each year there are some factors that will shift aggregate supply down to the right while others will shift it up to the left. The net effect

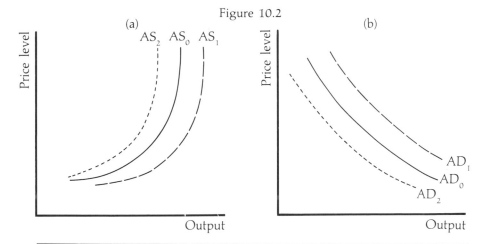

Figure 10.2

It is important to know if aggregate supply or demand will shift if there is no change in government policy.

Increases in investment, productivity increases or cost reductions may increase aggregate supply to AS_1. Wage or cost increases, falling capital stocks and increasing inefficiency can reduce aggregate supply to AS_2.

Increases in injections (investment, government spending and exports) or reductions in withdrawals (taxes, savings and imports) will increase aggregate demand to AD_1. Increases in injections or increases in withdrawals will decrease aggregate demand to AD_2.

depends on the balance between the two sets of forces and can in principle go either way.

Changes in aggregate demand

Aggregate demand will also change each year and changes will be caused by shifts in withdrawals and/or injections. Little need be added to what has already been said about savings (or consumption) and investment and detailed consideration of exports and imports is deferred until Part III but it may be worth saying a little more about taxation and government expenditure. The important point to make is that unchanged tax and expenditure policies do *not* necessarily mean unchanged levels of tax receipts or of amounts of government expenditure. If tax rates are constant tax receipts will rise if either real or monetary income rises. It is probably easier to think the position through if we concentrate on real magnitudes. If the economy is growing real tax receipts will rise. This is represented by a movement along a withdrawals function. If the tax system is a progressive one in which the proportion of income tax is higher for rich households than for poor households then tax receipts will rise by a larger proportion than the increase in income. If tax receipts rise then a higher level of expenditure can be financed with the same tax rates. If government expenditure is increased following higher tax receipts this would be represented diagrammatically by an upward shift to the injections function. Government expenditure plans are usually drawn up looking 4 to 5 years ahead and it is often the case that government expenditure plans show a rise each year. There are various reasons why this should be, ranging from the fact that the public likes to enjoy the benefit of higher expenditure (but does not like paying the taxes to finance it) to the fact that capital expenditure now for new schools, hospitals etc. often requires higher costs in future for running the new facilities. These points are illustrated in Figure 10.2(b). The net effect of the changes in aggregate demand might be to increase aggregate demand (to AD_1) or to decrease it (to AD_2).

Changes in both aggregate supply and demand

We now look at the implications of both supply and demand changing. In Figure 10.3 the current year's aggregate supply and demand curves are shown in parts (a) and (b) as solid lines. Parts (c) and (d) show the labour market with the solid lines again representing the current position. The broken lines show the position for next year assuming no change in government policy. In parts (a) and (c) there is a clearly unhealthy outlook. Aggregate supply is decreasing perhaps because of some combination of higher money wages, low investment, increasing structural unemployment and increasing slack. Aggregate demand is also falling due perhaps to falling investment, falling exports, and previously announced government expenditure cuts. If nothing is done then next year the economy will have higher prices (up to P_1 from P_0)and lower output (down to Y_1 from Y_0). Falling (or stagnant) output combined with rising prices has led to this situation being called **stagflation**.

In parts (b) and (d) the position is very different. Suppose that high investment is increasing aggregate supply because it is raising the marginal product of labour thus increasing labour productivity. As a result the demand for labour increases from D_{L0} to D_{L1} in Part (d). Increases in money wages are also low. The higher investment also stimulates aggregate demand which may also be helped by increases in exports or by previously announced increases in government expenditure. The second case is one with growth and a lower price level.

Policies clearly need to be very different for the two cases and are the subject matter of the next three chapters. What we have established here is

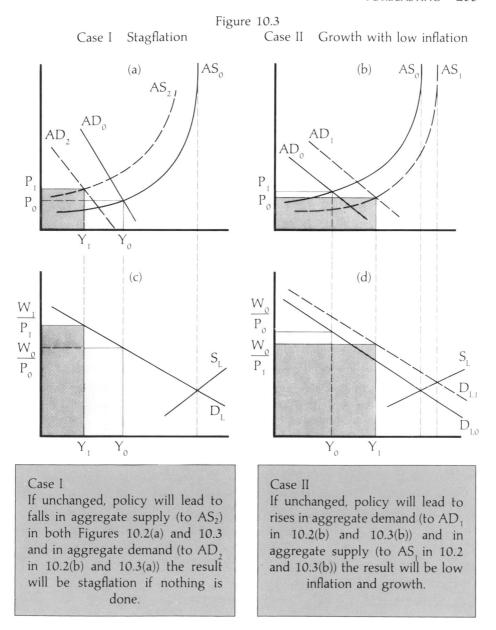

Figure 10.3

Case I   Stagflation   Case II   Growth with low inflation

Case I
If unchanged, policy will lead to falls in aggregate supply (to AS$_2$) in both Figures 10.2(a) and 10.3 and in aggregate demand (to AD$_2$ in 10.2(b) and 10.3(a)) the result will be stagflation if nothing is done.

Case II
If unchanged, policy will lead to rises in aggregate demand (to AD$_1$ in 10.2(b) and 10.3(b)) and in aggregate supply (to AS$_1$ in 10.2 and 10.3(b)) the result will be low inflation and growth.

the importance of being able to forecast changes in aggregate supply and demand so as to be in a position to make the necessary policy changes.

B   LAGS

We have already seen that the timing of fiscal policy changes is critical (see

TABLE 10.1 (a)   AUGUST 1982 GDP FIGURES

Gross domestic product at factor cost
At 1975 prices (1975 = 100)

Based on		Expenditure data	Income data	Output data	Average estimate
1980	1	108.8	112.0	109.9	110.2
	2	106.5	109.5	108.2	108.1
	3	106.1	107.4	106.4	106.6
	4	105.6	106.5	104.9	105.6
1981	1	105.6	105.6	104.4	105.2
	2	104.8	104.9	104.1	104.6
	3	..	106.0	104.6	..
	4	105.5	106.6	105.0	105.7
1982	1	105.8	106.9	104.8	105.8

Percentage change, quarter on corresponding
quarter of previous year

Based on		Expenditure data	Income data	Output data	Average estimate
1980	1	+1.9	+2.9	+1.4	+2.0
	2	−3.7	−3.3	−3.5	−3.5
	3	−2.7	−3.6	−3.3	−3.3
	4	−3.4	−4.0	−5.2	−4.6
1981	1	−2.9	−5.7	−5.0	−4.5
	2	−1.6	−4.2	−3.8	−3.2
	3	..	−1.0	−1.8	..
	4	—	+0.1	+0.1	+0.1
1982	1	+0.2	+1.2	+0.4	+0.6

TABLE 10.1 (b)   AUGUST 1983 GDP FIGURES

Gross domestic product at factor cost
At 1975 prices (1975 = 100)

Based on		Expenditure data	Income data	Output data	Average estimate
1980	1	108.8	110.7	110.1	109.9
	2	107.8	110.3	108.4	108.8
	3	107.3	107.0	106.7	107.0
	4	106.6	107.4	105.3	106.4
1981	1	106.3	105.9	104.9	105.7
	2	104.8	106.1	104.6	105.2
	3	104.0	106.1	105.4	105.2
	4	105.7	107.6	105.6	106.3
1982	1	106.2	107.4	105.5	106.4
	2	106.0	107.4	105.8	106.4
	3	106.3	107.3	106.3	106.6
	4	108.3	107.6	106.7	107.5
1983	1	110.1	109.3	107.2	108.9

Percentage change, quarter on corresponding
quarter of previous year

Based on		Expenditure data	Income data	Output data	Average estimate
1980	1	+0.8	+1.2	+1.4	+1.2
	2	−2.9	−2.7	−3.8	−3.2
	3	−3.0	−4.5	−3.5	−3.7
	4	−3.2	−4.0	−5.1	−4.1
1981	1	−2.3	−4.3	−4.7	−3.8
	2	−2.8	−3.8	−3.5	−3.3
	3	−3.0	−0.8	−1.3	−1.7
	4	−0.9	+0.2	+0.3	−0.1
1982	1	−0.1	+1.4	+0.5	+0.7
	2	+1.1	+1.2	+1.2	+1.1
	3	+2.2	+1.1	+0.9	+1.3
	4	+2.4	0.0	+1.0	+1.1
1983	1	+3.7	+1.8	+1.6	+2.4

TABLE 10.1 (c)   NOVEMBER 1983 GDP FIGURES

Gross domestic product at factor cost
At 1980 prices (1980 = 100)

Based on		Expenditure data	Income data	Output data	Average estimate
1980	1	101.3	102.7	102.7	102.3
	2	100.3	101.4	100.7	100.8
	3	99.3	98.2	98.9	98.8
	4	99.1	97.7	97.7	98.2
1981	1	100.0	96.8	97.4	98.0
	2	97.7	96.7	97.4	97.3
	3	98.2	98.4	98.4	98.3
	4	99.9	101.1	98.6	99.9
1982	1	100.1	100.3	98.6	99.6
	2	100.4	99.6	99.1	99.7
	3	100.9	100.0	99.8	100.2
	4	103.4	99.8	99.9	101.0
1983	1	105.1	102.8	100.7	102.9
	2	102.8	102.3	100.7	102.0

Percentage change, quarter on corresponding
quarter of previous year

Based on		Expenditure data	Income data	Output data	Average estimate
1980	1	1.7	3.1	1.7	2.2
	2	−4.0	−1.6	−3.9	−3.2
	3	−4.7	−4.6	−4.3	−4.4
	4	−3.6	−5.2	−6.0	−4.9
1981	1	−1.3	−5.7	−5.2	−4.2
	2	−2.5	−4.6	−3.3	−3.5
	3	−1.1	0.2	−0.6	−0.5
	4	0.8	3.5	0.9	1.7
1982	1	0.1	3.6	1.2	1.6
	2	2.7	3.0	1.8	2.5
	3	2.7	1.6	1.5	1.9
	4	3.5	−1.3	1.4	1.1
1983	1	5.0	2.5	2.2	3.3
	2	2.4	2.7	1.6	2.4

Figure 10.1). To achieve acceptable timing it is usually necessary to try to keep lags to a minimum. It is worth distinguishing four kinds of lags.

Recognition lags

Before we can attempt to solve a problem we have to recognize that the problem exists. This is called the **recognition lag.** We have established that what we would like to know is what will happen next year. Unfortunately we do not even know what is happening now. One reason for this is that statistics are not produced instantaneously. Some, like foreign exchange reserves, can be produced at very short notice. Others, like industrial production, money supply, price rises, unemployment, exports and imports, are usually made available about a month after the period to which they refer. Estimates of national income and the balance of payments are made quarterly and are usually available 6–8 weeks after the end of the quarter so that the last available data will refer to a quarter that may have begun up to $7\frac{1}{2}$ months ago. Census data are only available once a decade. The fact that statistics are late means that the only way to know where we are now is to make a forecast!

Once data are available they have to be interpreted. If the latest data show a sharp increase (decrease) in some series is this the signal for a change of direction that will continue for months or years? Perhaps it was caused by special factors such as strikes, or the weather. Perhaps it is a temporary fluctuation that will reverse itself next month or quarter. Perhaps it simply did not happen! Table 10.1 shows a selection of official statistics showing original and revised estimates for GDP for the early 1980s. The table shows index numbers of GDP in the UK for the early 1980s. Each part of the table shows GDP at factor cost based on expenditure, income and output data and an average estimate. We know from Chapter 1 that these estimates should in principle all be the same but in practice differ. Two general lessons emerge from the table. First at any point in time the statistics may not present a clear picture. Second that picture may change as revised statistics become available.

To illustrate the first point I want to draw your attention to two features of the table. (1) It can be seen from part (a) that if you had wanted to know in August 1982 the expenditure based estimate of GDP that referred to the third quarter of 1981 you would have been out of luck. This illustrates the special factors argument – in this case the absence of overseas trade statistics. (2) Suppose that in November 1983 you wanted to know what was happening to GDP in the year to last quarter of 1982. According to the expenditure data GDP *rose* by 3.5% whereas according to the income data

GDP *fell* by 1.3%! This means there was no certainty as to whether GDP was going up or down.

To illustrate my second point about the revision of data I again take two illustrations. (1) Suppose you wanted to know the income measure of GDP in the first quarter of 1980 (where the index is based on 1975 prices = 100) it can be seen from part (a) that it was 112.0. A year later the same figure had been revised down to 110.7 as part (b) shows. In part (a) the first quarter income figure was 2.9% higher than a year earlier (see right-hand half of (a)). In part (b) it was only 1.2% higher than a year earlier. (2) As a second illustration let us look at the same figure in part (c). It can be seen that the figure is now 102.7. The main reason for the change is that between August and November 1983 the index was rebased – from 1975 prices = 100 to 1980 prices = 100. The reason why rebasing is necessary is similar to those given for rebasing the retail price index in Chapter 5. Because of the rebasing it would *not* be appropriate to compare figures in part (c) *directly* with those in parts (a) and (b). What can however be seen is that the first quarter 1980 income figure is 3.1% above the figure for a year earlier which by chance is quite close to the equivalent percentage change in part (a). The moral, of course, is that it may well be several years before government statisticians have a clear picture of what is happening to the economy at the time you read this chapter.

Decision lags

Once a problem has been recognized there may be a **decision lag** before something is done about it. The length of this lag is very variable and is highly dependent on constitutional and institutional arrangements. In the US where there is a sharp separation of powers between the executive and the legislature a proposed change in taxes will first go to the House of Representatives where it may be discussed for months by the Ways and Means Committee. It will then go the full House and if passed will then go to the Senate. If after full debate there, a different version is passed the House version and the Senate version will have to be reconciled by the Joint Economic Committee of both Houses. The Houses will then have to ratify the compromise and the President approve the bill. Delay can be very long, especially if the executive and legislature are of different political persuasions.

In the UK the decision lag can be much less. Cabinet, or the Chancellor, can make a decision and the Chancellor can make an announcement putting the change into effect – in some cases immediately – see next sub-section. If the decision is made as part of the normal annual budgetary process this may introduce some delay until the annual budget is due but this is avoidable through the process of mini-budgets which can take place at any time.

Implementation lags

After a decision is made there may be **implementation lags**. In the UK changes in duties are often implemented on the same day they are announced. This is possible only because it is almost unimaginable for a British government to be defeated on a major budgeting item. If it were defeated on a major item there would be strong calls for the government to resign. Even in the UK, however, instantaneous implementation is not universal. Most income tax changes take at least a couple of months to implement and changes in social security payments take longer. In some cases an implementation delay is deliberately introduced, for example to allow time for consultation, to allow people time to adapt to new circumstances or to delay the effect of the measure.

Effect Lags

Once a policy has been implemented there are **effect lags** before its effects are fully felt. The length of this lag is variable. Changes in the tax or benefit position of poor people with a high marginal propensity to consume are probably reflected quite quickly in changes in consumption expenditure. On the other hand changes in investment incentives may not affect actual levels of investment for many months. Once the change in spending starts multiplier effects come into operation and it is estimated that 18–24 months may elapse before the full multiplier effects work through.

C   AN OFFICIAL FORECAST

The detailed mechanics of making actual forecasts are very complex. They involve a mixture of mathematical modelling of theoretical economic relationships, studying the recent data on the relationships between economic variables (e.g. between consumption and income) and judgement. Forecasting bodies differ in their views about the way the economy works and not surprisingly the models on which their forecasts are built reflect these differences. Some of the ways in which five of the major UK models work are summarized in Table 10.2. The models of the National Institute of Economic and Social Research (NIESR), The Cambridge Economic Policy Group (CEPG), The London Business School (LBS) and HM Treasury (HMT) are all broadly similar to each other at least in comparison with the Liverpool model. For example in the Liverpool model the private sector's expenditure decisions are related to its wealth not its income. The actual models are all

TABLE 10.2   CHARACTERISTICS OF MODELS (CURRENT VERSIONS)

Demand effects	Wage formation	Price setting	Impact of inflation on expenditure	Impact of interest rates on expenditure	Role of the exchange rate	Role of the money supply	Impact of bond financing
NIESR (version VI) Average	Long-run real wage target; rates change in response to expected inflation (partial compensation) and unemployment.	Based on costs plus weak pressure of demand effect.	Negative on personal consumption via real balance effect; positive on stockbuilding.	Effects on investment in dwellings, consumers' expenditure on durables and stockbuilding.	The real exchange rate responds to the real current account, NSO reserves and real interest differentials which cause continuous appreciation/depreciation; trade flows are less sensitive to prices.	Only direct role is on personal consumption; otherwise indirect role via interest rates.	Sales of bonds are constrained by private sector portfolio balance, therefore exert significant upward pressure on interest rates.
CEPG (Sept. 1982) Stronger than others because private sector savings do not rise in the long term.	Target real 'take-home' wage, influenced by unemployment and export cost competitiveness.	Constant mark-up on normal costs.	None.	Only transitory effects on private expenditure.	Adjusts to fully offset relative inflation.	None.	Bond sales absorbed by foreign sector; interest rates are linked to foreign rates and to domestic inflation.
LBS (Dec. 1982) Low	Earnings respond to inflation (partially), direct taxation, competitiveness, output and short-term interest rates.	Cost-related, plus adjustment to restore profit margins.	Negative impact due to real balance effects on private expenditure.	Only impact is on investment in dwellings.	Partly determined by relative excess supplies of money; partly by interest rate differentials, OPEC capital flows and NSO reserves.	Direct effects on the exchange rate and on personal expenditure; otherwise indirect role via interest rates.	Modelled only indirectly; interest rates forecast by a policy reaction function.
HMT (version 4) Average	Real private sector earnings linked to output, public employment, and tax deductions. In short run do not compensate fully for inflation.	Variable mark-up normal unit labour costs, fluctuating with the pressure of demand.	Negative impact on personal consumption via real wealth effect.	Weak impact on several categories of private expenditure.	Responds to long-run competitiveness factors and to short-run interest rate differentials.	Main influence is on long-run equilibrium exchange rate.	Modelled only indirectly; interest rates depend on excess demand for money.
Liverpool Determined by changes in wealth rather than income.	Equilibrium real wage determined by labour, taxes, benefits, union power, productivity and world trade; unexpected inflation reduces real wages.	Mark-up on costs.	Negative impact on private expenditure via changes in real wealth.	(i) Changes in nominal rates cause revaluation of private financial wealth. (ii) Changes in real interest rates cause substitution between real and financial assets.	Responds immediately to offset inflation; deviations occur in response to interest rate differentials. Trade flows influenced by future expected exchange rate.	Main influence is on inflation via expectations. Unexpected money shocks affect real wages, and so real exchange rate and output.	Sales of bonds constrained by private sector portfolio balance; attempts at pure bond financing are limited by overseas willingness to lend at world rates.

Source: M. Brech, 'Comparative structures and projectives of 5 macroeconomic models of the UK', NEDO Economic Working Paper No. 10.

TABLE 10.3 FORECASTS OF EXPENDITURE, IMPORTS AND GROSS DOMESTIC PRODUCT

	(1) Consumer expenditure	(2) General government consumption	(3) Total fixed investment	(4) Exports of goods and services	(5) Change in stocks	(6) Total final expenditure	(7) Less imports of goods and services	(8) Less adjustment to factor cost	(9) Plus statistical adjustment	(10) GDP at factor cost	(11) GDP index 1975 = 100
1980	71,550	24,300	20,450	33,050	−1550	147,800	34,100	12,200	200	101,700	108.0
1981	71,850	24,300	18,600	32,300	−1850	145,200	33,900	12,100	0	99,200	105.4
1982	72,750	24,550	19,250	32,500	−700	148,350	35,550	12,350	−550	99,900	106.1
1983	74,650	24,700	19,950	32,800	300	152,400	37,400	12,650	−500	101,850	108.2
1981											
First half	35,950	12,100	9300	15,900	−1400	71,850	15,950	6100	−200	49,600	105.3
Second half	35,900	12,200	9300	16,400	−450	73,350	17,950	6000	200	49,600	105.4
1982											
First half	35,950	12,250	9500	16,400	−50	74,050	18,050	6050	−150	49,800	105.8
Second half	36,800	12,300	9750	16,100	−650	74,300	17,500	6300	−400	50,100	106.4
1983											
First half	37,100	12,300	9900	16,200	0	75,500	18,450	6300	−250	50,500	107.3
Second half	37,550	12,400	10,050	16,600	300	76,900	18,950	6350	−250	51,350	109.1
1984											
First half	38,000	12,450	10,250	17,000	250	77,950	19,400	6450	−250	51,850	110.2
Percentage changes											
1981 to 1982	1	1	3.5	0.5		2	5	2		0.5	
1982 to 1983	2.5	0.5	3.5	1		2.5	5	2.5		2	
1983 first half to 1984 first half	2.5	1	3.5	5		3	5	2		2.5	

*GDP figures in the table are based on 'compromise' estimates of gross domestic product.
Figures in millions of pounds are rounded to 50 million pounds.
Percentage changes are calculated from unrounded levels and then rounded to ½%.

The GDP index in the final column is calculated from unrounded numbers.
Source: *Financial Statement and Budget Report, 1983/84.*

very complex typically having hundreds of equations.

While the ways in which forecasts are made are very complex, the forecasts themselves should be readily comprehensible and so I have included a recent British forecast. An official forecast for expenditure, imports and GDP for the British economy is given in Table 10.3 which was prepared for the March 1983 Budget. It is a forecast of aggregate demand at constant prices.[2]

This forecast of demand is laid out in a way that is similar to the leakages and injections framework of Chapter 3. Total expenditure (E) in column (6) is the sum of private consumption (C) (in 1), government consumption (part of G) (in 2), private and public fixed investment (fixed I and the remainder of G) (in 3), exports (X) (in 4) and changes in stocks (non-fixed I) (in 5). From total expenditure at market prices in column 6 one reaches GDP at factor cost in column 10 by subtracting imports (IM) (in 7), the adjustment to factor cost (mainly taxes and subsidies on goods) (in 8), and the statistical adjustment (in 9). Ignoring the statistical adjustment and the adjustment to factor cost this states that

$$E = C + I + G + (X - M)$$

which you recall from Chapter 3 (Figure 3.7). It should be noted that the forecast is made in constant prices (of 1975 vintage despite the forecast being made in 1983). The top part of the table shows the figures in £m and the bottom half shows percentage changes. It can be seen that total expenditure was forecast to rise by £2450m (col. 6) between the first half of 1983 and the first half of 1984 with the following components contributing to that total C = £900m (col. 1), G (consumption only) = £150m (col. 2), I = £600m (cols 3 and 5) and X = £800m (col. 4). GDP was expected to grow more slowly (at $2\frac{1}{2}$%) than total expenditure (at 3%) mainly because imports were expected to grow (at 5%) more rapidly than expenditure.

There is also a brief discussion of factors affecting aggregate supply. The key passage in this discussion shows that it is very much less quantitative than the aggregate demand forecasts.

---

2.   As suggested earlier very little is done to forecast supply although the 1983 Forecast did provide some historical information on unit labour costs which is given below.

	Percent changes on a year earlier	
	1981 Q3	1982 Q3
Labour costs per unit of output	8	3
of which earnings	10	8
less productivity growth	−4	−4
plus other labour costs including NIS	1	−1

(Source: 1983 Budget forecast)

In 1982 there was evidence that the period of exceptionally rapid productivity gains in manufacturing was giving way, as had been expected, to more moderate gains. Growth of total output in the range 2–2½ per cent, if sustained for a period and accompanied by no major shifts in financial pressures on employers, is probably consistent with no great change in unemployment.[3]

Given the very wide publicity given to forecasts by the media it is of considerable interest to know how accurate the forecasts are. Some information on this point is given in Table 10.4 for the performance of three of the models in the early 1970s. The table shows both average rate of growth of GDP and of consumers' expenditure and the average absolute errors in the forecasts. It can be seen that the errors are quite large relative to average changes in the variables being forecast. Not surprisingly the errors increase in magnitude the further into the future the forecast looks.

TABLE 10.4   AVERAGE ABSOLUTE ERRORS OF PERCENTAGE GROWTH
FORECASTS (based on 16 forecasts made between 1970 and 1975)

	Treasury	LBS	NIESR
Gross domestic product (annual average growth rate 1.7%)			
First half year	1.12	1.62	1.30
Second half year	2.04	1.62	2.32
First full year	1.36	1.22	1.57
Third half year	2.88	2.54	2.32
Consumers' expenditure (annual average growth 2.1%)			
First half year	0.72	0.60	0.82
Second half year	1.20	0.86	1.74
First full year	0.87	0.56	1.19
Third half year	1.87	1.61	1.42

Source: Committee on Policy Optimization *Report* (Chairman R. Ball) London HMSO, Cmnd. 7148. Quoted in Stuart Sayer, *An Introduction to Macroeconomic Policy*, Butterworth Scientific, London, 1982.

The purpose of this chapter is to discuss forecasts and not policy *per se* but it may be worth commenting very briefly on the Budget changes that accompanied the forecast we have just looked at. The Chancellor announced changes in taxes and expenditure that were designed to add less than 1% to overall demand. Given the very high levels of unemployment (which were

3. 1982 *Financial Statement and Budget Forecast, 1983/84.*

still rising) the Chancellor might have been expected to give a larger stimulus to aggregate demand. However he explicitly rejected this course. He said:

> It is sometimes suggested that countries which have made most progress against inflation should speed the recovery process by a resort to reflation. But nothing could be more dangerous for recovery.
>
> Lower inflation and lower interest rates are themselves the right foundations for economic recovery, a recovery which can be sustained. The days when governments by spending more could guarantee to boost activity are far behind us. (1983 Budget Speech).

The Chancellor did not expect there to be a significant fall in unemployment (see quotation in note at the start of this section). His view that stimulation of aggregate demand would not 'boost activity' only makes sense if the aggregate supply curve is inelastic but the Chancellor offered no reason for believing that to be the case. If he did believe that the aggregate supply curve was very inelastic it would still be possible to 'boost activity' by taking measures to shift aggregate supply to the right. While some of the tax concessions in the 1983 Budget such as additional incentives for small businesses should have that effect, the main stimulus in the Budget came through the increase in income tax allowances which affect demand much more than supply. This is one reason why imports were forecast to rise faster than demand (see Table 10.3).

D   PRIVATE SECTOR FORECASTING

In addition to government forecasts for the purpose of its own policy making forecasts are both made and used by the private sector. As we saw in the last section some of the private sector forecasts are made on models that are broadly similar to official models and both private and official forecasts receive wide press attention. Other forecasts of varying degrees of sophistication are made by international organizations, by some stockbroking firms and in often much less formal ways by many companies, trade unions and even individuals.

It may seem odd to suggest that small companies, trade unions and individuals forecast but clearly it is in almost everyone's interest to have a view on what will happen to some or all of the following; prices of individual items (for example to decide whether to buy a bottle of whisky before or after the Budget), the general price level (to decide whether or not to purchase granny bonds or other index-linked assets), one's own nominal wage (to help decide if you can afford a new car), the exchange rate (should you buy foreign exchange for purchasing raw materials – or for your holiday – now or later). Clearly the list could be greatly extended but the point is that we all have an interest in forecasting what everyone else in both the public and private sector will do.

The exercise of forecasting may be formal as in the large forecasting models; or it may be based on some simple model such as the one discussed in the next chapter which predicts that inflation depends on the rate of change of the supply of money; or forecasting can be based on a mere hunch. We will see in Chapter 14 that one of the current controversies in modern macroeconomics concerns the way in which forecasts influence the way we behave.

CONCEPTS FOR REVIEW

	page nos.
decision lags	207
effect lags	208
implementation lags	208
recognition lags	206
stagflation	204

QUESTIONS FOR DISCUSSION

1   How is it possible for prices to rise and for output to fall at the same time?
2   Why do we need to have a forecast in order to learn what is happening to the economy now?
3   Why do all sections of society have an interest in forecasting?
4.   What did HM Treasury think would happen to aggregate supply and aggregate demand in the UK in 1983/84?

5   Evaluate the 1983 Budget changes in the light of your answer to (4) and your knowledge of what has been happening in the UK economy (e.g. to prices, wages and unemployment).

11

Effects of Monetary Changes

This chapter considers the effects of monetary changes on the real economy – that is on the levels of real output and prices. In principle monetary changes may affect both aggregate demand and aggregate supply. Most texts concentrate exclusively or almost exclusively on the demand effects of monetary changes but I wish to consider the supply effects as well.

Economists differ in their views about the way in which monetary changes affect the real economy. The differing schools of thought can conveniently be labelled Keynesian and monetarist. Keynesian and monetarist economists differ in two important ways: (1) they differ in their view as to *how* monetary changes affect aggregate demand although both agree that an increase in the money supply will affect aggregate demand; (2) they differ in their views about the most likely shape of the short run aggregate supply curve. The plan of this chapter is as follows: in section A Keynesian and monetarist views about *how* monetary changes affect aggregate demand are considered; in section B Keynesian and monetarist views about the *shape* of the aggregate supply curve are discussed, and Part C is devoted to a discussion of the effects of monetary changes on the *position* of the aggregate supply curve. Another recent view of effects of monetary changes is embodied in the rational expectations hypothesis and is discussed in Chapter 14.

A   MONETARY EFFECTS ON AGGREGATE DEMAND

Keynesian and monetary economists agree that monetary changes will affect aggregate demand but disagree as to how aggregate demand is affected. Keynesian economists emphasize the role of investment in explaining *how* aggregate demand is affected by monetary changes. Monetarist economists see a more general connection between monetary changes and aggregate demand.

Figure 11.1

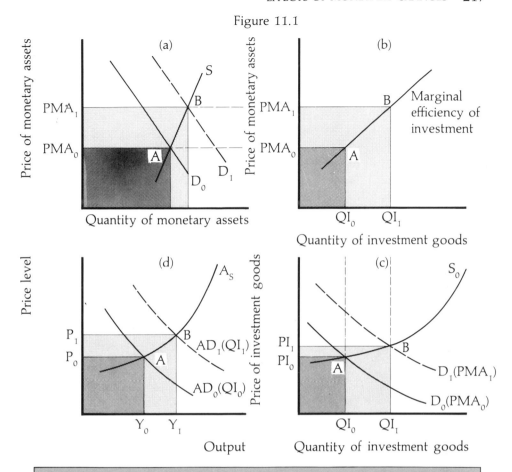

The money supply is increased by open market purchases of monetary assets. These purchases raise the price of monetary assets. As a result the demand for investment goods rises and the amount of investment goods purchased rises from QI_0 to QI_1. This increase in investment has multiplier – and possibly accelerator – effects increasing the level of aggregate demand from AD_0 to AD_1. The increase in aggregate demand raises output (from Y_0 to Y_1) and prices (from P_0 to P_1).

The Keynesian view

The **Keynesian transmission mechanism** view is as follows: a change in the money supply will affect the price of monetary assets. A change in the price of monetary assets will affect investment and a change in investment will have multiplier effects which alter the level of aggregate demand.

The argument is illustrated with the aid of Figure 11.1. Parts (a), (b) and (c) repeat Figure 9.2. If you remember the argument of Chapters 7 and 8 you will recall that the principal ways of altering the stock of money are (1) through commercial banks altering their deposits by altering their advances, and (2) through the central bank altering the liquid asset base of the commercial banks by intervening in the market for monetary assets. If the authorities want to stimulate investment they would increase the stock of money. They could do this by purchasing government securities on the open market thereby raising the demand for monetary assets from D_0 to D_1 in part (a) of Figure 11.1.. This would raise the price of monetary assets from PMA_0 to PMA_1. This in turn would lead to an upward shift in the demand curve for investment goods from D_0 to D_1 in part (c). The demand for real assets would rise because (1) they are now relatively cheaper and (2) more bank finance for investment will be available. We saw in Chapter 9 that bank finance of investment goes up for three reasons. First banks' capacity to lend increases because their liquidity increases (this shifts the vertical segment of the supply curve of bank assets to the right in Figure 9.3). Second the demand for bank advances shifts to the right (from D_0 to D_1 in Figure 9.3) because the demand for real assets increases. Third the cost of bank advances falls (from LR_0 to LR_1 in Figure 9.3). This means that the net result of the increase in the money stock is to increase the quantity of investment goods purchased from QI_0 to QI_1. This higher level of investment is an increase in injections which will have multiplier and possibly accelerator effects raising the level of aggregate demand. This is represented in part (d) of Figure 11.1. The initial aggregate demand curve AD_0 is drawn with the initial level of investment (QI_0). When investment is increased to QI_1 demand increases to AD_1. The effects on output and prices depend on the shape of the aggregate supply curve. This is discussed in section B but first we look at monetarists views.

Monetarist views

It is convenient to divide the **monetarist transmission mechanism** into the old quantity theory and the new quantity theory.

The old quantity theory of money

The **old quantity theory** can be represented by the equation

$$MV = PY \tag{1}$$

where M is the stock of money, V is the income velocity of the circulation of money, P is an index of prices, and Y is the level of real income. The **income velocity of money** is the ratio of the nominal value of income to the nominal stock of money. The money stock is less than nominal income because a unit of money passes from hand to hand several times in a year and can therefore finance several income-generating transactions. The equation MV = PY represents a *theory* about the relationship between the stock of money (M) on the one hand and the level of money income (PY) on the other hand. I have stressed the word theory to indicate that if the equation is written with 3 bars instead of 2 it becomes the identity

$$MV \equiv PY \tag{2}$$

The identity is by definition true. It states no more than that the stock of money multiplied by the average number of times that money is used for the purchase of money income will be precisely equal to the level of money income. The identity $MV \equiv PY$ is true but not very interesting. What would be interesting if it were true is the theory MV = PY which postulates that when the stock of money (M) changes there will be an equi-proportionate change in money income (PY). If, as monetarists tend to believe, Y is fixed then this leads to the prediction that prices will change in the same proportion as a change in the money stock. The fixity of Y is a proposition about the elasticity of the aggregate supply curve and is discussed in section B.

Monetarist theory is based on the assumption that there is a demand for money which is a constant proportion K of money income. Thus

$$M_D = KPY \tag{3}$$

The stock of money M_S is determined by the monetary authorities (at $\bar{M}_S$): thus

$$M_S = \bar{M}_S \tag{4}$$

The equilibrium condition is that

$$M_D = M_S \tag{5}$$

If the stock of money exceeds the demand for money ($M_S > M_D$) equilibrium can only be restored by an increase in money income until the demand for money and the stock are again in equilibrium. There is no very clear explanation as to *why* money demand will increase when the stock of money exceeds the demand. Note moreover that a very precise relationship is required. Money income (PY) must change by K times the change in the stock of money. It is easy to see that V in (1) is identically equal to the inverse of K in (3) i.e.

$$V = 1/K \tag{6}$$

The quantity theory of money thus requires that V, the income velocity of money, is constant. Figure 11.2 shows the income velocity of money which is found by dividing money income by the stock of money. It can be seen that

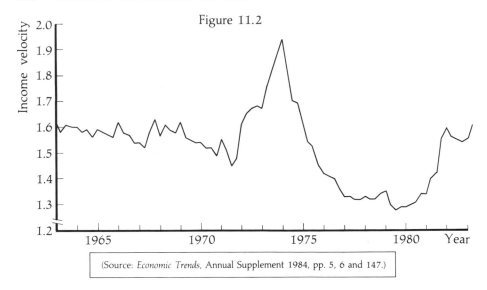

Figure 11.2

(Source: *Economic Trends*, Annual Supplement 1984, pp. 5, 6 and 147.)

V varies quite a lot in the figure. Monetarists do not deny that, if you divide money income by the stock of money that you will find that the ratio (V) varies. They argue, however, that this variation in the ratio represents short-term disequilibrium behaviour and that in the long term the ratio is constant. An enormous amount of effort has been expended in trying to find statistical tests that will conclusively support or reject the monetarist view. Both sides claim victory in a lengthy and heated debate that those of you who do more economics will have a chance to read about, and, if you wish, to join in.

The new quantity theory

The **new quantity theory** is more sophisticated than the old. In terms of its predictions for the level of aggregate demand it shares with the Keynesian view the idea that increases in the money stock will increase aggregate demand. The monetarist view differs in its explanation as to how aggregate demand increases. The Keynesian view, you will remember, is that aggregate demand changes because investment changes. The monetarists' view is more general. When the money stock is increased, the price of monetary assets rises. This alters not only relative prices between monetary assets and investment goods but it also alters relative prices between monetary assets and consumption goods. The extra bank finance that monetary expansion makes possible provides extra funds not only for the purchase of investment goods but also for the purchase of consumption goods. Monetarists would therefore argue that the aggregate demand curve in part (d) of Figure 11.1 would shift up and to the right not only because of an increase in investment but also because of an increase in consumption. In terms of the argument in Chapter 3 the increase in investment would increase (shift upwards) the injections function and the increase in consumption would decrease (shift downwards) the leakages function. Both changes would lead to increases in aggregate demand.

To conclude this section we have seen that monetarists and Keynesians agree that an increase in the stock of money will increase aggregate demand but the monetarists' explanation of the transmission mechanism is more general than the Keynesian one which concentrates on income changes being brought about by the multiplier process caused by an increase in investment.

B   SHORT-RUN MONETARY EFFECTS ON PRICES AND OUTPUT

More important than the divergence in view about how changes in the stock of money affect aggregate demand is the difference in views about how the change in aggregate demand will affect prices and output in the short run. The disagreement represents a difference of view about the likely shape of the aggregate supply curve. The Keynesian view is that most or all of the effect will be on output not prices – except at or near full employment and the monetarist view is that all or almost all of the effect will be on prices not output.

Keynesian views

There are really two Keynesian views corresponding to the two Keynesian models we have discussed.

Fixprice Keynesian view

If wages and prices are fixed as in the model presented in Chapter 3 we have seen that the aggregate supply curve is ⌐⌐ -shaped. By assumption any change in aggregate demand brought about by an increase in investment caused by monetary expansion will affect output and not prices, so long as the economy is on the horizontal section of the AS curve.

Flexiprice Keynesian view

If prices are not fixed by assumption we have a supply curve that rises gently when the level of output is low but which becomes less elastic as full employment is approached (see Figure 11.1d). In these circumstances an increase in aggregate demand brought about by an increase in investment induced by monetary expansion will have a large effect on output and little effect on prices when unemployment is high and output low. As output expands and full employment approaches the effect on output diminishes and the effect on prices increases.

Monetarist views

It is also convenient to separate monetarists into the old monetarist view and the new monetarist view.

The old monetarist view

We have seen that the old monetarist view can be represented by the equation

$$MV = PY \qquad (1)$$

It predicts that aggregate demand – here represented by PY – will change in proportion to the change in M given that V is assumed to be constant. Now the 'classical' model (see Chapter 4) predicts that employment is determined at the full employment level by the interaction of the demand for labour and the supply of labour. We have seen (see Figure 4.4) that this implies a perfectly inelastic aggregate supply curve. If the aggregate supply curve is inelastic it means that both V and Y are fixed in equation (1) so that we have the prediction that prices will change in the same proportion as the changes in the money stock.

The new monetarist view

The new monetarist view reaches a very similar conclusion by a rather different route. The new monetarist view is that there is a **natural rate of unemployment** and that the economy will in due course settle at that level of unemployment so that once again variations in aggregate demand caused by monetary variations will affect prices and not output. The argument is normally presented in terms of the expectations-augmented Phillips curve[1] but I think the argument is clearer if it is presented using the theoretical

---

1. A. W. Phillips found a statistical relationship between the level of unemployment and the rate of change of money wages represented by the curve PP in the figure. His data showed that if unemployment was above A money wages did not rise. If unemployment was below A money wages rose. This Phillips curve was interpreted to imply that there was a trade-off between unemployment and wage stability. As stable wages would also lead to stable prices it was thought by some that there was a trade-off between unemployment and inflation. Economics could opt for point A or they could choose points such as B or C with lower levels of unemployment but with higher rates of increase of wages and of prices. The Phillips curve fitted the facts quite well up to the mid-sixties but has broken down since when it has been quite common for both unemployment and wages to rise at the same time. The breakdown in the predicted relationship was attributed to the role of expectations. Using analysis similar to that in Chapter 4 (see Figure 4.7) it was argued that points like B and C could only be obtained if prices were expected to be stable. If price increases were fully anticipated the Phillips curve rotated to the vertical line P'P' and the trade-off became a trade-off between point A and points D and E. One could therefore choose no inflation (at A) or higher levels of inflation (at D or E) but the level of unemployment could only be affected in the short run when inflation was not fully anticipated.

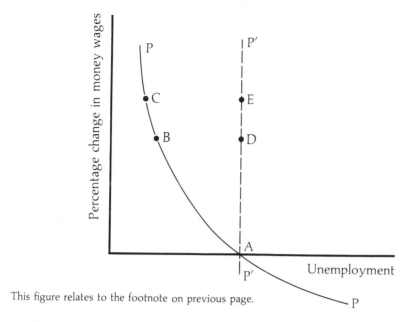

This figure relates to the footnote on previous page.

model of this book. There are two parts to the argument: one concerned with structural unemployment and the other concerned with inflationary expectations.

Structural unemployment[2]

Structural unemployment exists when the labour force and the capital stock are not well matched to each other and in Chapter 4 the argument was illustrated (in Figures 4.14 and 4.15) by assuming that there are two sectors of industry, old and new. It will be remembered that the structural unemployment persists because relative wages do not adjust to levels required to equate supply and demand in the two sectors. If there were no structural unemployment and if money wages are flexible the economy could operate where the supply and demand for labour intersected in Figure 11.3b. However if structural unemployment does exist (and is represented by $H_S^O -$ H_D^O in Figure 4.14) we have to deduct the amount of structural unemploment (H_{SU} in Figure 11.3b). This means that the effective full employment level is $H_F - H_{SU}$ rather than H_F.

It is my belief that this argument is substantially correct but that monetarists present it in a misleading way. It *is* correct that if the only unemployment is structural unemployment and if a 'cure' is attempted by

2. The minor complications of frictional and seasonal unemployment are assumed away. Some interpretators of the natural rate of unemployment would not include structural unemployment in the natural rate. They might prefer the use of the term non-accelerating-inflation rate of unemployment.

Figure 11.3

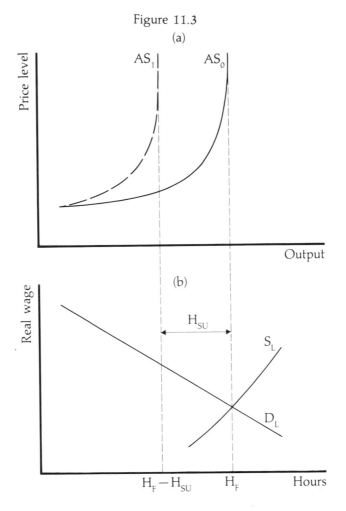

If there is structural unemployment of H_{SU} full employment for the economy will occur at output corresponding to employment of $H_F - H_{SU}$ rather than H_F.

raising aggregate demand the effect will be to raise prices and not output. If the problem is structural then structural remedies are required rather than remedies involving higher levels of aggregate demand (see section C of this chapter and Chapter 13). Monetarists confuse the issue and mislead people by referring to unemployment of a structural nature as the 'natural' rate of unemployment. If something is natural the implication is that nothing can be done about it whereas, as we will see, things can be done about structural unemployment.

Inflationary expectations

The second strand in the new quantity approach concerns the role of expectations about prices. We saw in Chapter 4 that, if people do not expect prices to increase and believe that an increase in money wages makes them better off even when prices are rising by the same proportion, they suffer from money illusion. This shifts the supply curve of labour to the right so long as the expected rate of inflation is less than the actual rate of inflation (see Figure 4.7). We saw in Chapter 4 that as a result the **expectations augmented aggregate supply curve** becomes more elastic. In Figure 11.4 AS_0 represents the aggregate supply curve when price changes are fully anticipated. If price changes are not fully anticipated the aggregate supply will become the expectations-augmented aggregate supply curve AS_1. If aggregate demand is increased from AD_0 to AD_1 there will be a movement along the expectations-augmented aggregate supply curve which means a large change in output $(Y_1 - Y_0)$ for a small change in prices $(P_1 - P_0)$. This

Figure 11.4

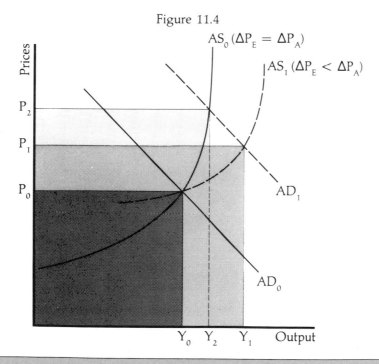

If workers suffer from money illusion they will increase their labour supply when *money* wages rise. The effect of this is to flatten the aggregate supply curve to the expectations-augmented supply curve AS_1. If money illusion disappears and price changes are fully anticipated the supply curve returns to AS_0.

occurs because workers suffer from money illusion. If the inflation is fully anticipated there will be a smaller increase $(Y_2 - Y_0)$ in output (or none if we are already on the vertical segment of AS_0) and a large increase in prices $(P_2 - P_0)$. It is my belief that it is right to emphasize the importance of both structural unemployment and inflationary expectations. Low levels of structural unemployment coupled with money illusion in the labour market made it possible to combine low levels of unemployment with low rates of inflation in the first two decades after World War II. The monetarist position is that monetary changes will lead (a) to proportionate changes in aggregate demand and (b) to proportionate changes in prices. Even if (a) is correct (b) will only be correct if the aggregate supply is perfectly vertical. It has been suggested here that the aggregate supply does have a vertical segment and that the presence of structural unemployment means that this segment may occur at levels of unemployment that are high relative to the first couple of decades after World War II. This is however entirely consistent with a segment of the aggregate supply curve that is *not* perfectly inelastic (for the reasons given in Chapter 4). When the economy is operating on this non-vertical segment of the aggregate supply curve, increases in aggregate demand will increase output as well as prices.

C MONETARY CHANGES AND THE POSITION OF THE AGGREGATE SUPPLY CURVE

The argument as presented so far neglects the possibility that monetary changes will affect the position of the aggregate supply curve. This possibility is particularly important for Keynesians who see investment as having a special role in the monetary transmission mechanism. Omitting from the discussion the effects of investment on the position of the aggregate supply curve is normally justified as follows. Our interest is in what is happening in the short run. In the short run the total capital stock is very large relative to investment. It does very little damage to neglect the effects of the change in the capital stock if the economy is operating a long way below the full employment level.

The argument as presented means that the short-run model refers to a period which is long enough for the multiplier and accelerator processes to work their way through but simultaneously short enough for the capital stock not to change significantly. It is usually assumed that the time taken for the capital stock to alter is longer than the time taken for the multiplier process to work through. If the investment under consideration were a new hydroelectric scheme or a new integrated steel works that assumption may well be correct. On the other hand if the investment consisted of purchases of new machines which have already been produced the argument would be wrong. This means that it is difficult to know *a priori* whether the lags on the supply side will be longer or shorter than the lags on the demand side.

My own view is that it is a mistake to neglect the effects of investment on aggregate supply. We have seen that net investment represents an increase in the capital stock. We saw in the last chapter that net investment will cause the aggregate supply curve to shift to the right. An increase in net investment will therefore increase the amount by which the aggregate supply curve shifts to the right. An increase in the capital stock will increase the amount that can be produced with a given amount of labour. The amount of extra output will depend on the capital–output ratio (discussed in Chapter 9 in connection with the accelerator). If capital–output ratio were 3 then net investment of £300m would increase capacity output by £100m.

The argument is illustrated in Figure 11.5. We start from point A where AS_0 and AD_0 cross given the initial stock of capital and the initial level of

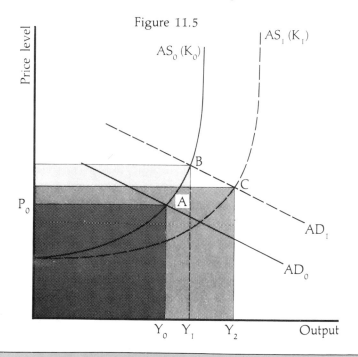

Figure 11.5

Investment increases the capital stock from K_0 to K_1 and this increase in the capital stock shifts the aggregate supply curve to the right. This means that output rises both because the increase in investment raises aggregate demand from AD_0 to AD_1 (which raises output from Y_0 to Y_1) and because investment shifts aggregate supply from AS_0 to AS_1 (which raises output from Y_1 to Y_2).

investment. Monetary expansion raises investment and shifts the aggregate demand curve to AD_1. This same net investment increases the capital stock from K_0 to K_1 and shifts the aggregate supply curve from AS_0 to AS_1. The economy thus moves from A to C rather than from A to B. It can readily be seen that output is higher and prices lower at C than at B.[3]

In one sense the argument about the effects on aggregate supply is more important in a Keynesian model but in another sense it is more important in a monetarist model. The sense in which it is more important in a Keynesian model is because the Keynesian model puts more emphasis on the role of investment in the monetary transmission process. The sense in which it is more important in a monetarist model is that *some* net investment *will* take place and that *that* investment will shift the aggregate supply curve to the right. To the extent that the aggregate supply curve shifts to the right there will be an increase in output which means that monetary expansion will affect output as well as prices even if the aggregate supply were vertical. This means that the monetarist view that monetary expansion will affect only prices and not output is wrong.[4]

CONCEPTS FOR REVIEW

QUESTIONS FOR DISCUSSION

1　How do (a) Keynesians, (b) monetarists believe that changes in the money stock affect the position of the aggregate demand curve?

2　What are (a) Keynesian, (b) monetarist explanations of monetary changes on output and the price level?

3.　What are the effects of monetary changes in aggregate supply?

3.　Whether prices are lower at C than at A depends on the relative shifts in the AS and AD curves.
4.　Or more charitably – too short run.

12

Demand Management Policies

The purpose of this chapter is to extend the discussion of demand management policies that was started in Chapter 5 and which continued in Chapter 11 where the effects of monetary changes were considered. In this chapter it is assumed that forecasts of aggregate supply and aggregate demand have been made and that it has been decided by how much it is desirable to change the level of aggregate demand in the light of these forecasts. In section A of the chapter we consider the way in which fiscal policy affects the level of aggregate demand. **Fiscal policy** refers to the level of government spending on the one hand and of government taxation on the other hand. Monetary policy has already been fairly fully considered in Chapter 11 but in section B we consider the interaction between monetary and fiscal policy.

In this chapter we are considering demand management policies in the context of a closed economy so we can for the moment ignore exports and imports (these are considered in part III). In a closed economy injections are investment and government spending, and leakages are savings and taxation. This means that in a closed economy changes in level of demand will involve changes in savings, taxes, government spending, or investment. We saw in Chapter 3 that aggregate demand can be raised by increasing government expenditure or investment and/or by decreasing savings or taxes. Likewise aggregate demand can be reduced by reducing government spending, reducing investment, increasing taxes, or increasing savings. These matters were fully considered in Chapter 3 and in Chapter 5 the effects of changes in aggregate demand on output, prices and employment were considered (see section F – especially Figure 5.6).

A   FISCAL POLICY

Fiscal policy can change the level of aggregate demand either directly by changing the levels of government expenditure and/or taxation or indirectly by attempting to influence the levels of savings and/or investment.

The purpose of this section is to consider a number of issues in the use of fiscal policy for stabilization purposes. The first issue considered is whether it is more appropriate to vary government spending or taxes.

Variation in government spending versus taxes

To increase aggregate demand we either increase government expenditure or reduce taxes or both. To decrease aggregate demand we reduce government expenditure, increase taxes or both. Is it more satisfactory to vary government expenditure or taxes? I first consider variation in government expenditure.

The problem is to find aspects of government expenditure which can readily be increased or decreased depending upon the needs of aggregate demand. It is instructive to consider government expenditure under three headings: transfer payments, government expenditure on current goods and services, and government fixed capital formation.

Transfers are payments which are not made in exchange for goods and services. Examples are the old age pension and unemployment benefit. The amount that is spent on financial payments is, of course, the product of the average amount each eligible person is entitled to and the number of eligible people. We consider here the effect of variation in the amount that people are entitled to (the question of the number of people entitled to receive payment is considered under automatic stabilizers below). Most people would consider it objectionable if the amount paid to old age pensioners or to the unemployed were to be decreased when the government wished to decrease levels of aggregate demand. For this reason variations in the levels of transfers are not widely used although in an inflationary period the real value of state benefits is not always fully adjusted to take account of inflation.

Government spending on goods and services includes mainly the salaries of civil servants, teachers, workers in nationalized industries, etc. It also includes the costs of running government offices, schools, etc. It is, of course, very much easier to increase the number of civil servants and/or their pay than it is to decrease the number of civil servants or their pay. Aside from the obvious fact that sacking workers is unpopular with the workers themselves it is also clearly disruptive of the service that the employees would provide. The public would, for example, not like to see large changes in the pupil/teacher ratio depending upon the state of the economy.

The component of government expenditure that has in fact been subject to the greatest variation has been government investment. This is in fact very much in line with Keynes' own thinking. The idea was that in times of severe recession one would undertake public works projects and that these would be discontinued in times of excess aggregate demand. While variation in government capital projects has probably been the main form of changes in government expenditure it is nevertheless open to two serious objections. First is the question of lags. As was pointed out in Chapter 10 it is very important to have the right policy at the right time. Lags can be very long in the construction of a new motorway or in building a new power station, to take only two examples. It frequently takes several years to draw up detailed plans,to hold planning enquiries and to obtain the necessary planning permission. Once this is done tenders have to be sought and contracts let. The construction phase is then often several additional years. With such large-scale projects it would be very easy to have government expenditure becoming seriously out of phase with the need for changes in the level of aggregate demand. The problem can be somewhat reduced, but not eliminated, by having a 'shelf' of projects which have been fully planned and costed and which can be undertaken at relatively short notice. It seems likely that there are a number of relatively minor public works which can meet these criteria. The second objection is that investment affects aggregate supply as well as aggregate demand. Cuts in public sector investment for demand management purposes have disrupted the investment programme of nationalized industries. The effect of investment on aggregate supply was considered in Chapter 5 and in the preceding chapter.

Because of the problems of changing levels of government expenditure the main way of changing aggregate demand has been through changes in the level of taxation (see quotation from J. C. R. Dow in Chapter 5).

Changes in the level of taxation have the following advantages over changes in the level of government expenditure.

(1)   Lags are often shorter than with changes in expenditure.
(2)   The effects on aggregate supply are likely to be very much less than changes in government investment. (This does not mean they can be totally ignored – see next chapter.)

Despite these advantages changes in taxation have the following disadvantages.

(1)   Continual changes in taxation create a climate of uncertainty making it difficult for businessmen and for private individuals to plan sensibly.
(2)   While decreases in taxes are fairly popular with the electorate increases are very unpopular and may not be implemented when they are required.

Another consideration in the choice between government expenditure and taxation concerns the desirable role of government in the economy. At any moment in time some people are likely to be very conscious of the number of useful things that government could be doing but is not. These people will wish to increase government expenditure when an increase in aggregate demand is called for. On the other hand when a reduction in aggregate demand is called for they will not want to reduce government spending and will prefer to see the change made by variation in taxes. Other people believe that the extent of government influence on the economy is already too great. They will wish to see any stimulus to the economy brought about by tax reductions and will tend to favour reductions in government spending when it is time to reduce the level of the aggregate demand. It is right that this important issue should be a matter of debate amongst the political parties.

The balanced budget multiplier

The purpose of this subsection is to consider a simultaneous and equal increase (or decrease) in both public expenditure and taxation. The effect of this is to raise (lower) the level of aggregate demand and is termed the **balanced budget multiplier**. The reason that an increase in government expenditure matched by an equal increase in taxes will increase the level of aggregate demand is because of the differences in the first round effects. If the government spends a hundred million pounds more, then in the first round aggregate demand will go up by one hundred million pounds. If at the same time the government raises one hundred million pounds more in taxes consumption will fall, but typically by less than one hundred million pounds. The reason that consumption will fall by less than one hundred million pounds is because the marginal propensities to consume and to save are both less than one. The extra hundred million pounds will reduce people's disposable income (income after taxes). As a result people will reduce both their savings and their consumption. It is the reduction in savings that means that the first round effect of the tax change will be less than the expenditure change. The *difference* between the increase in expenditure and the cut in consumption provides a stimulus which affects the equilibrium level of income through the normal multiplier process.

Automatic versus discretionary fiscal policy

In this subsection we consider automatic versus discretionary fiscal policy. **Automatic fiscal policy** refers to changes in government receipts or spending which come about without any changes in tax rates or expenditure plans. **Discretionary fiscal policy** involves deliberate acts of government policy. We have seen that there are two fundamental difficulties with discretionary policy. First there is the problem of lags. We saw in the chapter on forecasting that if one's forecasting is wrong, or if one does not estimate lags correctly, the effects of fiscal policy may be perverse. The second set of objections are those just outlined in discussing changes in government spending and taxation. We have seen that there are objections to almost all of the possibilities that we have looked at. For these reasons many people have favoured partial or total reliance on automatic stabilizers.

When income rises government tax receipts will rise even if tax rates are left unchanged. If the income tax system is a progressive one in which people with high incomes pay a larger proportion of their incomes in income tax than those with low incomes then as incomes rise tax receipts will go up by a larger proportion than the increase in income. Other forms of tax receipts will also go up, but less dramatically. If higher real incomes lead to increased spending on goods and services then tax receipts from taxes on these goods and services will also increase. In an inflationary period the tax receipts will go up particularly quickly if the nominal rates of tax are not changed to bring them into line with inflation.

A similar effect occurs on the expenditure side particularly with unemployment benefit. Total expenditure on unemployment benefit is, of course, the product of the rate of unemployment benefit and the number of people who are unemployed. If the unemployment benefit is kept the same then expenditure on unemployment benefit will depend upon the number of people who are unemployed. We have seen that when aggregate demand falls there will be a reduction in both output and employment, that is to say unemployment will rise.

What this means is that when aggregate demand rises both tax receipts will rise and government expenditure will fall. Conversely when aggregate demand falls tax receipts will fall and government expenditure will rise. These changes in taxation and government expenditure are in the direction that is required to stabilize the level of aggregate demand. The presence of automatic stabilizers means that the difference between government expenditure and taxation **the public sector borrowing requirement (PSBR)** will automatically tend to fall as aggregate demand rises and will automatically rise as aggregate demand falls.

The medium-term financial strategy

In 1979 the new Conservative government in the UK adopted a set of targets for demand management that cut across the distinction made in the last subsection between automatic and discretionary stabilizers. As we will see the implication of the **medium-term financial strategy (MTFS)** is to require government to take discretionary action to *counteract* the stabilizing function of automatic stabilizers! In the MTFS the government adopted a series of targets for the money supply and for the PSBR. The implications of the PSBR targets are examined here. The connection between the PSBR and the money supply is examined in the second half of this chapter.

In the fiscal year 1978/79 the PSBR was $5\frac{1}{2}$% of GDP at market prices. In the 1980 Budget the government announced that the target for the PSBR would be reduced in each of the following few years until it reached $1\frac{1}{2}$% of GDP at market prices in 1983/84. In subsequent budgets the target PSBR was slightly relaxed but the policy of sharply reducing the PSBR continued. What makes the MTFS a complete departure from previous practice is that the targets have been more or less adhered to despite the very deep recession with very high levels of unemployment. We saw in the previous subsection that in a depression when aggregate demand falls there will be a fall-off in tax receipts and a rise in government expenditure for things such as unemployment benefits. As a result the PSBR would rise. But the MTFS called for a fall in the PSBR. This means that government was set upon reducing the PSBR at a time when it would naturally be rising in order to help stabilize the economy. In order to keep to the the MTFS the government had to use discretionary policy. However it had to use the discretionary policy in the opposite way from that which would be required to stabilize the level of aggregate demand. In order to keep to its financial strategy the government had to cut some public expenditure and raise taxes in real terms at a time when the Keynesian prescription would have been to reduce taxes and/or increase government expenditure. Critics of the government's policy believe that the MTFS served to deepen the recession rather than to ease it. These critics believe that the fall in the PSBR led to an extra loss of output, and extra unemployment from what it would have been if the automatic stabilizers had not been consciously overridden.

Indirect fiscal controls

Thus far we have talked about fiscal policy as a direct way of controlling the level of government expenditure and the level of taxation. However in addition fiscal policy can be used to attempt to influence other leakages and injections in the economy. The most important of these are probably incentives to investment. There are a variety of ways in which government can encourage investment. These include things like tax holidays and capital allowances, provisions for accelerated depreciation, grants, loans on favourable terms, the creation of special development areas, etc. Many of these have implications for aggregate supply and are discussed in the next chapter. One measure that has been used for counter-cyclical fiscal policy has been varying the terms for home improvement grants, both for the installation of basic facilities and for the provision of insulation. Increased grants in a recession can provide a useful stimulus to work available to small builders.

Other considerations in fiscal policy

The main purpose of this chapter is to consider policies in terms of their effects on aggregate demand. There are however two other considerations in fiscal policy which should be mentioned briefly. These are the redistributive effects of fiscal policy and the allocative effects of fiscal policy. Fiscal policy affects the distribution of income both in macroeconomic terms, that is between the owners of labour and the owners of capital, but also in microeconomic terms, i.e. between rich households and poor households. The allocative effects of fiscal policy arise because fiscal policy distorts choices between different goods, between goods and leisure (the work/leisure choice) and between consumption and savings. The consideration of these issues is a large part of the subject matter of what used to be called public finance and what is now more commonly termed public sector economics.

B   THE RELATIONSHIP BETWEEN FISCAL AND MONETARY POLICY

Fiscal policy and monetary policy have now been discussed separately and the purpose of this section is to discuss the relationship between them. You will remember that fiscal policy is concerned with the levels of taxation and government expenditure and that monetary policy is concerned with the control of the money supply and with the prices of monetary assets. As we will see monetary and fiscal policy cannot be decided entirely independently of each other. The first task is to look at the formal relationship between fiscal policy and monetary policy and then we will look at the implications of this relationship.

Financing the public sector borrowing requirement

The basis of the link between fiscal policy and monetary policy is through the government deficit or the public sector borrowing requirement (PSBR) as it is officially called. If the government spends more revenue than it raises in taxes then the additional expenditure has to be somehow or other financed. Neglecting minor items of revenue such as charges for museums, swimming pools and parking meters, if the government does not raise the money it requires through taxation then it must borrow the money. That is why the government's deficit is called the borrowing requirement. The relationship between the Public Sector Borrowing Requirement and the money supply is set out in Table 12.1. The formal relationship between the columns in the table is as follows:

$$\text{column } 1 - \text{column } 2 + \text{column } 3 = \text{column } 4$$
$$\text{and} \quad \text{column } 4 + \text{column } 5 + \text{column } 6 = \text{column } 7.$$

Understanding these formal relationships is easier if we think in terms of a series of approximations. For the first approximation let us assume that the money stock consists entirely of currency and that changes in the money stock are equal to the PSBR. If this were true it would mean that if the government did not raise the money it needed in the form of taxation it would finance expenditure by issuing additional currency. We know from our discussion of central banks in Chapter 8 that the currency is a liability of the central bank, that is of the public sector. Therefore inducing the public to hold additional currency is one form of borrowing from the public. As we will see the matter is rather more complicated than simply changes in the money stock being equal to the PSBR but that relationship nevertheless contains the core of the relationship and is in all probability why the medium term financial strategy contains both money supply targets and PSBR targets. If the world were indeed as simple as this then monetary and fiscal policy would be two sides of the same coin. The determination of the size of the PSBR by fiscal policy would also determine the size of the change in the money stock, i.e. it would determine monetary policy.

For our second approximation it is recognized that there are other forms of lending to government than of issuing more currency. If the government issues securities (monetary assets) these are paid for with money so the need to increase the money supply is correspondingly reduced. That is why column 2 is subtracted from column 1 in Table 12.1. The principle that is now introduced is that forms of borrowing other than currency issue means that the government can run a deficit without increasing the money supply. Of course if the government wants to sell a large amount of monetary assets (government securities) it will have to sell them at a low price so as to make the price attractive. You should remember from Chapter 8 that a low price for government securities (high interest rates) may reduce investment. This issue is discussed more fully in the section on crowding out at the end of this chapter.

For the third approximation we need to recall from Chapter 8 that government purchase or sales of government securities alters the banks' monetary base and can alter their own ability to lend. There may in addition be scope for changes in lending with a given monetary base. Putting these two factors together we have to recognize that, as we saw in Chapter 7, that

TABLE 12.1 PUBLIC SECTOR BORROWING AND THE MONEY STOCK,
SEASONALLY ADJUSTED DOMESTIC COUNTERPARTS (£ MILLION)

	1 Public sector borrowing requirement	2 Net acquisition of public sector debt by UK non-bank private sector	3 Sterling lending to UK private sector	4 Sub-total domestic counterpart	5 External and foreign currency counterparts	6 Non-deposit liabilities (net)	7 Money stock sterling M_3
1976	9175	5755	3407	6827	−2120	−1142	3565
1977	5988	8453	3188	723	3849	−442	4130
1978	8357	6021	4698	7034	658	−920	6772
1979	12,608	10,877	8585	10,316	−3120	−557	6639
1980	12,189	9318	10,025	12,896	−474	−1373	11,049
1981	10,582	11,192	11,217	10,607	255	−1741	9121
1982	5428	10,385	17,861	12,904	−2489	−2088	8327

(Source: *Financial Statistics*, various years.)

commercial banks can alter the money supply. This is what is shown in column 3 of the table.

This completes the major aspect of the relationship between the PSBR and the stock of money for our present purposes. Two aspects remain. The first of these is that there is a foreign sector component. Monetary flows from overseas can affect the domestic money supply. The second point is technical and refers to column 6 of the table. An increase in bank lending (an asset of commercial banks) is not always matched by an increase in those deposits which are counted as part of the money supply (a liability of commercial banks). The increase in lending may be matched by some change in non-deposit liabilities and that is what is shown in column 6.

To sum up, if we neglect the foreign element and the change in non-deposit liabilities we are left with the fundamentals of the formal position: the money supply will increase by the amount of the PSBR less any amounts borrowed by the government from outside the banking system plus any amounts lent by the banks to the non-government sector.

We now turn to the implications of this formal relationship for the conduct of monetary and fiscal policy. For the present we concentrate entirely on the relationships in terms of their effects on aggregate demand. We have seen that government tax and expenditure policies affect the level of aggregate demand directly through altering the levels of leakages and injections. Fiscal policy may also affect demand indirectly as we have seen through things like incentives for investment. We saw in Chapter 11 that monetary policy also affects the level of aggregate demand and we have also seen that monetarists and Keynesians differ in the way in which they expect changes in the stock of money to influence aggregate demand. Let us now look at various combinations of fiscal and monetary policy.

Expansionary monetary policy and expansionary fiscal policy

If both monetary and fiscal policy are expansionary there will be an increased (PSBR) and there will be little or no attempt made to finance the borrowing requirement by borrowing from the non-bank public. In these circumstances the increase in the money supply is likely to be larger than the PSBR. This is the most expansionary of all of the possible policies. It has the advantage, particularly if one believes in the Keynesian transmission mechanism, of making it possible to keep the price of government securities high (interest rates low) which will encourage additional investment. Its primary disadvantage in a closed economy (there are other disadvantages in an open economy – see Part III) is that it may lead to an over-expansion of aggregate demand. Monetarists would also see the objection to this as an increase in the stock of money will in their view lead to an increase in prices. (The mechanism for this is not often fully explained.)

Expansionary fiscal policy and tight monetary policy

A second possible combination of fiscal and monetary policy is to have an expansionary fiscal policy and to have a tight monetary policy. This implies usually trying to finance as much as possible of the PSBR by borrowing from the non-bank private sector. That in turn means reducing the price of government securities (monetary assets) to make them attractive. This will reduce the extent of expansion of aggregate demand relative to a policy which is expansionary in both fiscal and monetary policy. Monetarists would argue that the reduction in aggregate demand would be general whereas Keynesians would argue that the reduction would tend to be concentrated on investment which would be choked off by the lower prices of monetary assets (see Chapter 9). Once again as we will see there are other considerations in an open economy.

Tight fiscal policy and expansionary monetary policy

A third alternative is to have an expansionary monetary policy combined with a tight fiscal policy. This would mean a decreased PSBR (or possibly even a zero or negative PSBR). In this case little effort would be made to borrow from the non-bank public and some government debt might be repaid. This would make the price of government securities (monetary assets) high, stimulating investment.

Tight fiscal and monetary policy

A final possibility is to have tight fiscal and monetary policy which implies a small or at least a falling PSBR and much or all of the PSBR being financed by the sale of government securities to the non-bank public. In this case both fiscal and monetary policy would be reducing the levels of aggregate demand.

Crowding out

Crowding Out is the term which is used to describe how additional expenditure by the public sector may result in a reduction in – a crowding out of – expenditure by the private sector. This is most likely to happen when fiscal policy is expansionary and monetary policy is tight. In these circumstances there would be a large PSBR but attempts would be made to finance as much as possible of this by borrowing from the non-bank public. In order to finance the borrowing requirement the prices of government

securities would have to fall and this would have the effect of reducing the
level of investment. Additional government spending would have crowded
out some investment due to the effects of the change in the price of
government securities.

It is important to recognize that crowding out does *not* imply that
increases in government spending always cause an equal reduction in private
spending. There are several points to be made. First: if the economy is at full
employment an increase in one component of national income will necessarily cause another component to fall unless the economy is growing.
However if the economy is not at full employment, or is growing, increases
in injections will have multiplier effects on the level of income. Second the
weaker proposition that increases in government borrowing will crowd out
an equal amount of private sector investment is also wrong. Higher
borrowing will lower security prices (raise interest rates) and, *other things
remaining equal*, this will reduce private sector investment. It will not however
reduce private sector investment by the full amount of the increase in
borrowing. This would only happen if the total amount of money available
for lending were fixed. An increase in government borrowing will lower
security prices (raise interest rates). The extent to which this will reduce
private sector spending will depend on how sensitive spending is to security
price changes. Third, if higher government spending raises the level of
income —by shifting the aggregate demand curve — there will be a higher
level of income that will increase savings and make more funds available for
lending. The increase in aggregate demand may also increase investment
opportunities which will *increase* investment. This effect is called crowding in
and may partially or fully offset crowding out.

Aggregate demand, output and the price level

In this chapter the emphasis has been on alternative ways of changing
aggregate demand. It is important for you to remember that the effects of a
given change in aggregate demand on output, employment and the price
level will depend on aggregate supply. You should remember that it will
depend *both* on any shifts in aggregate supply (see section A of Chapter 10)
and on the shape of the aggregate supply curve. If the aggregate supply
curve is vertical or if it shifts up to the left there will be little if any increase in
output and a large increase in price. The more elastic the aggregate supply
curve and the more it shifts down to the right the larger the effect on output
will be and the smaller the effect on price.

If the argument in the last paragraph is not clear draw AS and AD
diagrams for yourself. If it is still not clear go back to section A of Chapter 10.

Some economists would wish to qualify the above argument by saying that only unexpected changes in aggregate demand will affect output. This argument is examined in Chapter 14 after looking at policies to change aggregate supply in the next chapter.

CONCEPTS FOR REVIEW

QUESTIONS FOR DISCUSSION

1   If the government wished to stimulate demand what considerations should guide a choice between cuts in taxes and increases in expenditure?
2   Discuss the choice between discretionary fiscal policy, automatic stabilizers and the medium-term financial strategy.
3   Explain why it is not possible for the authorities to control each of the following independently: the PSBR, changes in the stock of money, and the price of government securities.
4   Does it matter if the PSBR is financed by borrowing from the public or by printing more bank notes?

13

Supply Management Policies

The purpose of this chapter is to consider various ways of managing aggregate supply. It is assumed that it is generally desirable to increase aggregate supply – that is to shift the aggregate supply curve down and to the right. This is in contrast to aggregate demand which it may be desirable to increase in order to reduce a deflationary gap or to reduce in order to decrease an inflationary gap. I have divided the discussion of measures to increase aggregate supply into three main groups which will be considered in turn. These are

A   Measures to reduce cost
B   Measures to reduce structural unemployment
C   Measures to increase capacity

While this division is convenient it is somewhat arbitrary and there is interaction between the various heads.

A   COST REDUCTIONS

In this section we consider measures that can increase aggregate supply by reducing costs. It is of course the case that any measures which increase unit costs will cause the aggregate supply curve to shift up to the left, while any measures which decrease costs will cause the aggregate supply curve to shift down to the right. There are a number of possible kinds of cost reduction. These include the reduction in the cost of imported goods, and the reduction in taxes which are treated as part of the costs. In this connection the reduction in the national insurance surcharge is a very good example. The national insurance surcharge which was introduced in 1977 was an increase in the national insurance levy for each worker. When it was introduced it was probably passed on largely in the form of higher prices which caused the

242

aggregate supply curve to shift up to the left. When it was reduced in a series of stages in the early 80s the effect may have been to cause the aggregate supply curve to shift down to the right.

Wages policies

The most widely discussed policy to control costs has been a wages policy. **Wages policies** have a long and chequered history and have been called things like wages policies, incomes policies, prices and incomes policies, national economic assessments etc. What wages policies attempt to do can be illustrated very simply in Figure 13.1. Suppose that AS_0 and AD_0 represent the aggregate supply and the aggregate demand curves for the current year. Suppose further that it is forecast that aggregate demand will increase from AD_0 to AD_1. Suppose it is further forecast that productivity will increase by 3%. On its own this would shift the aggregate supply curve down by 3%. However suppose that it is also forecast that money wages will increase by 8%. The net effect of the productivity increase and the money wage increase would be to shift the aggregate supply curve up by 5% say from AS_0 to AS_1 in the figure. If that were to happen the economy would move from A to B on the diagram. Suppose however that there was a wages policy that

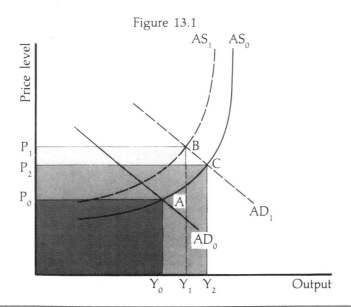

Figure 13.1

A successful incomes policy keeps the aggregate supply curve from shifting from AS_0 to AS_1. As a result the economy can have higher output (Y_2 rather than Y_1) and lower prices (P_2 rather than P_1).

succeeded in containing wage incrases to 3%. If that were to happen then the 3% in money wages and the 3% increase in productivity would just offset each other and the aggregate supply curve would remain at AS_0. That would mean that over the coming year the economy would move from A to C, rather than from A to B. At C output would be higher than at B (Y_2 rather than Y_1) and prices would be lower (P_2 rather than P_1). The objective, then, of an incomes policy is to allow the economy to be operated at a higher level of output with lower levels of prices and unemployment.

There are, however, a number of difficulties or potential difficulties with incomes policies. One difficulty concerns the length or duration of the policy. Some people would argue that wages policy should be very **short-lived**. The policy should be introduced in times of very high rates of wage increases as a temporary measure. The objective should be to bring down these rates quickly in the hopes that this would change expectations about the rate of inflation and hence about wage increases. The counter argument to this particular point is that it takes rather longer than a year or two to change expectations. This would suggest that perhaps an incomes policy should be semi-permanent or **permanent**. The objection to the more permanent incomes policies is that they will tend to freeze wage differentials and this will prevent the changes in relative wages which are necessary to mitigate structural unemployment. This point is discussed further in the next section of this chapter.

Another question about wages and incomes policies is whether they should be expressed in **percentage** terms or in terms of the same **absolute amount** for all or some mixture of the two. Suppose one had a norm of 5%. This would mean that someone on £30,000 a year would be entitled to an increase in their income of £1500. Someone on £3000 a year would be entitled to increase of £150. The person on £3000 a year might well resent the fact that the £30,000 a year person would have an increase equal to half the total income of the £3000 a year person. This has led to arguments that all increases should be the same absolute amount. Indeed a policy to pay a flat rate increase for everybody was suggested by the Heath government in the early 1970s but was never adopted. An absolute increase of the same amount for every person would have quite radical effects in altering the distribution of income. If the absolute increase were £300 a year it would represent a 10% increase for the £3000 a year person, but only a 1% increase for the £30,000 a year person. If inflation were also 10% a year this would mean a large fall in real income for the £30,000 a year person. Another objection to a flat rate increase is that it will vastly reduce differentials and this will exacerbate structural unemployment.

Sometimes more sophisticated forms of wages policy have been advo-cated. One such variant is to have a very low norm but to allow increases above the norm when they can be justified on productivity grounds. Wage increases which are covered by genuine productivity increases are not inflationary. However experience suggested that some or perhaps many of the alleged productivity deals turned out to be hopes or aspirations which were not, in the event, fulfilled.

There is also the question as to whether incomes policies actually succeed in reducing wages. There are two variants to the argument that incomes policies do not reduce wages. First there is the argument that the temporary incomes policy succeeds in reducing wages temporarily but that when the temporary policy ends there is a flood of wage increases that result in the overall level of wage increases being at least as high as it would have been had there been no incomes policy in effect. The second variant of this argument is that there is a danger that a wages policy will not even have the effect of reducing the overall level of wages in the short run. The argument is that if the incomes policy norm is set too high its effects will be to increase the overall level of money wage settlements rather than to decrease it. The reasoning is as follows. The wages norm becomes just that; something that everyone expects to receive. In the absence of a wages policy some workers might in fact have been willing to settle for less than the norm, but because a norm has been announced they insist upon achieving it. This argument can be illustrated with reference to the two sector model introduced in Chapter 4 (see Figure 4.14). In the old industry where there is a great deal of excess of supply of labour workers might be willing to settle for a very small increase in wages or none at all. The overall effect could thus be to increase overall wages if wage increases in the new industries equal the norm.

A further difficulty with all the incomes policies discussed above, is the effect that they have in weakening the allocative role of wages (discussed in the next section), and this combined with the dislike of wages policies particularly amongst many trade union leaders, has led to incomes policies becoming somewhat unpopular. One view is that the only way that wages can be controlled is by having a high level of unemployment. This, however, appears to be a very expensive way of obtaining money wage stability. At the time of writing in early 1984 money wage increases were still running above price increases despite a level of unemployment in excess of three million.

Meade's wages policy

These difficulties have led to people searching for alternative forms of wages policies. An interesting alternative has been proposed by Nobel Laureate Professor James Meade. **Meade** has proposed that governments should increase the level of aggregate demand in money terms by some fixed percentage. This would mean that the aggregate demand curve would be shifting outward by a constant amount each year. Wage settlements would be done on the following basis. No one would be expected to have a decrease in money wages. Increases in money wages would however run from zero to whatever figure could be justified by the rules below. The general proposition in deciding on the increase in money wages would be to have that increase in money wages which maximized the level of employment for that particular group of workers. The way that this would work can be illustrated with reference to Figure 4.14. In the new industry it can be seen that the actual level of employment is determined by the supply of labour at H_S^N. Employment would be maximized by increasing the wage to 7. In the old industry on the other hand the level of employment is limited by the demand for labour at H_D^O. In these circumstances no increase in money wages would be justified at all. The difficulties with these proposals are likely to arise when employers and employees could not agree upon the employment maximizing change in money wage. In these circumstances a tribunal would have to adjudicate. A serious problem would arise if the tribunal's findings were not accepted. Despite this difficulty Meade's proposal has the great advantage of combining some control over the overall level of wage settlements, while at the same time, allowing relative wages to change. As we will see in the next section changing relative wages is one of the prerequisites for reducing the level of structural unemployment.

B   MEASURES TO REDUCE STRUCTURAL UNEMPLOYMENT

You should remember from the discussion in Chapter 4 that structural unemployment arises when the stock of labour is not well matched to the stock of capital. The mismatch may be because the levels and types of skills of the labour force may not be well matched to the needs of employers. There may also be a geographical mismatch which may be reflected in the differing rates of unemployment by region (see Table 4.3).

As we saw in Chapter 5 the effect of structural unemployment is to shift the aggregate supply curve up and to the left meaning that less can be produced and typically at a higher cost of production. There are four main strategies which can be used to try to reduce or eliminate structural unemployment. These are changes in relative wages, retraining, reducing the geographical gap between the supply of labour and the demand for it, and increasing entrepreneurship. These are considered in turn.

Changes in relative wages.

We saw in Chapter 4 that one of the causes of structural unemployment is relative wage structures which do not adapt to the changing needs of the labour market. We saw in the previous section of the present chapter that incomes policies which are fixed in terms of a given percentage increase for everyone or which are fixed in terms of the same absolute increase for everyone (or some combination of the two) make the existing wage structure even more rigid. Incomes policies which are specified in terms of the same absolute increase for everyone may be particularly harmful in this respect. The reason for this is, as we saw in the previous section, that such an incomes policy reduces differentials and may therefore make people less willing to improve their labour market skills. One of the major advantages of James Meade's incomes policy is that it appears to offer a way round this difficulty.

We have thus far been thinking of relative wage changes as a change in the permanent wage as a way of inducing people to overcome the skill and/or geographic disadvantages that prevent them from being employed. An alternative to this is to provide people with lump sums which can wholly or partially compensate them for the time and money cost of skill acquisition and moving homes. This naturally leads us on to my next subsection.

Education and training

Most people in Britain finish their formal **education and training** at the official school leaving age: now 16, but twice increased from 14 during the post-war period. This is four to five decades before people come to the end of their normal working life. To put the matter another way most people retiring during the 1980s will have finished their formal education before World War II. In the 1930s there were no computers, and for all practical purposes no television. Cars and aeroplanes were much less common than they are now and far more rudimentary. Many modern service industries were far less important than they are today. On the other hand heavy industries, including steel making, shipbuilding and mining, were more important than they are today, as was the manufacture of clothing, footwear etc. Looking at it from this perspective it is hardly surprising if people who left school in the 1930s were ill equipped for jobs of the 1970s and 1980s. There is no reason to think that the pace of change of the last 50 years will prove to have been any greater than the pace of change in the next 50 years. If this is so it is necessary to stop thinking of education and training as something that one does entirely before one starts work. Periodic re-training probably needs to become the norm.

There are re-training facilities available but often the financial sacrifice involved in attending them is very large in the absence of the kind of financial incentives that are, for example, available to people who want to go into further or higher education immediately after they leave school. Quite a lot of re-training is, of course, done by industry itself. However one of the difficulties of a period of severe recession is that firms cut back on their training and re-training programmes. Another way of encouraging mobility is to end restrictive practices that reduce labour mobility. If a job requires an unnecessary paper qualification, or it requires an unnecessarily long apprenticeship, labour mobility will be reduced. It is of course vital that people have whatever training is necessary for them to be able to do the job safely and adequately. It is, however, often the case that both professional bodies and skilled workers insist upon qualifications or apprenticeships which are easier to justify in terms of maintaining high earnings for their members than they are in terms of the genuine needs of the job.

Bridging the geographical gap

When there is a geographical mismatch between jobs and workers two solutions are possible: move the **jobs to the workers**, or move the **workers to the jobs**. In Britain much more attention has been paid to the former rather than to the latter. Indeed much of regional policy in Britain has been concerned with attempts to persuade industry to move into areas of high unemployment. The creation of special development areas, and of agencies such as the Welsh and Scottish Development Agencies that try to attract jobs to areas of high unemployment, are discussed in the next section.

Jobs to people rather than people to jobs has been emphasized for two main reasons. People frequently dislike moving and movement of people often creates an imbalanced infrastructure. For example, if one started off with reasonably equal roads, schools, hospitals, etc., throughout the country, and if people then left areas of high unemployment to move to areas of low unemployment, the areas of high unemployment would be faced with a surplus of roads, schools, etc, which would then have to operate at less than capacity which would be expensive. The parts of the country that were receiving workers would also have to spend additional money on infrastructure because they would find that their existing facilities were overcrowded and inadequate.

Despite these advantages of the jobs to the people strategy it is my view that more could be done to encourage people to move to jobs. In part what is required is information. With computers it should be relatively easy to have a central store of available jobs which would mean that people in one area could find out not only about employment opportunities in their own area but also about employment opportunities in other areas. People could be encouraged to look more widely for jobs by the use of central funds to defray a proportion of costs involved in travel for job search or by allowing these to be claimed against income tax (as is done in some other countries). The availability of housing is another obstacle to geographical mobility. Particularly in the council house sector it is often necessary to go on to waiting lists in order to obtain satisfactory accommodation. Measures to help incomers to find suitable housing would obviously be of considerable importance. An example of an imaginative scheme is that in some cases people moving to new areas are being allowed to buy part of a house if they cannot afford a whole house. Under this scheme they might start by purchasing a quarter of a house with a mortgage, and paying rent on the remaining three quarters. As their circumstances improve they can increase the proportion of the house they own up to 100%. Another obstacle to mobility is the lack of full transferability of private pension rights in many cases. If people lose part or all of their pension rights when they move jobs this can be an important incentive against mobility particularly amongst older workers.

Increasing entrepreneurship

When there is structural imbalance the very fact of imbalance may create possibilities for **entrepreneurship**. Entrepreneurs may see possibilities for profit making by exploiting genuinely new ideas or, less glamorously, by introducing products or services which are new to the area, or by exploiting new technology to improve products or services or to reduce costs.

Some of this entrepreneurial activity is doubtless best undertaken by large firms with adequate finance and well backed up with a variety of technical skills necessary for the product as well as a wide range of accounting, legal and secretarial skills. However big organizations often become bureaucratic and find it difficult to grasp new opportunities.

Small firms have potential advantages of flexibility, speed of response and the dedication that sometimes comes from working for oneself. They have the disadvantages to mirror the advantages of large firms: lack of finance and of the full range of technical skills. Small firms are often swamped by the requirements of official form filling.

Courses to improve entrepreneurial skills are now available and a number of government agencies exist that can provide technical and financial support if certain criteria are met. One of the problems of small firms is that criteria concerning locations, type of product, method of production, etc. can vary so much that information can be hard to come by and the aid may not be forthcoming if the precise criteria cannot be met.

The Conservative government after 1979 took a number of initiatives which were designed to create a more favourable climate for the growth of business, particularly of small businesses. The best known of these measures is a scheme which enables individuals to gain tax relief on money that they invest in young businesses.

C   MEASURES TO INCREASE CAPACITY OUTPUT

In this section measures to increase capacity output are considered under two headings: investment and labour.

Investment

Both the quantity and the quality of investment are important.

Quantity of investment

Increased investment is almost certainly the most important way in which aggregate supply can be increased. We have already spent a great deal of time stressing the importance of investment. In Chapter 2 the British record on investment was compared with the record of its main competitors and found to be deficient. In Chapter 5 the effect of investment on capacity output, demand for labour, and aggregate supply were all considered. As this is the single most important aspect of policies designed to increase aggregate supply section D of Chapter 5 should be reviewed. In Chapter 9 the inducement to invest was considered and in the last section of this chapter structural imbalances were considered.

The most important determinants of investment (see Chapter 9) are the objective factors influencing the potential profitability of investment, the subjective interpretation of these factors (animal spirits), the price of monetary assets and the availability of finance. Changes in aggregate demand can affect objective factors influencing profitability. For example an increase in demand will make many investments potentially more profitable. These same policy changes may affect animal spirits. The inducement to invest can be increased by raising the price of monetary assets (government securities) as we saw in Chapter 9.

There are however a number of more specific ways in which investment may be encouraged. These include provisions to encourage investment through tax incentives by, for example, giving capital allowances for investment, by making provision in the tax law for accelerated depreciation, and by granting tax holidays. There are a variety of other types of measures designed to encourage investment. For example in the UK there are a wide range of schemes designed to encourage investment. These include the creation of special development areas with particularly attractive grants, the erection of advanced factories, renting factories at subsidized rates or providing rent-free accommodation for a period of years. Special help may be provided for particular kinds of investment. For example there are special investment incentives in the UK for industrial robots. There also may be special grants or loans for research and development and there are a number of government agencies which are designed to bring investment into particular areas. Examples of these include the Highlands and Islands Development Board, the Scottish Development Agency and the Welsh Development Agency. Any of these measures will, if successful, lead to an increase in investment leading to increased capacity and, often, to reductions in cost. This means that the aggregate supply curve is shifted down and to the right (see Figure 13.1 on page 242).

Quality of investment

The quality of investment is as important as the quantity. There is no point in investing in factories to build things no one wants to buy. Where the capital stock is not well matched to the labour force and there is structural unemployment investment can have a crucial role in restoring the balance. We must have the correct distribution of investment as well as the correct total. This is why entrepreneurial activity is so important.

Another aspect of the quality of investment concerns the degree of technological sophistication. Capital deepening investment (discussed in Chapter 2) often embodies more recent technology than the capital it is replacing. This often creates the opportunity for improvements in the product – for example by the inclusion of more reliable microelectronic components – or reductions in cost – perhaps by reducing labour requirements or by using cheaper components.

The labour-saving opportunities that arise from new investment can of course create problems both in securing agreement for the investment to be used and in creating structural unemployment.

Labour

Once again both the quantity and quality of labour may be important.

Quantity of labour

Let us consider how a decrease in taxation could shift aggregate supply as well as aggregate demand. The argument is illustrated in Figure 13.2, which is similar to the figures used in Chapter 5. Part (a) shows aggregate supply and aggregate demand curves and the intersection of AD_0, the initial aggregate demand curve (AD_0) and the initial aggregate supply curve (AS_0) at A give the initial price level (P_0) and the initial level of output (Y_0). Part (b) shows the labour market with the real wage on the vertical axis and hours of work on the horizontal axis. When output is at Y_0 the demand for labour is for H_0 hours and the real wage rate is W_0/P_0. There is a substantial level of unemployment. Suppose that income tax is now cut. This will increase the

Figure 13.2

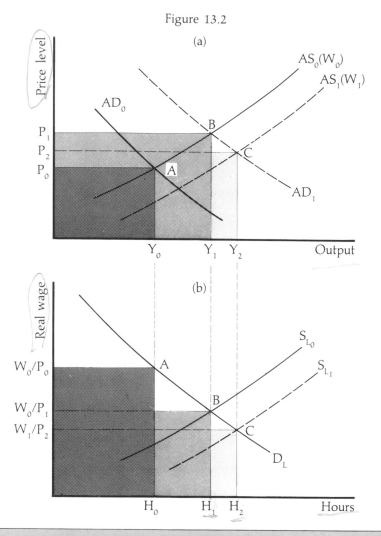

NB

Tax cuts that shift the aggregate demand curve alone will move the
economy from A to B. Tax cuts that also increase labour supply will shift
the aggregate supply curve, as will moving the economy to C rather than
B. The result is higher output and lower prices. Evidence for tax cuts
increasing labour supply is, at best, weak.

level of aggregate demand from AD_0 to AD_1. If there were no effects on
labour supply that would mean that the economy moved to point B with the
price level of P_1 and output at Y_1.

It is possible that the decrease in taxes would not only affect aggregate
demand but would also affect aggregate supply. It is possible in *theory* that
the cut in income tax would shift the supply curve of labour from SL_0 to SL_1.
This would also increase the full employment level from H_1 to H_2. If that

were to happen it would *increase* the level of unemployment for any given level of aggregate demand below the full employment level. That increase in the level of unemployment *could* reduce the level of the money wage from W_0 to W_1.[1] The lower money wage would mean that the aggregate supply curve in part (a) would shift downwards from $AS_0(W_0)$ to $AS_1(W_1)$. *If* the aggregate supply curve were shifted from $AS_0(W_0)$ to $AS_1(W_1)$ then the result of the tax change would be to move the economy from point A in Figure 13.2(a) to point C rather than to point B. The result would be higher output (Y_2 rather than Y_1) and lower prices (P_2 rather than P_1) than would have been the case had there been no effect on the supply of labour.

While they have not spelled the arguments out it may be that an argument something like this lay behind the attractiveness to the Thatcher government in the UK and the Reagan government in the US in their policy of wishing to encourage reductions in income taxation. While it is conceivable that the argument just outlined could be correct the evidence that is available does not lend very much support to it. Fully conclusive evidence on the effects of taxation on labour supply is not yet available and would in any case depend on the exact form of the tax cut but preliminary evidence suggests that the effects of income tax changes on labour supply would be small and that, if anything, reductions in taxation would decrease rather than increase labour supply. There are a variety of reasons why there might be a small decrease in labour supply as a result of tax cuts. The most important of these reasons is the strength of income effects (see Chapter 4). The conclusion then is that while there is a possible theoretical argument that cuts in income tax will increase aggregate supply as well as aggregate demand the evidence to date is not supportive.

If the objective of policy is to increase labour supply a more successful – and perhaps less costly policy might be to increase facilities for the care of young children to make it easier for their mothers to work.

Quality of labour

Once again there is little point in increasing labour supply unless it both has the necessary skills and is in the right place – or prepared to move. Measures to improve labour quality were discussed in section B.

D   SUMMARY AND CONCLUSION

One of the themes of this book is that British government policy has put too

---

1.   More realistically it would prevent the money wage from rising as fast as it would otherwise have done.

much emphasis on demand management and too little emphasis on supply management. Important exceptions to this generalization are the attempts to bring jobs to the people under regional policy and wages and incomes policy. However we have seen that wages and incomes policy has possibly had only limited effect on reducing the overall levels of wages and has at the same time frozen relative wage structures.

One of the alleged panaceas of 'supply side economics' — tax reductions to increase the incentive to work — is almost certainly not a panacea, although tax reductions may encourage risk taking and lead to higher investment.

The analysis in Chapter 2 suggests that higher investment is critical. This requires a concerted combination of special incentives, higher prices of monetary assets (lower interest rates), refraining from using variations in public sector investment to vary the levels of aggregate demand and a level of aggregate demand which is high enough to provide prospects for enhanced profitability. Profitability is necessary to finance much of investment and yet too often profits are regarded as something which is undesirable.

Despite the difficulties of enforcement I am attracted personally to James Meade's incomes policy as a way of combining changes in relative wages with a modest overall level of wage settlements. Grants and/or tax relief for re-training, for moving house, for liberal transferability of pensions, and easier access to housing would all help.

One worry is that the high and increasing levels of unemployment will not have produced a general excess supply of labour in all areas and in all skills. If this is so an increase in level of demand will soon lead to bottlenecks. This would mean that the aggregate supply curve is quite inelastic even at present high levels of unemployment. If that is so increases in aggregate demand will lead to higher prices in a closed economy or to repercussions in the foreign sector in an open economy. Part III of this book is devoted to a discussion of the foreign sector.

CONCEPTS FOR REVIEW

QUESTIONS FOR DISCUSSION

1 What do wages policies attempt to do? Why do they not always succeed?
2 Assess the view that wages policies increase structural unemployment. Would the Meade proposals avoid this problem?
3 How can structural unemployment be reduced?
4 How can we best ensure adequate amounts of investment of the right quality at the right time in the right place?

14

Rational Expectations[1]

*The Rational Expectations Hypothesis asserts that individuals do not make
systematic mistakes in forecasting the future.*[2]

Rational expectations is a recent development in macroeconomics which
hypothesizes that people make *full* use of *all* available information in making
their decisions. At least in its strictest form it leads to the prediction that
government attempts to control the economy will result in changes in the
price level and no change in output *if the policy changes are foreseen*. Output
can be altered only by unforeseen policy changes.

  The purpose of this chapter is to provide an introduction to the rational
expectations approach to macroeconomic policy. For most of the chapter the
rational expectations approach is explained as a development of the 'classical'
model outlined in Chapter 4. The most pessimistic conclusions of rational
expectations about the impotence of anticipated policy depend on this model
as we will see. The plan of the chapter is as follows. In section A the new
'classical' view of the labour market, in which the role of price expectations
are crucial, is outlined. This new 'classical' view of the labour market is then
extended to give a 'classical' expectations-augmented aggregate supply
curve. In section B the connection between expectations about the price level
and the actual price level are explored. It is only at this stage that a more
formal definition of rational expectations is employed. In section C the policy
implications of rational expectations are explored and in section D the
rational expectations hypothesis is evaluated.

---

1. This chapter may be omitted without loss of continuity.
2. David K. H. Begg, *The Rational Expectations Revolution in Macroeconomics: Theories and Evidence*,
   Philip Alan, Oxford, 1983. p. xi.

A   THE NEW 'CLASSICAL' VIEW OF THE LABOUR MARKET AND
    THE EXPECTATIONS AUGMENTED AGGREGATE SUPPLY
    CURVE.

The labour market

The first building block in explaining rational expectations is to explain the derivation of the expectations augmented supply curve associated with the new 'classical' view of the labour market. The new 'classical' model takes as its point of departure the 'classical' model of the labour market outlined in Chapter 4 where you should remember that the supply and demand for labour – both functions of the real wage – interact to determine both wages and the level of employment. Given the capital stock this level of employment determines the level of output in the economy. It should also be remembered that in the 'classical' model it is assumed that the only influence on labour supply is the real wage.

In the 'classical' model money wages are assumed to adjust to whatever level is required in a competitive market. In the **new 'classical' labour market** it is recognized that labour market information is incomplete. It is assumed that

(1)   firms know the price at which they will be able to sell their own output;

(2)   individuals do not know what the general price level will be; and

(3)   nominal wage bargains adjust to maintain labour market equilibrium.

The implications of the assumptions for the demand for labour are absolutely standard. The demand for labour is a function of the real wage. The supply of labour depends on the *expected* price level. When individuals enter into a contract to supply labour at a given money wage they are assumed to have some expectation about the general price level. It is of course easy to calculate the real wage associated with any given level of expected prices. This means that there is a labour supply curve – showing the amount of labour people wish to supply for each level of expected prices.

It should be remembered from Chapter 4 and Chapter 11 (see Figure 11.4) that price expectations in the labour market will affect the shape of the aggregate supply curve. In order to understand rational expectations it is necessary to formalize the relationship which is done with the aid of Figure 14.1. Part (b) shows the labour market. It has hours on the horizontal axis and the real wage on the vertical axis. The demand for labour D shows the amount of labour firms will wish to hire at each real wage. The solid supply curve of labour $S^E_{Pe=P0}$ shows the amount of labour workers will wish to supply at each money wage if the *expected* price level P_e is equal to the original price level (P_0). The expectations-augmented aggregate supply curve will be derived in part (a). The vertical solid line 'C'AS shows the 'classical' aggregate supply curve.

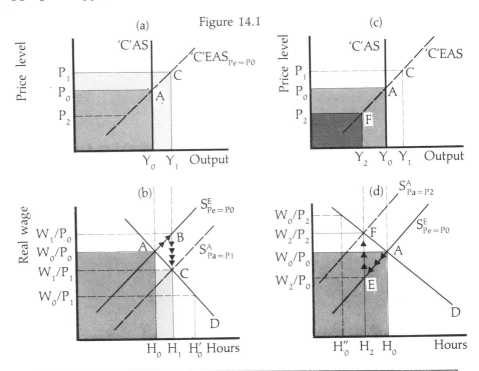

Figure 14.1

The 'classical' expectations-augmented supply curve ('C'EAS) shows the amount that will be supplied for a given level of expected prices. If the expected level of prices is $Pe = P0$ and the actual level of prices is P_1 the real wage will fall and the demand for labour will increase. Because expected prices remain at $Pe = P0$ the expected supply curve of labour remains the same. To reduce the shortage of labour money wages are bid up to W_1. At the expected real wage of W_1/P_0 workers wish to supply H_1 hours at B. Because the actual level of prices is P_1, H_1 hours are in fact supplied at a real wage of W_1/P_1. This point is labelled C, as is the corresponding point in part (a).

If the actual price level were below the expected price level at $P_2 < P_0$ there would be a surplus of labour so that the money wage would fall to W_2. The fall in the money wage would be less than the fall in the real wage so that the real wage would rise to W_2/P_2 and equilibrium would be at H_2 hours. This point and the corresponding point on the 'C'EAS are labelled F.

The 'classical' expectations augmented supply curve

We are now set to derive the **'classical' expectations-augmented aggregate supply curve ('C'EAS)**. The 'C'EAS shows the total amount that will be supplied at various actual price levels given that the expected price level is P_0 in Figure 14.1. To follow the derivation we start with the actual price level being equal to the expected price level at P_0. The money wage in Part (b) adjusts to W_0 and there is full employment with a real wage of W_0/P_0 and hours worked of H_0. This determines the position of the 'classical' aggregate supply curve 'C'AS in part (a). It also determines point A on the 'C'EAS.

Suppose now that the actual price level were higher – at P_1 – but the expected price level remained at P_0. If the money wage remained at W_0 the real wage would fall to W_0/P_1 and the demand for labour would rise to H_0'. Given the money wage of W_0 and the expected price level of P_0 workers are only willing to supply H_0 of labour. There is a potential labour shortage of $H_0' - H_0$. Because of the shortage of labour the nominal wage is bid up. Because workers expect the price level to be fixed at $Pe = P0$ an increase in the nominal wage leads workers to believe their real wage is higher. If the nominal wage required to remove the labour shortage is W_1 the *expected* real wage will be W_1/P_0 and workers will attempt to move out along the supply curve $S^E_{Pe=P0}$ from A to B increasing labour supply from H_0 to H_1. Because the actual price level is now P_1 not P_0 the actual real wage is W_1/P_1 so that workers have supplied H_1 hours at an actual real wage lower than the real wage they had expected. The dashed line $S^A_{Pa=P1}$ shows the actual labour supply curve. Workers thinking they were moving from A to B have actually moved from A to C.

It should be noted that D and $S^A_{Pe=P1}$ intersect to provide the new position of equilibrium at C. It should also be noted that the money wage has risen by less than the price level so that the real wage has fallen from W_0/P_0 to W_1/P_1. Because the real wage is lower the demand for labour is higher at H_1. The new 'classical' economists refer to C as a position of overfull employment. Employment at H_1 is above the full employment level because expected prices at P_0 are below actual prices at P_1.

Corresponding to point C in part (b) of the figure is point C in part (a) which gives a second point on the 'classical' expectations-augmented supply curve.

To find a third point on the 'C'EAS let us take a price level – P_2 – which is lower than P_0 the expected price level. To avoid clutter on the diagram I use new parts (c) and (d) which are identical in construction to (a) and (b). If the price level falls to P_2 firms will wish to hire H_0'' units of labour but households will wish to supply H_0 units, money wages will therefore need to fall to W_2

reducing the real wage to W_2/P_0 and as a result households will expect to move down their expected supply curve from A to E reducing hours to H_2. The actual price level at P_2 is however lower than the expected price level so that the actual real wage is W_2/P_2 on $S^A_{Pa=P2}$. The position of equilibrium at F shows a reduced demand for labour because money wages have fallen by less than prices $(W_2/P_2 > W_0/P_0)$. Point F represents a position of underemployment equilibrium. Corresponding to point F in part (d) is a point on the 'C'EAS in part (c) also labelled F.

It should be noted that in contrast to the other aggregate supply curves in the book the 'C'EAS has changes in money wages built into it. The reason for this is that in this model money wages are assumed always to adjust to equate supply and demand. In the remainder of this book it is recognized that money wages may not so adjust – see Chapter 4.

Effects of an increase in aggregate demand with constant expected prices

If prices are expected to remain constant an increase in aggregate demand will cause both output and prices to rise in the new 'classical' model as can be seen with the aid of Figure 14.2. We start from the positions labelled A in both parts of the figure. Aggregate demand then increases from AD_0 to AD_1 – perhaps as a result of some change in fiscal policy. This increases output from Y_0 to Y_1 and the price level from P_0 to P_1. The final position is labelled C in both parts of the figure.

B   RATIONAL EXPECTATIONS AND THE PRICE LEVEL

The purpose of this section is to explore further the relationships between expectations and the price level in the new 'classical' model and to explain the rational expectation of the price level. In the previous section expected prices remained constant. In detail the purpose of this section is

(1)   to show how a change in the expected price level shifts the 'C'EAS;
(2)   to show how the expected price level influences the actual price level;
(3)   to explain more fully the meaning of rational expectations;
(4)   to explain the rational expectation of the price level.

How changes in expected prices shift the 'C'EAS

In the last section the 'C'EAS was derived for a given set of expectations about the general price level. If the expected price level changes, both the labour supply curve and the 'C'EAS will shift. Figure 14.3 will aid the

Figure 14.2

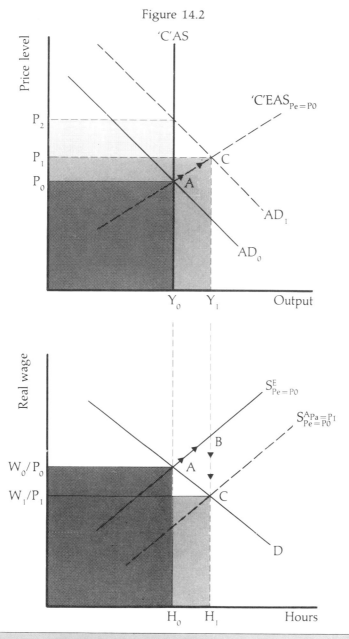

In the expectations augmented 'classical' model an increase in aggregate demand from AD_0 to AD_1 raises output to Y_1 and price level to P_1 if prices are expected to remain constant – at P_0. Higher prices increase the demand for labour and the money wage rate is increased from W_0 to W_1. The increase in money wages is less than the increase in the price level so that the real wage falls to W_1/P_1 and employment rises to H_1 hours. In the pure 'classical' model the same increase in aggregate demand would have raised the level to P_2 and output would have remained at Y_0.

Figure 14.3

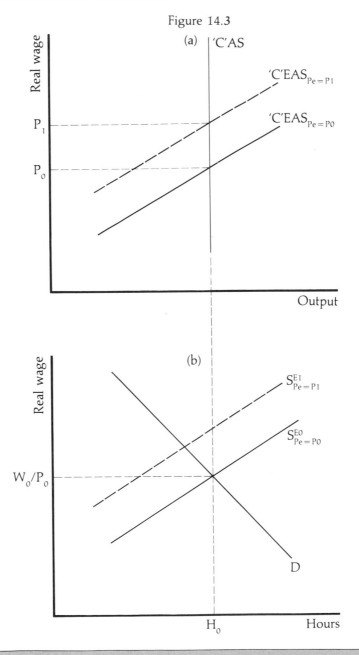

If the expected price level is $Pe = P1$ rather than $Pe = P0$ the supply curve of labour will shift to the left because the higher *expected* price level means a lower expected wage. As a consequence the expectations-augmented 'classical' supply curve also shifts up to the left.

exposition. The solid lines (D, $S^{E0}_{Pe\,=\,P0}$, 'C'AS, and 'C'EAS$_{Pe\,=\,P0}$) are the same as in Figure 14.1. Suppose now that people expect the price level to be higher at Pe = P_1 rather than Pe = P_0. If $P_1 > P_0$ the expected real wage will be lower for any nominal wage. If workers will work longer for a higher real wage then a lower real wage means workers will wish to work less. The $S^{E1}_{Pe=P1}$I curve is thus to the left of the $S^{E0}_{Pe=P1}$I. At every nominal wage workers will now wish to work less. Just as we were previously able to derive a 'C'EAS for Pe = P_0 so we can now derive a 'C'EAS for Pe = P_1. The resulting curve is shown in part (a) of the figure. Check that you understand this derivation – going back to the previous section if necessary.

How the expected price level influences the actual price level[3]

One of the complicating factors in economics is that our expectations about events may influence the events themselves. If the weatherman forecasts rain and everyone puts on a raincoat the actual probability of rain is unaffected, we all believe. If a reputed financial analyst predicts that the shares of the ABC company are seriously undervalued and should rise, people considering buying shares are likely to purchase shares in the ABC company causing the price of ABC shares to rise. The financial analyst's prediction has become self-fulfilling.

Our immediate task is to examine how the actual price level is influenced by the expected price level. In the new 'classical' model prices are determined by the expected level of aggregate demand and the 'C'EAS. Suppose that in Figure 14.4 aggregate demand is expected to remain at AD$_e$. If the expected price level were Pe = P_0 the actual price level would be P_1 (where AD$_e$ and 'C'EAS$_{Pe\,=\,P0}$) intersect. Suppose that the expected price level were P_2. This would shift the aggregate supply curve to 'C'EAS$_{Pe=P2}$ and the actual price level would rise to P_3. The actual price level depends in part on the expected price level.

It should be noted that the expected aggregate demand curve depends in principle on expectations both about things like injections, leakages and the stock of money that influences aggregate demand and also the part played by these influences in determining the shape and position of the aggregate demand curve. It is not however necessary that every individual go through the forecasting process personally. Our own expectations may be wholly or partly determined by published forecasts.

---

3. In this exposition it is assumed there is only one future time period. In fact with rational expectations it is necessary to have expectations for all future time periods. For example undergraduates reading this book would be assumed to have expectations about prices even after they retire.

Figure 14.4

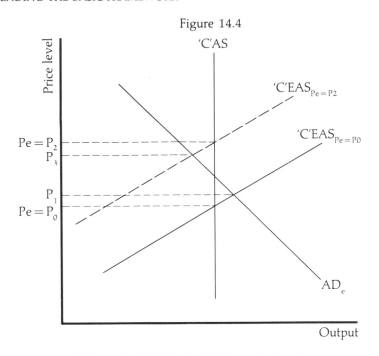

The actual price level depends on the expected price level. If the expected price level is Pe = P0, the actual price level will be P_1 where the expected level of aggregate demand AD_e intersects 'C'EAS$_{Pe=P0}$. If the expected price level were Pe = P_2 the actual price level would be determined at P_3 by the intersection of AD_e and 'C'EAS$_{Pe=P2}$. It should be noted that the expected aggregate demand curve AD_e depends in principle on expectations about both the influences on aggregate demand (injections, leakages, stock of money, etc.) *and* how these influences interact to determine the expected aggregate demand. For many individuals such expectations could be formed from published forecasts.

Rational expectations

In the quotation at the start of this chapter it was stated that the **rational expectations hypothesis** is that people do not make systematic mistakes in forecasting the future. We are now in a position to see more precisely what this means. *People's expectations are rational if they coincide with expectations based on all available information.* Note that I did not say that to be rational an individual has to process all available information personally. Nevertheless people on average have to behave as if they had done this.[4] In order to

4.   In microeconomics an analogy would be the MC = MR rule for profit maximization. For this to be a useful way of analyzing firms' behaviour does *not* require either that firms go through the MC = MR calculations or even that they understand the terms marginal cost and marginal revenue.

process information and to use it in order to forecast future behaviour we must have a theory that explains how economic variables are related. A theory which is wrong may of course give predictions that are systematically wrong. The avoidance of systematic mistakes requires us to behave *as if* we know the correct theory. In the next subsection the rational expectations approach is illustrated by deriving the rational expectation of the price level.

The rational expectation of the price level

The purpose of this subsection is to explain the **rational expectation of the price level**. As has just been said this requires us to have the correct theoretical model of price level determination. *For the purposes of this explanation* it will be assumed that the correct model is the new 'classical' model as outlined in this chapter.

    The rational expectation of the price level is the price level predicted by theory. We have already seen that the actual price level is influenced by the expected price level. How then is this rational expectation formed? Suppose that the expected aggregate demand curve is AD_e in Figure 14.5. The rational expectation of the price level is that it will be $P*$ where AD_e and 'C'AS intersect. To see why this is the rational expectation of the price level it is necessary to demonstrate that other expectations are not rational as they would not be predicted by the theory which is being assumed to be correct. Suppose that the expected price were $Pe = P_0$ which is well below the rationally expected price $P*$. If the expected price were $Pe = P_0$ we would be on $'CEAS_{Pe=P0}$ and the actual price level would be P_1. However if the actual price level were P_1 then that is what we would expect. If the expected level of prices were P_1 the expectations augmented supply curve would shift to $'CEAS_{Pe=P1}$. Note that $'CEAS_{Pe=P1}$ and AD_e intersect at P_2. We should therefore expect prices to be P_2 giving us $'CEAS_{Pe=P2}$. With AD_e this determines the new price level at P_3 causing 'CEAS to shift etc. Note that at each stage the price rise becomes smaller and the series comes to an end when $Pe = P*$. To insure you understand this argument work it through assuming that the initially expected price level is above $P*$.

C   POLICY IMPLICATIONS OF RATIONAL EXPECTATIONS IN THE NEW 'CLASSICAL' MODEL

Effect of an anticipated change in aggregate demand

We are now in a position to explain why it was asserted at the start of this chapter that fully anticipated changes in aggregate demand will change prices

Figure 14.5

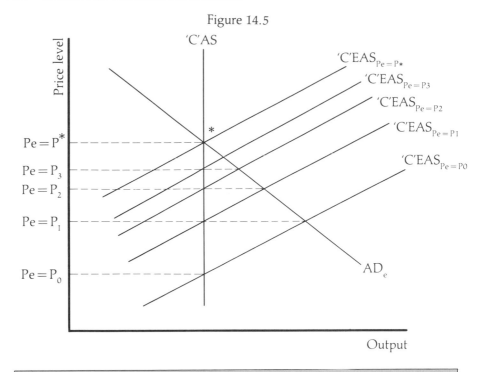

The rationally expected price level is P* given by the intersection of the 'classical' aggregate supply curve 'C'AS and the expected aggregate demand curve AD_e. To see this suppose the expected price level were quite different, say, $Pe = P_0$. If expected prices were $Pe = P_0$ the actual price level would be P_1. If we predicted prices would be $Pe = P_1$, prices would in fact be P_2 and if that level of prices were expected, prices would be P_3. Only when expected prices are P* is the actual level of prices equal to the expected price level.

but not output in the new 'classical'/rational expectations model. The task is straightforward as all of the necessary building blocks have been assembled. We know how the 'classical' expectations-augmented supply curve is formed. We know how price expectations influence actual prices given the anticipated level of aggregate demand and the 'C'EAS. We know the rational expectation of the price level.

Suppose we start from point A in Figure 14.6 which is similar in construction to Figure 14.5. Point A is determined by an initial level of expected aggregate demand AD_{e0}, the 'C'AS and the 'C'EAS$_{Pe = P0}$. It should be immediately obvious that point A corresponds to point * in Figure 14.5. If the anticipated level of aggregate demand were to rise from AD_{e0} to AD_{e1} the rational expectation of the price level would rise from P_0 to P_1. (If the reasons for this are not clear re-read the immediately preceding subsection.)

Figure 14.6

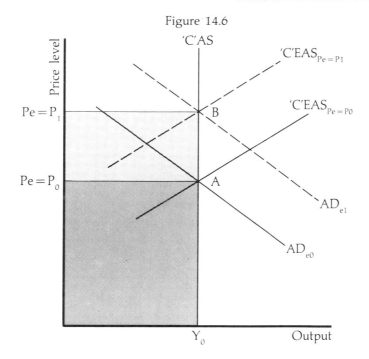

A fully anticipated change in aggregate demand affects the price level but not output in the new 'classical' model. If the economy starts with expected aggregate demand of AD_{e0} the expected price level is $Pe = P0$. However if there is a fully anticipated increase in aggregate demand to AD_{e1} the rational expectations price level would be $Pe = P1$. As a result the 'classical' expectations-augmented supply curve shifts up to the dashed line and actual prices rise to the expected level P_1 leaving output unchanged at Y_0.

With the expected price level at P_1 the 'C'EAS shifts from $'C'EAS_{Pe=P0}$ to $'C'EAS_{Pe=P1}$ (see Figure 14.3). The actual price level will, as before, be determined by the intersection of the 'C'EAS and the anticipated aggregate demand curve; in this case by the interseaction of $'C'EAS_{Pe=P1}$ and AD_{e1}. The economy moves from A to B. Prices have risen from P_0 to P_1 but output remains at Y_0.

Effect of an unanticipated change in aggregate demand

According to the new 'classical'/rational expectations model it is only an unanticipated change in aggregate demand that can affect output. The argument is presented with the aid of Figure 14.7. As in the last Figure 4.6 we start at position A where output is Y_0 and both the expected and the actual price level are P0. An unexpected increase in demand raises the actual level of

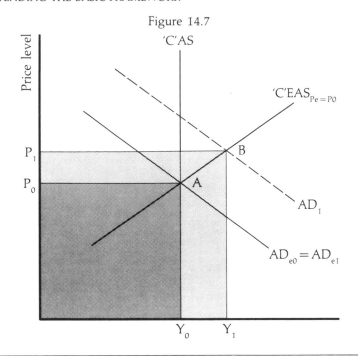

Figure 14.7

We start from A with the output at Y_0 and the price level P_0. An unanticipated increase in aggregate demand shifts the aggregate demand curve to AD_1. *Because* it is unanticipated expected prices remain at P_0 and the economy moves to B with prices rising to P_1 and output rising to Y_1.

demand from AD_{e0} to AD_1. However, by assumption the expected level of aggregate demand remains at AD_{e0}; that is $AD_{e1} = AD_{e0}$. Because the expected price level remains at P_0 the 'C'EAS does not shift. The actual level of prices rises to P_1 – determined by the intersection of the 'C'EAS at AD_1. Output rises to Y_1.

The central proposition of the rational expectations approach for macroeconomic policy is contained in the last two results. This proposition is that changes in economic policy will only affect output if they are unexpected. Anticipated changes will only affect prices.

There are a number of reasons why I think this central policy conclusion is too pessimistic about the possible role for macroeconomic policy. These are considered in the next section.

D   EVALUATION OF RATIONAL EXPECTATIONS

There are a number of reasons why we may wish to question the very pessimistic conclusion that anticipated changes in output affect only prices not output. Some of these reasons are consistent with the basic rational expectations framework but others are not.

The position of the aggregate supply curve

The discussion so far in this chapter has assumed that the ordinary – i.e. not augmented – aggregate supply curve is both vertical and fixed. If expectations are rational they are based on the correct theory and it has been argued in this book that the correct theory allows for both a positively sloped aggregate supply curve *and* one that may shift.

I start with the latter. We have seen in Chapter 13 that many types of policy will affect aggregate supply. Suppose we are considering the anticipated effects of a policy of incentives to investment. We know that if successful the policy will increase both aggregate demand because of higher injections – and aggregate supply – because of a larger capital stock. The initial position is shown by the solid lines in Figure 14.8 and is labelled A. The effects of the higher investment are expected to lead to higher aggregate demand – up to AD_{e1} – and higher aggregate supply – up to AS_{e1}. As the

Figure 14.8

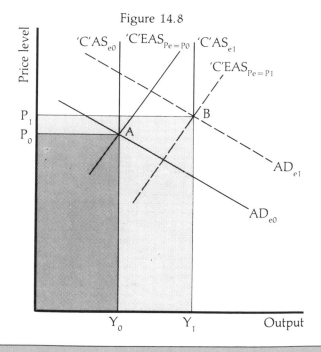

If the policy is anticipated to increase both aggregate supply – to $'C'AS_{e1}$ in the figure – and aggregate demand to AD_{e1} then an anticipated policy will have increased output as well as prices.

diagram is drawn the rationally expected price level rises to P_1 as does the actual price level. The new equilibrium at B has not only higher prices but also higher output. Failure to allow for policy shifting aggregate supply can only be justified in a very short-run model. Concentration on a model which is too short run would be obtaining the result that output cannot change by assumption rather than by argument.

Shape of the aggregate supply curve

It was argued in Chapter 4 that the (unaugmented) aggregate supply curve would be positively sloped rather than vertical because of interest rate effects, real balance effects, sticky money wages and possibly because of money illusion. If the (unaugmented) aggregate supply curve is positively sloped then a policy that affects only anticipated demand will still raise output as well as prices as can be seen from Figure 14.9. The construction of Figure 14.9 is the same as the previous figures in this chapter except for the slope of the (unaugmented) aggregate supply curve and the reader is left to work out why the economy moves from A to B with prices rising from P_0 to P_1 and output rising from Y_0 to Y_1.

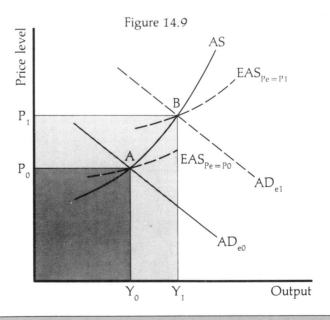

Figure 14.9

If the (unaugmented) aggregate supply curve is positively sloped an anticipated increase in aggregate demand will raise both prices (from P_0 to P_1) and output (from Y_0 to Y_1).

Working of the labour market

As was stated in section A of this chapter it is assumed in the new 'classical' analysis that money wages adjust to equate the supply and demand for labour. If money wages do not adjust – because of union pressures or sticky wage hierarchies – then the labour equilibrium described in section A may not occur. If wages do not adjust to equilibrium levels this can give rise to unemployment. The level of this unemployment and the associated level of output can be affected by anticipated changes in economic policy as well as by unanticipated ones.

Objections to the rational expectations hypothesis

The objections just given to the conclusion that anticipated policy changes will affect only prices and not output are objections to the new 'classical' versions of rational expectations, not to the rational expectations hypothesis *per se.*

There are however a number of objections to the rational expectations hypothesis which are discussed below.

Costs of acquiring information

The rational expectations hypothesis assumes people analyze all relevant information. It is objected that this is far too costly for individuals. Supporters of rational expectations argue that all that is required is that a few bodies process the information and publish the results – other people can base their expectations on these findings. Whether enough people take these forecasts seriously is an open question.

Knowing policy

The conclusion that anticipated policy has no effects on output depends on being able to anticipate policy. It is possible that a government will both announce clearly what it intends to do and then carry out its intentions. After a few years we might have a clear idea of what policy it would follow. But would a new government have such a clear policy? Would it in fact be able to carry it out or would events blow it off course?

Finding the correct model

There are two issues here. The first is what is the correct model; for example is it Keynesian or monetarist? We have already seen that this can be accommodated within the broad rational expectations framework. The second issue is that even if we know what the correct model is how do we know the precise coefficients? For example the correct model may be one in which consumption depends on income. How do we find the correct value for the marginal propensity to consume if the observed relationships between income and consumption depend on expectations which may have been wrong.

In my view this is perhaps the most telling objection. The Director of the National Institute of Economic and Social Research – one of the leading UK forecasting bodies – put it this way. Rational expectations implies

> that agents in the past have behaved as if they already knew the structure, and even the parameters, of the models now being built to describe their behaviour. It is surprising how seriously this view has been put forward. It seems to imply that the public has access to quantified knowledge of the economy, free of all systematic bias, which is not available to professional economists.[5]

It was pointed out in the chapter on forecasting that forecasting errors are quite large. Unless all of these errors are random even the professional forecasts are not free of systematic bias.

Adaptive expectations

To my mind the main lesson from the rational expectations literature is that expectations are important. To reject rational expectations is not to reject the idea that we may be able to learn from our mistakes – although perhaps not in as formal a way as implied by rational expectations. Nor is the rejection of rational expectations the rejection of the importance of expectations. If expectations are not formed rationally how are they formed? Perhaps the leading alternative to rational expectations is the adaptive expectations hypothesis. The adaptive expectations hypothesis has people learning from past behaviour. The adaptive expectations hypothesis about the price level would be that people expect prices to go up next year by an amount reflecting price changes in recent years, probably putting greatest weight on the most recent changes.

---

5.   Andrew Britton 'Introduction' to A. Britton (ed.), *Employment, Output and Inflation: The National Institute Model of the British Economy*, Heineman, London, 1983.

Conclusion

The new 'classical' version of rational expectations appeals to monetarists who find in it support for a basically monetarist position because of its conclusion that policy is most likely to affect prices rather than output. For this reason the terms new monetarist and new classical are sometimes used in place of rational expectations.

CONCEPTS FOR REVIEW

QUESTIONS FOR DISCUSSION

1   How do expectations about the price level influence the actual price level?
2   What is the rational expectation of the price level?
3   Explain why the rational expectation school believes that an anticipated increase in aggregate demand will affect prices not output.
4   Explain why an anticipated increase in aggregate demand may increase output.

PART III
THE OPEN ECONOMY

15

International Trade

The purpose of Part III of this book is to discuss the macroeconomic implications of economic relationships with other countries. We will see that these relationships offer the potential for all countries to become better off and we will also see that the same international trade complicates the conduct of economic policy.

The purpose of the present chapter is to provide the background for that discussion: to discuss the principles underlying international trade, to discuss quotas and tariffs which tend to limit trade, and to describe the institutions which are designed to promote it.

A THE PRINCIPLES OF INTERNATIONAL TRADE

The purpose of this section is to explain the principles of international trade. As we will see the application of these principles is not confined to the international arena and in fact they are often easier to understand if we start with domestic examples.

Arbitrage and speculation

Arbitrage and speculation are terms which are used to describe buying in a market where the price is low and selling in a market where the price is high. The term **arbitrage** is used when prices in the markets are known and the term **speculation** is used when the prices in one of the markets are not known.

Arbitrage

It has just been said that arbitrage refers to buying in a market where the price is low and selling in another market where the price is higher. When I was an undergraduate, a fellow undergraduate was driving along a road and noticed that a road-side stall was selling watermelons. A few miles down the road he noticed another road-side stall also selling watermelons. In the second stall the price of watermelons was twice as high as in the first stall. He asked the owners of the second stall what they had to pay for watermelons and found it was more than watermelons were being sold for in the first stall. He took an order from the owner of the second stall, drove back to the first stall, bought a number of watermelons and returned to the second stall where he sold them for a profit. While he was still an undergraduate he developed this into a thriving business where he had two trucks and two drivers employed buying fruit and vegetables where it was inexpensive, transporting it and selling it where it was more expensive.

Figure 15.1

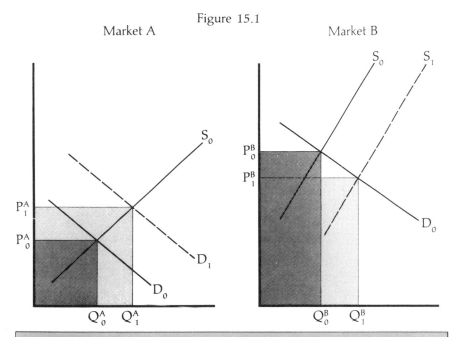

Arbitrage involves buying at a low price in market a and selling at a high price in market b. Speculation is similar except that the future price is unknown.

The argument about arbitrage in competitive markets with many buyers and sellers can be illustrated in Figure 15.1. The same commodity, which might be watermelons, is sold in two markets, market A and market B. Before arbitrage the position is as represented by the solid lines. In market A the price is low at P_0^A and in market B the price is high as P_0^B. Traders will notice the price differential and buy in market A, shifting the demand curve from D_0 to D_1 raising the price from P_0^A to P_1^A. Purchases will be $Q_1^A - Q_0^A$. This quantity is then sold on market B. This shifts the supply curve in market B from S_0 to S_1. Notice that the price in market B falls from P_0^B to P_1^B. Notice that the effect of arbitrage is to reduce the price differential in the two markets very substantially. Notice, however, that as the diagram is drawn, the price differential is not entirely eliminated (i.e. P_1^B is higher than P_1^A). The reason for this is that traders will have certain costs in buying and selling goods and in transporting them. The principles of arbitrage are precisely the same whether the markets concerned are all located in one country or whether they are located in more than one country.

'Law' of one price

Arbitrage means that only one price will rule in a market if we neglect distortions such as transportation costs (and quotas and tariffs – see section 8). We saw in the preceding subsection that if there is more than one price people will buy in the lower price market and resell in the higher price market until the price differential becomes equal to transport differentials. This is straightforward in application in domestic markets and explains why homogeneous products like wheat or common bricks will have a common price ignoring transport costs.

In international markets the same principles should operate but there are complications in practice. The first of these complications is multiple currencies. If a ton of steel costs $1500 in the US and an identical amount of steel costs £1200 in the UK, and if price of £1 is $1.50, that is the exchange rate is $1.50 = £1, then the steel will be cheaper to buy in the US. People will wish to buy US steel rather than British steel so long as these conditions remain. **The 'law' of one price** predicts that prices or the exchange rate will change so that prices become equalized (see subsection on purchasing power parity in Chapter 16). A second complication is that the costs of acquiring and acting on information may outweigh the potential profits from arbitrage. A third complication is non-price barriers to trade. In the early 1980s many kinds of automobiles were cheaper on the continent than in the UK even after allowing for differences in taxes. The differential was easier to maintain in this case because of the complications caused by driving on different sides of the road and detailed differences in safety requirements. Manufacturers recognizing the higher profits in UK markets did little to make it easier for people to buy cars on the continent. Non-price barriers also prevented the importation into Britain of cheaper UHT milk from the continent until late 1983.

Speculation

The idea behind speculation is basically the same as the idea behind arbitrage. The difference is that with speculation the price in one of the markets is unknown. Perhaps the most common form of speculation is to buy in the present when the price is low and sell in the future when it is hoped that the price will be higher. When this happens the argument can be illustrated again with Figure 15.1. Market A is now the present market and market B is the future market. A fundamental difference between arbitrage and speculation is that with arbitrage the trader knows precisely what the prices are in both markets. With speculation on the other hand the trader can only know the present price. He can clearly only make guesses about the future price. However in some circumstances these guesses are likely to be fairly well founded. For example if one considers the prices of agricultural crops the price is likely to be low immediately after the harvest and then is likely to increase throughout the year until it reaches its peak just before the next harvest. This pattern is illustrated by the solid line in Figure 15.2. It will be noted that Figure 15.2 has price on the vertical axis and time on the horizontal axis. At the time of the first harvest the price is low and then gradually increases until the time of the second harvest when it falls down and a new cycle starts. It is clearly fairly easy for the trader to forecast the general pattern of prices although of course there will be uncertainty about the precise pattern of price movements in any particular year. Nevertheless what the speculator does is to buy the crop at the time of the harvest, store

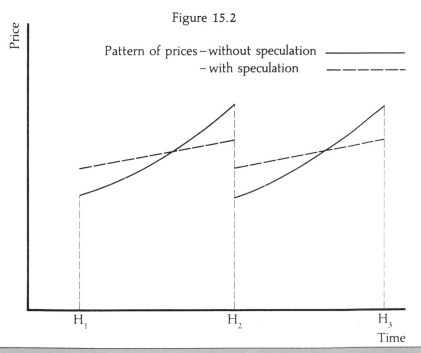

Figure 15.2

Pattern of prices – without speculation ————————
– with speculation — — — — — —

The solid line shows the assumed time path for the price of an agricultural commodity between harvests. If speculators predict this pattern they will buy soon after one harvest and sell soon before the next. The effect is to make prices more stable as is shown by the dashed line.

it[1] and then sell it later in the year when the price is higher. The result of the speculator's activity is to raise the price over what it would have been just after the harvest and to reduce it below what it would have been just before the next harvest. The dashed line in Figure 15.2 shows the assumed price movement including the effect of the speculator.

Speculation has just been described as purchasing in the present when the price is low in order to sell in the future when it is hoped that the price will be higher. Conversely if the speculator believes that the price will fall he will sell in the present and buy later. The activities of speculators, as they have been described so far, have been to stabilize both prices and quantities. Many people would think this is a very valuable economic activity. Why then is speculation so often viewed as an undesirable activity? The answer to that may in part be prejudice, but the activities of speculators are not helpful when their price forecasts are wrong. If a speculator expects the price to rise he will buy now. Suppose, however, that he is wrong and the price is about to fall. The act of speculation increases the present price, when the speculator buys, and decreases the price later when the speculator sells. Thus when the speculator is wrong his activity is destabilizing. It is perhaps fortunate that speculators can only make profits when their activities are stabilizing.

The reader may have noted that no mention has been made of whether the markets are all in the same country or if they are in different countries. One can speculate on the price of American wheat both in Chicago and in London.

Gains from trade

Both individuals and countries can gain from trade. Some of these gains arise purely from trade and some involve both production and trade.

Gains from pure trade

Even in a world in which there was no production people could gain from trade and people certain find it *mutually* advantageous to exchange goods that have been produced. Two youngsters may swap or barter, say, an old pocket knife for five marbles. Both may feel better off as a result. Trade makes it possible for countries without some resource – say iron ore, or petroleum or a tropical climate, to acquire what it does not have in exchange for something else.

Trade also makes it possible to exchange goods to make us better off even if we already have some of each of the goods to be traded. Two youngsters, one with two red marbles and eleven green marbles, the other with five red

---

1. The actual storage need not be done by the speculator who may never actually see the crop.

and one green marble, may both find trade in marbles is advantageous.[2] At the international level the same principle explains in part why nations with similar economies still find trade advantageous.

Gains from production and trade: comparative advantage

So far we have considered pure trade only. However trade becomes even more advantageous when it is combined with specialization in production. Subsistence farmers show that it is possible to produce most things that are absolutely necessary for bare survival, but of course if we specialize and produce a limited range of goods we can be much better off.

The most important principle underlying international trade is the principle of **comparative advantage** and it is that principle that is explained in this subsection. The principle of comparative advantage is about specialization and the division of labour. Like the other principles of trade, the principle of comparative advantage has both domestic and international applications, and once again it is easiest to grasp if we begin with a domestic application. One of the best known stories of the principle of comparative advantage concerns the organization of work within a lawyer's office. Suppose that the entire staff of the office consists of the lawyer and a secretary. Suppose further that the work in the office consists of doing law and typing. We might expect to find that the secretary was the best typist in the office and that the lawyer knew the most law. If these expectations were fulfilled then it would obviously be a straightforward matter that the lawyer would do the law and the secretary the typing. Suppose, however, that it happened that not only was the lawyer better at law than the secretary, suppose also that the lawyer was a better typist than the secretary. How should the work be organized when the lawyer was both a better lawyer and a better typist? Once again it seems highly probable that the most efficient arrangement will be for the secretary to do the typing and the lawyer the law. Why is this? The probability is that the lawyer is very much better than the secretary at law and only a little better than the secretary at typing. The secretary has a *comparative* advantage at typing, the lawyer a *comparative* advantage at law. That simple example is worth thinking about because it contains in it the basis of the principle of comparative advantage which is the principle that underlies much of the potential gain which can be made from international trade. The essence of the example would not change if we called the lawyer country A and the secretary country B and referred to law and typing as two commodities in international trade. That is indeed the basis of the example which is to follow. To keep the illustration of the principle of comparative

2. Micro texts show that trade will be advantageous until the relative prices of the products are equal to the marginal rates of substitution between the products.

advantage as simple as possible it will be assumed that there is no money (which means that goods are bartered), no transportation costs, and that countries can produce as much or as little of commodities as they wish to at constant costs.

Absolute advantage

Let us further assume that there are two imaginary countries which we can name Shangrai La and Utopia and that there are two products that are produced in both countries, namely Longevity Pills and Bliss Pills. The assumptions that have been introduced simplify the argument without affecting its essentials. All that remains is for assumptions to be made about the real costs of production of Bliss Pills and Longevity Pills in the two countries. Suppose that the numbers that can be produced are as given in Table 15.1. In Shangrai La a worker can produce 10 boxes of Bliss Pills or 16 (boxes of) Longevity Pills per week whereas in Utopia the worker can produce 5 Bliss pills or 20 Longevity Pills per week.

TABLE 15.1   PRODUCTION: BOXES PER WORKER PER WEEK

	Shangrai La	*Utopia*
Bliss Pills	10	5
Longevity Pills	16	20

It is easy to see with the aid of Table 15.2 that world production of both commodities can be increased if Shangrai La specializes in the production of Longevity Pills. The movement of workers to the production of Longevity Pills in Utopia and to the Bliss Pill industry in Shangrai La increases total 'world' production of both products. How this increase in world production might be divided is considered after looking at comparative advantage. Having specialized Utopia would export Longevity Pills to Shangrai La in exchange for Shangrai La exporting Bliss Pills. The results of this example are straightforward because Utopia has an absolute advantage in the production of Longevity Pills whereas Shangrai La has an absolute advantage in the production of Bliss Pills. **Absolute advantage** means that one producer can produce more for a given amount of resources than another producer.

TABLE 15.2   PRODUCTION: BOXES PER WEEK

	Shangrai La: effect of moving 10 workers from LP to BP	Utopia: effect of moving 10 workers from BP to LP	World production
Bliss Pills (BP)	+ 100	− 50	+ 50
Longevity Pills (LP)	− 160	+ 200	+ 40

TABLE 15.3   PRODUCTION: BOXES PER WORKER PER WEEK

	Shangrai La	Utopia
Bliss Pills	10	15
Longevity Pills	16	20

Comparative advantage

Suppose, however, that we complicate the issue slightly by changing the assumption about the costs of production in the two countries. Table 15.3 shows the new assumed production figures. A comparison of Tables 15.2 and 15.3 shows that the production possibilities in Shangrai La remain unchanged whereas in Utopia it is now possible to produce 15 Bliss Pills where before it was only able to produce 5 a week. It can be seen that in Utopia a week's work will produce more Bliss Pills than in Shangrai La *and*, a week's work will produce more Longevity Pills than in Shangrai La. Utopia can produce more Bliss Pills *and* more Longevity Pills, which means it has an absolute advantage in the production of both Bliss Pills and Longevity Pills. Does this mean that trade will not be advantageous? The answer to that is no. The reason why Shangrai La can benefit from trade despite being able to produce less per worker than Utopia in both products is that Shangrai La has a comparative advantage in the production of Longevity Pills. Comparative advantage arises whenever there is a difference in *relative* production capabilities between the two producing countries. In the present example the ratio of production of Bliss Pills to Longevity Pills in Shangrai La is 5–8 whereas in Utopia it is 3–4. This means that Utopia has a comparative advantage in producing Bliss Pills and Shangrai La a comparative advantage in producing Longevity Pills. To see this let us look at Table 15.4. Suppose that in Shangrai La we take 8 workers off the production of Bliss Pills and move them on to the production of Longevity Pills. Output of Bliss Pills falls by 80 (= 8 × 10)) whilst the output of Longevity Pills rises by 128 (= 8 × 16). Suppose that in Utopia we shift 6 workers from making Longevity Pills into making Bliss Pills. The production of Longevity Pills will fall by 120(= 6 × 20) whereas that of Bliss Pills will rise by 90 (= 6 × 15). The final column of Table 15.4 shows the position of the world, i.e. for the two countries combined. It can be seen that the total world output of Bliss Pills has risen by 10 a week and the total output of Longevity Pills has risen by 8 a week. There is the possibility of both countries benefiting from specializing in the commodity where they have the comparative advantage and then entering into trade.

TABLE 15.4   PRODUCTION: BOXES PER WEEK

	Shangrai La: effect of moving 8 workers from LP to BP	Utopia: effect of moving 6 workers from BP to LP	World production
Bliss Pills (BP)	− 80	+ 90	+ 10
Longevity Pills (LP)	+ 128	− 120	+ 8

The principle of comparative advantage does not tell us what the distribution of the potential gains will be. They might be go all, or largely to Shangrai La or conversely mainly to Utopia. Table 15.5 illustrates one possibility. Suppose that Shangrai La and Utopia get together and agree that Shangrai La will sell, i.e. export, 124 Longevity Pills to Utopia each week and in exchange will import 85 Bliss Pills from Utopia. If that were to happen then the gains after trade would be as shown in the table. Both countries would have 5 more Bliss Pills per week than before trade and 4 more Longevity Pills a week than before trade, although once again, it should be stressed that this equal division of the gains is by assumption only.

TABLE 15.5   CHANGE IN CONSUMPTION: BOXES PER WEEK

	Shangrai La	Utopia
Bliss Pills	+ 5	+ 5
Longevity Pills	+ 4	+ 4

Having illustrated the basic principles in the simplest possible case it is now worth thinking about the assumptions that were made earlier. It was assumed that both countries could switch from the production of one good to another without affecting the cost per unit. This, however, may not be correct. One possibility is that there will be increasing returns to scale, if that is so then the gains from trade can be larger than the illustration given. Another possibility is that there will be decreasing returns to scale. If so, as the country tries to specialize in the commodities in which it has a comparative advantage the cost of production of these commodities will rise and this will have the effect of limiting the potential gains. We have also abstracted from transportation costs. Transportation costs must of course be paid, and these will tend to offset potential gains from trade. This explains why commodities like bricks which are heavy in relationship to their value do not feature prominently in international trade.

As the final complication to the principle of comparative advantage suppose that we recognize that goods are traded for money and not bartered. Suppose further that the currency of Shangrai La is roubles and that the currency of Utopia is the drachma and there is a fixed exchange rate of 2 roubles for 1 drachma. We can now look at the market for one of the commodities, say Bliss Pills, which is represented in Figure 15.3. Part A of the diagram shows the supply and demand of Bliss Pills in Shangrai La and it can be seen that the equilibrium price of Bliss Pills is assumed to be 8 roubles in the absence of trade. In part B the supply and demand of Bliss Pills in Utopia are shown and it can be seen that the supply and demand curves intersect, before trade, at a price of 2 drachmas. We have seen that the comparative advantage in the production of Bliss Pills is in Utopia. Utopia will increase its output of Bliss Pills from BP_0^u to BP_1^u. It will then export $BP_1^u - BP_2^u$. Shangrai La will import Bliss Pills (of the same amount that Utopia exports if there are only two countries). The arbitrage that this involves has the effect of reducing the price of Bliss Pills in Shangrai La from 8 roubles to 6 roubles and to raise the price of Bliss Pills in Utopia from 2 drachmas to 3 drachmas (in the absence of transportation costs).

The lessons are that people can have higher living standards through specializing where their comparative advantage lies and that trade makes it possible to have a wider choice. We can enjoy, for example, subtropical fruits in temperate climates. Even when commodities are basically the same the choice may be widened by, for example, having available different brands of clothing, domestic appliances, and automobiles. This wider choice also brings increasing advantages from competition. When domestic producers have to compete with foreign producers they typically have to pay more attention to their own efficiency and this ultimately benefits the consumer through lower prices and better products.

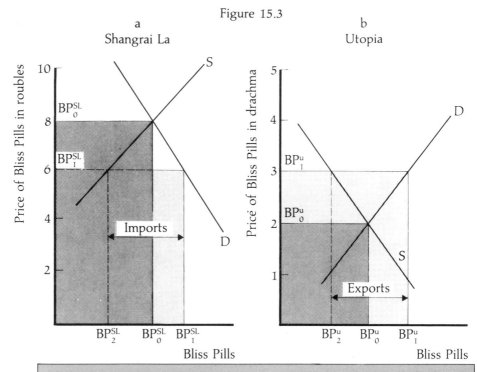

Figure 15.3

With fixed exchange rates (here 2 drachma = 1 rouble) Utopia, the country with the comparative advantage in Bliss Pills, exports Bliss Pills to Shangrai La. Arbitrage will result in equal prices in the two countries if there are no transportation costs.

We have seen that there is a general presumption that countries generally can benefit from specialization in areas where they have a comparative advantage. There is, however, one major drawback to this argument and that is that it is an entirely static one. By the nature of things countries do not have a comparative advantage in the production of something which they are not producing at all! It is also unlikely that countries will have a comparative advantage in something which they are just beginning to produce. It follows from this that countries should specialize in areas where they can expect to have a comparative advantage rather than in areas where they actually have a comparative advantage at the moment. More precisely countries should specialize where they can expect to have an **incremental comparative advantage**. A country may have a comparative advantage now in peanuts but it may have a greater incremental comparative advantage in microcomputers. It will grow faster if it specializes where it has the incremental comparative advantage. The effect of making the principle of comparative advantage dynamic is that its application is very much more difficult and very much more uncertain. As we will see dynamic comparative advantage is probably the most important justification for quotas and tariffs, a subject to which we now turn.

B   QUOTAS AND TARIFFS

We have seen that there is a general presumption that people will gain from international trade. A corollary of this proposition is that artificial restrictions on trade will generally be harmful. In this section we look at the two most important forms of restriction on trade: quotas and tariffs and we look at the circumstances under which these may be justified. Quotas are a restriction on the physical volume of trade, usually through restricting imports. Thus steel might be given a quota of so many million tons, or cloth a quota of so many million square metres. A zero quota would of course amount to a ban on that class of imports. A tariff is a tax, again usually on imports, and has the effect of restricting imports through raising their price. We will see that while both quotas and imports are generally undesirable the arguments against quotas are stronger than the arguments against tariffs.

In this section we look at trade restrictions on individual markets ignoring the effect of changes on imports and exports on leakages and injections and hence on overall levels of output and prices. We return to these more general issues in Chapter 17.

Quotas

Quotas normally take the form of a restriction on the physical amount of imports. Their effect is to decrease total consumption of the good, to increase domestic prices and, perhaps, to increase domestic production. The argument is illustrated with the aid of Figure 15.4 in which it is assumed that markets are competitive. The figure has the quantity of some good on the horizontal axis and price on the vertical axis. It is assumed that before the introduction of the quota that the good in question is both produced at home and imported. The supply curve of the home produced goods is shown at the line S_H. The supply curve of the imported goods is shown at the line S_{IM}. The supply curve of imported goods would generally be more elastic than the supply curve of home produced goods because imports in any one country are likely to be a small proportion of the total world output of the good in question. For convenience the supply of imported goods is shown here as being perfectly elastic. If we assume that markets are competitive and that consumers are indifferent between the purchase of home produced goods and charged more for what they do have. Even the gain to domestic producers is

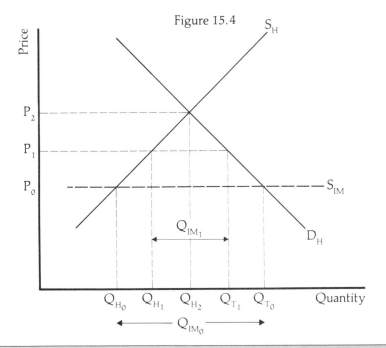

Figure 15.4

Before a quota is introduced Q_{H_0} is produced at home, Q_{IM_0} is imported so that Q_{T_0} is consumed at a price of P_0. Introducing a quota restricting imports to Q_{IM_1} enables domestic production to increase from Q_{H_0} to Q_{H_1}. Total consumption falls from Q_{T_0} to Q_{T_1}. The elimination of imports would mean home production equal to total consumption at Q_{H_2} and price up further at P_2.

imports then the consumer will buy home produced goods when they are cheaper (as occurs to the left of the intersection S_{IM} and S_H) and will buy imported goods when they are less expensive than home produced goods (which occurs to the right of intersection S_H and S_{IM}). The effect of this is that total consumption in the home market will be Q_{T_0}. The price will be P_0. This total consumption will be made up of Q_{T_1} produced in the home market and of Q_{IM_0} of imported goods. Suppose that a quota is now introduced that reduces imports from IM_0 to IM_1. The reduction in imports will have three effects. It will reduce the total quantity sold (from Q_{T_0} to Q_{T_1}), it will increase the quantity of home produced goods (from Q_{H_0} to Q_{H_1}), and it will raise the domestic price (from P_0 to P_1). If the quota was set at zero, and imports totally eliminated, price and quantity would be determined by the intersection of the domestic demand and supply curves at Q_{H_2} and P_2.

It can be seen that quotas cause domestic producers to be better off. But this is at the expense of consumers who have less to consume and who are charged more for what they do have. Even the gain to domestic producers is uncertain because it assumes that nothing happens to the ability of domestic producers to export. If the effect of one country introducing a quota is to cause other countries to retaliate, as is likely, then quotas in other countries would restrict the capacity of the first country to export. Quotas can thus cause everyone to be worse off by negating the gains from trade.

Tariffs

Tariffs normally take the form of a tax on imported goods. Their effects are in general similar to the effects of quotas. There is, however, the difference that with tariffs the government receives revenue. The argument is illustrated in Figure 15.5. The construction of Figure 15.5 is similar to the construction of Figure 15.4; and as before the position before the imposition of the tariff is total consumption of Q_{T_0} of which Q_{H_0} is home produced and Q_{IM_0} is imported. The price is P_0. If a tariff of t_1 is introduced on imported goods, its effect is to shift the supply curve of imported goods upwards by the amount of the tariff. That is to say the supply curve shifts from S_{IM_0} to S_{IM_1}. The reader should verify that the effect of the tariff is to reduce total consumption

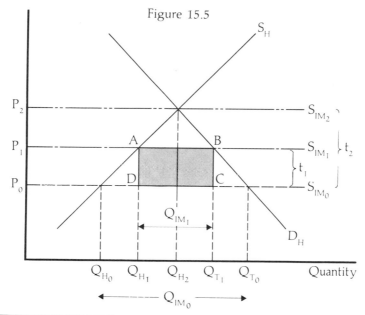

Figure 15.5

Before a tariff is introduced Q_{H_0} is produced at home, Q_{IM_0} is imported so that domestic consumption is Q_{T_0} at P_0. A tariff of t_1 per unit raises the supply curve of imports to S_{IM_1}. This reduces imports to IM_1 and prices rise to P_1. The tariff raises ABCD of revenue. A tariff of t_2 would eliminate imports and have identical effects to a zero quota – see Figure 15.4.

from Q_{T_0} to Q_{T_1}, to raise the price from P_0 to P_1, to reduce imports from Q_{IM_0} to Q_{IM_1} and to allow domestic production to increase from Q_{H_0} to Q_{H_1} (assuming no retaliation). This is very similar, as the reader can see, to the effects of a quota that we have recently examined. The main difference is that, with the tariff, the government collects some revenue. The tariff is a tax of t_1 per unit on the quantity of imported goods (Q_{IM_1}). This means that government revenue is equal to the rectangle ABCD in the figure. If the tariff were raised to T_2 the supply curve would shift up further to S_{IM_2}. This tariff of T_2 is just high enough to totally eliminate imports. Total domestic consumption would be reduced to Q_{H_2} and the price would rise to P_2.

Because tariffs are generally less undesirable than quotas we will in general talk about tariffs in what follows.

Arguments for tariffs

Tariffs are in general undesirable because, as we have seen, they undermine the principle of comparative advantage and reduce or eliminate the gains from trade. We have seen that they cause consumers to lose out due to higher prices and reduced consumption. Producers may gain, but only if foreign countries do not retaliate. Most arguments for tariffs are unsound for these reasons. For example it is commonly said that we should impose a tariff against the imports of country X because labour costs in country X are lower than they are here. The low wage country may conceivably have an *absolute* advantage in the production of all products. We could still benefit from exploiting our own comparative advantage. Despite the fact that many arguments for tariffs are specious there are a few which are well founded. Some of these are considered here.

National security is sometimes cited as a reason for restricting trade. The argument is that in time of war imports of strategic goods might be impossible and therefore a domestic industry should be kept in production. This is an argument essentially for buying insurance. The people of a country may possibly be willing to have a permanently lower level of consumption and higher prices in order to have this protection in the case of war. This is the argument used to support industries like steel, shipbuilding and aircraft building. In the days before electronic watches I once heard the President of an American watch company openly justify a tariff on watches on these grounds. He admitted that the Swiss had a comparative advantage in the production of watches and the effect of the tariff was to make watches in America more expensive than they would have been in the absence of a tariff. His justification was that the skills necessary to make watches were very similar to the skills necessary to make bomb sights. If the American domestic watch industry were not protected from the more efficient Swiss imports he argued that American watch companies would be driven out of business. This would benefit the consumer, but would mean that in time of war the skills necessary to manufacture bomb sights would have disappeared.

Another argument is the need for revenue. Particularly in less developed countries it may be difficult to find adequate ways of raising revenue for the government. The absence of modern social and commercial institutions, when coupled with low levels of literacy, may make it very difficult indeed to collect taxes. In these circumstances if trade is channelled through a few ports there may be an overwhelming administrative advantage in collecting government revenue through taxes on imports and exports.

Another argument in favour of tariffs is the so-called infant industry argument. A country may not have the comparative advantage in a particular industry for the very good reason that it has never produced that range of goods. The industry could not expect initially to stand up to the rigours of foreign competition. There is thus a dynamic comparative advantage argument for the temporary imposition of a tariff in order to provide the infant industry with a few years of breathing space with which to become efficient and reduce its costs, in order to compete on the open market. This is an argument which is clearly most (but not exclusively) applicable to countries which are beginning the process of industrialization.

A somewhat similar argument has recently been advanced in Britain – although it might better be termed the senile industry argument than the infant industry argument. The argument has been that imports should be restricted in Britain because British industry has proved incapable of meeting competition from abroad. Even if the probability of retaliation is set to one side this would leave the British consumer with fewer goods being sold at higher prices. However some of the advocates of quotas or tariffs in Britain argue for them very much as a temporary measure to allow time for new investment and industrial restructuring.

All of the arguments for tariffs suffer from the disadvantage that it usually proves politically difficult, if not impossible, to remove them once they are introduced.

C THE INSTITUTIONS OF INTERNATIONAL TRADE

During World War II officials and economists in the United States and United Kingdom, led by Dr White in the US and Lord Keynes in the UK, began to give serious thought to international institutions for the post-war period. It was their belief that the great inter-war depression was at least in part due to factors inhibiting international trade. They were also conscious that the devastation of the war would create a number of additional problems. To this end they sought to create a number of international institutions which would promote trade and development. The purpose of this section is to discuss three of these institutions: The International Monetary Fund (IMF), The International Bank for Reconstruction and Development (IBRD), also known as The World Bank, and The General Agreement on Tariffs and Trade (GATT). I will also discuss one regional institution, The European Economic Community (EEC).

In the summer of 1944, when the war was still going on, a meeting was held at a secluded hotel at Bretton Woods in the mountains of New Hampshire. There were representatives of some 45 countries at the Bretton Woods Conference and they founded two important institutions: The IMF and the IBRD.

International Monetary Fund (IMF)

The **International Monetary Fund (IMF)** which was founded at the Bretton Woods Conference came into formal existence in December 1945. Almost all countries of the non-communist world are now members and Hungary joined in 1982. The fundamental purpose of the IMF is 'the promotion and maintenance of high levels of employment and real income essential to an improvement in living standards'. To this purpose the IMF attempts to promote international monetary cooperation, to facilitate a balanced growth of trade, to encourage stability of exchange rates with a minimum of foreign exchange restrictions, to use its resources to mitigate the effects of maladjustments in the balance of payments of member countries and to help countries to reduce disequilibria in their balance of payments. The exchange rate system that the IMF introduced is discussed further in the next chapter.

Member countries of the IMF have to contribute a subscription (which varies with the size and wealth of the country concerned). These funds are used, amongst other things, to assist countries which are having balance of payments difficulties. Each country has the automatic right to borrow up to the amount of its subscription. As the subscription is paid in gold, this first borrowing is called the **gold tranche**. Additional borrowings from the IMF are called credit tranches. The first **credit tranche** is normally limited to 100–125% of its subscription. Countries which borrow from the IMF are at the same time expected to take steps to put their economic affairs in order. The first credit tranche is usually given fairly readily, but subsequent tranches require very substantial justification by the member country concerned and are often subject to fairly severe restrictions imposed by the IMF (as happened in the UK in 1976).

International Bank for Reconstruction and Development (IBRD)

The **International Bank for Reconstruction and Development** (IBRD or the World Bank) is, as its title implies, designed to promote reconstruction and development throughout the world. Like the IMF it was founded at the Bretton Woods Conference in 1944 and it came into existence at the end of 1945. Like the IMF its members include most of the countries of the non-communist world. Its role in reconstruction was completed within a few years of the end of World War II and it now concentrates on development. The main way in which the World Bank tries to promote development is by facilitating investment for productive capital projects. Whenever possible it promotes private investment, sometimes through the use of guarantees. It also makes loans to member countries and to private institutions within countries from its own resources or from borrowed funds. Loans can only be made when stringent conditions are met including the following. The Bank must be satisfied that the loan will make a substantial contribution to the development of the recipient country. It has to be satisfied that it is impossible to raise the necessary funds privately on reasonable terms and the bank has to be satisfied that the borrower will be able to repay the funds. The bank also has to be satisfied that the project is well designed and that the people borrowing money have the financial, technical and administrative competence to undertake the project.

General Agreement on Tariffs and Trade (GATT)

The World Bank is an example of an institution designed to promote world development through the promotion of aid. An alternative strategy is to try to promote development through encouraging international trade. The **General Agreement on Tariffs and Trade (GATT)** was established after a conference at Geneva in 1947. While the total membership is somewhat smaller than that of the IMF and the IBRD it nevertheless includes the major developed countries of the world, many less developed countries, and a few countries from the communist world (including Czechoslovakia, Hungary and Poland).

GATT attempts to promote trade by the elimination of non-tariff barriers to trade such as quotas, and by reducing tariffs. A fundamental principle of GATT is that trade has to be conducted on the basis of non-discrimination and the contracting parties to GATT are bound by a **'most favoured nation' clause** in the application of both import and export tariffs. The most favoured nation clause requires that reduction in the import duties of a GATT member must be applied unconditionally to imports from all other

GATT members. The most important of reductions achieved by GATT were the 'Kennedy round' and the 'Tokyo round' cuts. The Kennedy round was negotiated in the mid-1960s and the cuts were phased in over a 5-year period which ended in 1972. During that time the average level of tariffs in the world was reduced by about one third. This was followed by further tariff reductions in the Tokyo round of cuts in the mid-1970s.

European Economic Community (EEC)

Thus far we have looked at three of the main world institutions to promote international trade. There are, however, a number of regional institutions which are designed to promote trade within the regions. The most important are Customs Unions which have an agreement to reduce or eliminate tariffs amongst the member states while maintaining tariffs between member states and the rest of the world. This has two effects on the level of trade which are known respectively as **trade diversion** and **trade creation**. When the Customs Union is created some trade that formerly took place between the members of that union and other countries which are not members of the new union will be diverted to trade with members of the Customs Union because of reduced tariff barriers within the Customs Union. This is, of course, a change in the pattern of trade but does not in itself increase the level of trade. However in addition to trade diversion the presence of the Customs Union may lead to the creation of trade between member states in addition to existing levels of trade. This is trade creation and may occur because of growth and/or economies of scale within the Customs Union. There are a number of examples of Customs Unions in various parts of the world and not surprisingly their fortunes have been mixed.

The most important of these regional institutions is the **European Economic Community (EEC)** – better known in Britain as the Common Market. While the EEC includes the characteristics of a Customs Union its institutions go considerably beyond their limited functions. The EEC was created by the Treaty of Rome in 1957 and originally had six members: Italy, France, Germany, Luxembourg, The Netherlands and Belgium. In the early 1970s the membership was enlarged to include Britain, the Republic of Ireland and Denmark. More recently Greece has joined. In addition to reducing and eventually eliminating tariffs between member states the EEC is designed to eliminate non-tariff barriers to trade between countries and to promote economic development and cooperation. One of the most important forms of non-tariff barriers is the existence of different tax regimes in the different member countries. The EEC is promoting the harmonization of tax regimes to promote trade. For example shortly after Britain joined the EEC, purchase tax was abolished and was replaced by value added tax which is

TABLE 15.6 GEOGRAPHICAL ANALYSIS OF UK TRADE

	1971	1972	1973	1974	1975	1976	1977	1978	1979	1980	1981	1982
Visible trade on a balance of payments basis:												
Exports												
European Community*	2536	2849	3851	5546	6227	8936	11,674	13,348	17,310	20,427	20,862	22,991
Other Western Europe	1450	1551	1951	2623	2972	3862	4615	4385	5663	6844	6384	6731
North America	1422	1559	1879	2278	2316	3065	3773	4219	4788	5305	7139	8352
Other developed countries	1085	940	1209	1719	1835	1932	2075	2302	2485	2660	2925	3263
Oil exporting countries	584	641	794	1225	2275	3172	4335	4680	3667	4817	6005	6509
Rest of world	1966	1897	2253	3003	3705	4224	5256	6129	6774	7362	7662	7700
Total—all areas	9043	9437	11,937	16,394	19,330	25,191	31,728	35,063	40,687	47,415	50,977	55,546
Imports												
European Community*	2720	3441	5178	7680	8734	11,194	13,606	15,863	19,935	19,682	20,859	24,294
Other Western Europe	1470	1733	2462	3219	3240	4146	4795	5224	6908	6911	7432	7957
North America	1575	1633	2153	2964	2955	3887	4585	4953	5853	6958	7116	7603
Other developed countries	851	1083	1410	1615	1852	2040	2627	2714	2771	2892	3107	3907
Oil exporting countries	802	775	1122	3393	2948	3854	3421	3033	2963	3969	3480	3246
Rest of world	1425	1520	2198	2874	2934	3999	4978	4818	5706	5770	5975	6420
Total—all areas	8853	10,185	14,523	21,745	22,663	29,120	34,012	36,605	44,136	46,182	47,969	53,427
Visible balance												
European Community*	−184	−592	−1327	−2134	−2507	−2258	−1932	−2515	−2625	+745	+3	−1303
Other Western Europe	−20	−182	−511	−596	−268	−284	−180	−839	−1245	−67	−1048	−1226
North America	−163	−74	−274	−686	−639	−822	−812	−734	−1065	−1653	+23	+749
Other developed countries	+234	−143	−201	+104	−17	−108	−552	−412	−286	−232	−182	−644
Oil exporting countries	−218	−134	−328	−2168	−673	−682	+914	+1647	+704	+848	+2525	+3263
Rest of world	+541	+377	+55	+129	+771	+225	+278	+1311	+1068	+1592	+1687	+1280
Total—all areas	+190	−748	−2586	−5351	−3333	−3929	−2284	−1542	−3449	+1233	+3008	+2119

*Figures for all years relate to the nine countries.
Source: *United Kingdom Balance of Payments*, 1982 and 1983.

used in the other Community countries. In addition the EEC promotes the free movement of capital and of labour throughout EEC member countries. It is, for example, possible for a citizen of any one EEC country to work in any other EEC country. The Community budget is used in part to finance the Community institutions, and to finance the much-criticized Common Agricultural Policy. It is also used to fund projects in poor regions within the EEC member countries. Table 15.6 shows how the pattern of British trade has changed since Britain became a member of the EEC. In 1971 28% of exports were to nine countries that were EEC members in 1980. By 1982 the figure had risen to 41%. Comparable figures for imports are 31 and 45%.

CONCEPTS FOR REVIEW

QUESTIONS FOR DISCUSSION

1 Are the activities of speculators harmful?
2 Assess the argument that the UK should put a tariff on imports from the Far East because wages in the Far East are lower than in the UK.
3 It was stated in section A that bricks do not feature prominently in international trade because they are heavy relative to their value. Why

then does cement have a more important role in international trade given that it is also heavy relative to its value?

4   Why are tariffs less harmful than quotas?
5   Under what circumstances are tariffs justified?

16

International Payments

The discussion in the previous chapter was conducted almost entirely in real terms and we now have to recognize the fact that international trade involves the use of money. There are in fact two main purposes to this chapter. In section A we look at exchange rates and in section B we examine the balance of payments.

A   EXCHANGE RATES

In the previous chapter it was emphasized that arbitrage, speculation and comparative advantage all have domestic as well as international implications. Perhaps the most important characteristic distinguishing international trade from domestic trade is that different countries use different currencies. Exporters in each country of course want to be paid ultimately in terms of their own domestic currency. British exporters want to be paid in pounds sterling rather than in say US dollars or French francs or Indian rupees. Similarly if people in Britain buy goods from the US, France or India, the exporters of these goods will wish to be paid in dollars, francs or rupees respectively.

The fact of separate currencies in different countries means that transactions involving international trade normally require two transactions. One first has to buy the currency of the country concerned and then that domestic currency is used to buy the good in question. This of course means that there are markets for currencies just as there are markets for commodities. The price of one currency in terms of another currency is called the **exchange rate**, i.e. the rate at which one currency can be exchanged for another.

The exchange rate for a currency is determined by the supply of, and the demand for, that currency. It is helpful to depict the flows diagrammatically using supply and demand curves. Figure 16.1(a) shows hypothetical demand curves for pounds sterling in terms of dollars assuming only two countries.

The horizontal axis measures the quantity of pounds sterling and the vertical axis shows the price in dollars for each pound. The demand curve for pounds represents the demand by Americans for pounds used for importation of

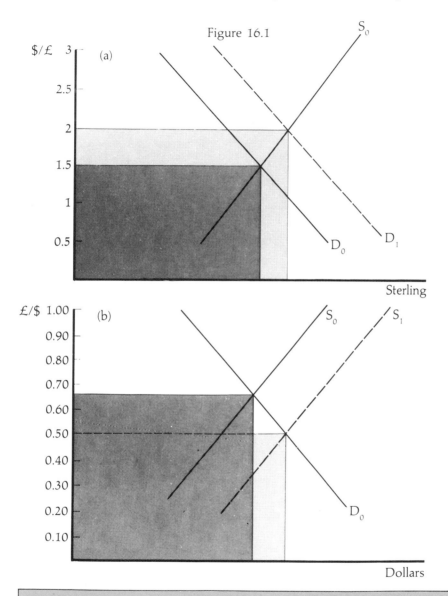

Figure 16.1

The exchange rate is determined by the demand for and the supply of currency. Americans supply dollars and demand sterling to buy British exports. The British supply sterling and demand dollars to buy imports from America. If Americans decided to buy more British goods the dollar price of sterling would appreciate in (a) while the sterling price of the dollar would depreciate by a corresponding amount in (b).

British goods and services or in order to purchase pounds sterling for investment purposes. Similarly the supply curve of pounds represents people in Britain's willingness to sell pounds in order to purchase dollars so that ultimately American goods and services could be purchased or again American investments can be made. As the diagram is drawn the supply and demand curve intersect at an exchange rate of $1.50. Essentially the same information is represented in Figure 16.1(b) where we look at the supply and demand for dollars with the quantity of dollars measured on the horizontal axis and the price in terms of pounds per dollar measured on the vertical axis. If it cost $1.50 to buy £1, then it costs £0.667 to buy $1.

Changes in exchange rates

When we draw supply and demand curves for currency we represent the amounts of that currency people would like to buy or sell each period at various prices other things remaining equal. Of course other things may not remain equal. Suppose for example that British goods gain an enhanced reputation for reliability and for being delivered on time. In these circumstances Americans would be very likely to increase their demand for British goods. In the first instance this would increase the demand for pounds sterling in Figure 16.1(a) and would also of course increase the supply of dollars in 16.1(b). As the figures are drawn this increases the exchange rate of the pound against the dollar from $1.50 to $2.00. This is of course equivalent to reducing the price of a dollar from £0.667 to £0.50. If this were to happen we would say that the pound had *appreciated* and the dollar had *depreciated*.

Changes in the price level

Suppose that prices in Britain rise relative to prices abroad. Goods produced abroad would now be relatively less expensive. People in Britain would tend to buy more imports again shifting the supply curve of sterling out to the right to S_1 in Figure 16.2. If as a result of higher British prices foreigners decide to purchase fewer British goods this would also shift the demand curve for sterling down to D_1 causing sterling to depreciate to $\$/£_1$.

Purchasing power parity theory

It will be remembered from the previous chapter that if the same product is selling at more than one price the 'law' of one price predicts that arbitrage will equalize prices to the maximum extent possible given the existing levels of tariffs, transport costs and other barriers to trade. We can combine the 'law' of one market with the effect of price level changes in the previous

Figure 16.2

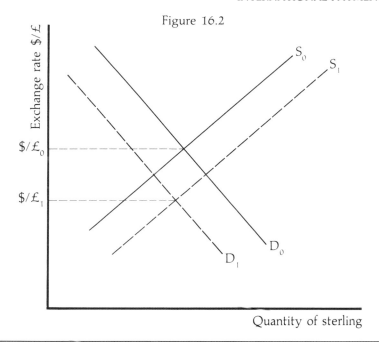

If the price level in Britain rises relative to prices in the US, imports of US goods would rise at the initial exchange rate increasing the supply of sterling from S_0 to S_1. It would also reduce US demand for British goods reducing the demand for sterling from D_0 to D_1. The result is a depreciation in the sterling exchange rate from $\$/£_0$ to $\$/£_1$. The purchasing power parity theory predicts that in the long run the exchange rate will adjust to whatever level is required to offset differences in changes in price levels.

section into the purchasing power parity theory. The **purchasing power parity theory** predicts that exchange rates will have to adjust in the long run to accommodate international differentials in price level changes. You will recall from the previous chapter that it was suggested that if the only traded good was steel costing $1500 a ton in the US and £1200 a ton in the UK and the exchange rate was $1.50 = £1 then people would purchase US steel so long as these conditions remained. One possibility in these circumstances would be for British steel manufacturers to reduce their prices to below £1000 a ton. Another would be for British steel producers to be driven out of business. A third possibility would be for the exchange rate to be reduced to £1.25 = £1 (or just lower) so that British steel becomes competitive. Why would this happen? If steel prices remained fixed it would pay people to sell sterling and to buy dollars in order to buy US steel. This would increase the supply of sterling causing the exchange rate to depreciate.

To extend the example suppose that initially the exchange rate was

£1.25 = £1. Suppose further that over the next 5 years US prices rose by 33⅓% so that the US steel now costs $2000 a ton. If British prices rise by 66⅔% a ton of UK steel will cost £2000. The purchasing power theory would predict that the exchange rate would be $1 = £1.

There are drawbacks to the purchasing power theory because for example many goods such as houses, factories and roads are not traded. Nevertheless purchasing power parity is a useful predictor of the long-run value of a currency.

Changes in the level of economic activity

The purchasing power parity theory is designed to predict long-run movements in the exchange rate. In the medium and short run other factors may swamp these long-run trends. In the medium term changes in the level of economic activity are likely to be particularly important. It will be remembered from Chapter 3 that imports are a leakage and so will rise as the level of economic activity rises. If people wish to import more they will require more foreign currency. To acquire this foreign currency they will have to supply more sterling, shifting the supply curve for sterling out to the right causing the pound to depreciate.

Changes in the price of monetary assets

People with surplus funds will normally wish to purchase monetary assets. If sums are large and there are no exchange controls to prevent it people will wish to purchase monetary assets in the country where they will get the best returns. Judging what is the best return is complicated because it depends on

(1)   The nominal return on monetary assets.
(2)   The present price of monetary assets in nominal terms.
(3)   The expected future price of monetary assets in nominal terms. The difference between the present and future price will give the expected nominal capital gain or loss.
(4)   The expected change in the price level. This will determine real returns to (1) and (3) above.
(5)   The expected change in the exchange rate.

Let us look at the choice between US and UK Treasury bills under the following simplifying assumptions

(1)   The money is now in an OPEC country and will be required there in a year's time.
(2)   There are no transactions costs.

(3)   Treasury bills have a life of 1 year, are sold at a discount, and are redeemed at 100 at the end of the year.
(4)   Prices are expected to be stable in both countries.
(5)   The sterling exchange rate against the dollar is expected to depreciate.

Suppose that in the UK the Treasury bill price is 90 (implying an interest rate of 11.1%) and that the US Treasury bill price is 92 (implying an interest rate of 8.7%). The UK Treasury bill price is lower. Is it the better buy? The answer depends on how much the sterling exchange rate is expected to depreciate. If the expected depreciation of sterling exceeds 2/90ths (the difference in the two prices) the US Treasury bill rate will be the better buy. The moral that comes out of this is that surplus funds – often termed hot money – can be expected to go to countries where the price of monetary assets is lower after allowing for both expected price changes and expected exchange rate changes.[1]

Money would tend to leave countries where the price of monetary assets was high (after expected price level and exchange rate changes) and to go to countries where the price was low. This would tend to equalize the price of monetary assets in the countries concerned (again allowing for expected changes in the price level and exchange rate). This may be termed **monetary asset price parity**.

Short-term fluctuations in exchange rates tend to be influenced by changes in the price of monetary assets. A country can raise its exchange rate by lowering the price of monetary assets (by, for example, open market operations).

This discussion of exchange rates has assumed that the exchange rate is free to change in response to pressures of supply and demand. That is a reasonable approximation to what happens with floating exchange rates but it is also instructive to consider alternative exchange rate regimes.

Exchange rate regimes

There have been a number of exchange rate systems or regimes in operation in the last century or so and it is instructive to consider three of these.

Gold standard

For about 50 years prior to the World War I some countries operated on a

---

1. If people were considering bonds with a life longer than a year and people wanted their money back in a year they would also have to consider the expected change in the price of the monetary assets.

Gold standard. Gold coins were in circulation and it will be remembered from Chapter 8 that central banks used to promise to redeem their notes in terms of gold and in 1914 the pound sterling was convertible into 0.257 ounces of gold. In 1914 the US dollar was convertible into 0.053 ounces of gold. The exchange rate was thus $4.86 to the £. If the exchange rate varied very much from this it would pay people to ship gold. Thus if the exchange rate went very much above $4.86 = £1 people would sell US dollars for gold and use this gold to purchase pounds sterling. Thus with $1000 one could buy 53 ounces of gold; 53 ounces of gold would buy 206.2 pounds sterling. If the exchange rate were $5.00 = £1 one could buy $1031 with 206.2 pounds, thus making a profit of $31 less the cost of shipping 53 ounces of gold across the Atlantic. Thus arbitrage would keep the price close to $4.86 so long as the countries remained willing to buy or sell their currencies for the same quantity of gold. The costs of shipping gold across the Atlantic meant that the exchange rate would fluctuate within a few cents of $4.86. The limits, called gold points, were determined by the cost of shipping gold.

In principle the gold standard was self-equililbrating. Suppose for example that American prices were stable and British prices rose. This would tend to cause British imports to increase as American goods would now be relatively cheaper in Britain. At the same time it would cause British exports to fall because British goods would now be dearer in America. The fall in the amount of British goods exported would mean a decline in the demand for sterling whereas an increase in the amount of goods imported would mean an increase in the supply of sterling. As a result both the supply and the demand curves would shift downwards which would mean that the price of sterling in terms of dollars would fall. When the exchange rate fell below the gold point it would pay people to convert their pounds sterling to gold and to buy dollars. The effect of this would be to reduce the stock of money in Britain which, as we saw in Chapter 10, reduces aggregate demand in Britain tending to lower prices. The conversion of the gold into dollars increases the American money supply and causes the aggregate demand curve in America to shift upwards. The fall in aggregate demand in Britain thus tends to decrease prices while increased aggregate demand in America tends to increase prices. Thus in principle one had a system which was self-regulating.

In practice the self-regulatory nature of the gold standard system did not work as well as it should in principle. In practice the adjustment process could be slow and painful with very high levels of unemployment. This could lead to countries adopting protective measures such as quotas and tariffs in an attempt to protect their own position. However when all countries did this the net result was a lower level of trade and a lower level of welfare, and as we saw in the previous chapter, it is thought that these measures contributed to the depths of the inter-war depression. As we also saw in the previous chapter considerable thought was given to ways of securing a more satisfactory system for international trade in the post-war period.

Adjustable peg system

At the conference at Bretton Woods, New Hampshire, where the post-war international institutions were discussed it was decided that international trade would benefit from stable exchange rates that were intended to avoid the difficulties surrounding competitive devaluations. They decided to recommend, and it was included in the IMF provisions, an exchange rate regime known as the **adjustable peg system** which is also sometimes called either the Bretton Woods system or the IMF system. Under the adjustable peg system each country announces a parity in terms of gold and is then expected to keep the currency 'pegged' at that rate until the peg is changed. If all currencies have a fixed relationship to gold then it is of course a simple matter to work out the exchange rate between any two currencies which are called the cross-exchange rates. In fact under the adjustable peg system there was not a single fixed rate but rather a narrow band above and below the official ratio. This narrow band is similar to the gold points of the gold standard. Once a country had fixed its currency in relationship to gold, and hence in relationship to other currencies, it was expected to maintain that rate until the IMF agreed to a change in the parity. It was envisaged that countries wishing to change the parity of their currency by more than 10% would consult with the IMF about it in advance. In practice this provision proved unworkable and countries simply informed the IMF when they wished to change the parity of their currrency. It was both the intention and the practice that the emphasis should be on the word 'peg' rather than on the word 'adjustable' in this system, and in fact parities tended to be changed quite infrequently. Thus the exchange rate of the pound sterling was changed only twice between the end of the war and 1970 (in 1949 and 1967). The great advantage of the adjustable peg system was that it provided a very considerable amount of stability and certainty. People engaging in international trade had a very clear idea of what the foreign exchange costs of their business transactions would be.

How was the rate maintained? If the market put upward pressure on the exchange rate the central bank or government of the country concerned simply sold its currency and accumulated foreign reserves. On the other hand if the market was putting downward pressure on the exchange rate the central bank was under the obligation to buy its own currency with its external reserves. If it had already exhausted or nearly exhausted its reserves the country had two alternatives. It could lower the parity of its currency or it could take direct measures to improve its balance of payments. The General

Agreement on Tariffs and Trade prohibited the use of quotas and tariffs for this purpose and in any event they would invite retaliation. The measures that were used in practice when there was downward pressure on the exchange rate were lowering prices of monetary assets to try to encourage an inward movement of foreign capital and a reduction in domestic demand to try to discourage imports. Both of these measures had the effect of reducing aggregate demand, lowering prices, output and employment. We have already seen in Chapter 3 that this stop–go procedure characterized much of British policy in the 1950s and 1960s.

While the adjustable peg system did provide for great stability in international trade, the international stability was purchased at a relatively high cost in terms of internal instability as a result of the stop phase of the stop–go cycle creating unemployment. The stability of the adjustable peg system was undoubtedly greatly enhanced by the low rates of inflation that occurred in the first two decades after the World War II. However, when inflation rates accelerated, and in particular when the rate of inflation was higher in some countries than in others, the strain on the adjustable peg system became very great and the system broke down in the early 1970s.

Floating exchange rates

When the adjustable peg system broke down it was replaced by a system of floating exchange rates. With a floating exchange rate the exchange rate of each currency is determined by the supply and demand of that currency as described earlier. If the rate is determined entirely by supply and demand without interference from the authorities the float is known as a **'clean' float.** If the authorities intervene in the currency market from time to time in order to control the rate the float is known as a **'managed' float** or sometimes as a **'dirty' float.** While monetary authorities are not always entirely open about whether their float is 'clean' or 'dirty' it does seem unlikely that many floats would be entirely clean. Even if a country is willing to see the trend of the external value of its currency determined by market forces it is unlikely to wish to see very sharp changes in its external value from day to day or from hour to hour. It does therefore seem likely that in most countries the authorities at least attempt to smooth the hour-to-hour fluctuations in the value of their currencies. This is termed **leaning against the wind**. The implications of the floating exchange system are considered in the next chapter.

B   THE BALANCE OF PAYMENTS

In this section we consider a country's balance of payments. A **balance of payments** is simply a record of financial transactions between one country and the rest of the world. As we will see the balance of payments can be a little bit confusing because there is a sense in which the balance of payments must always balance and another sense in which it may be out of balance.

To see the sense in which a balance of payments must always be in balance it is useful to go back to the circular flow and to remind ourselves that there are in fact two flows – a flow of goods and services going in one direction and a flow of money going in the other direction. This simply means that there are two sides to any transaction. A flow of goods and services, and a corresponding flow of money. Thus if I buy a loaf of bread one flow is the loaf of bread from the shopkeeper to me and the other flow is the money from me to the shopkeeper. It may of course be the case that, instead of paying cash for the loaf of bread, I charge it. If so, I receive a loaf of bread and the shopkeeper receives an increase in his accounts receivable. It is precisely because every transaction has two sides (the bread on the one hand and the cash or credit on the other hand) that the balance of payments must be in balance. This should become clear as we look at the way the UK balance of payments is actually constructed. This is done with the aid of Table 16.1 which shows UK balance of payments for several recent years. It is convenient to examine the layout of the table and the figures at the same time. It can be seen that the table is laid out in sections and what is meant by the expression the balance of payments being out of balance is that one or more sections of the table are not in balance. The balance of payments as a whole must balance but any one section may be out of balance. When people speak of the balance of payments being out of balance what they usually mean by this is that the current account is out of balance. However this usage is by no means universal and it would doubtless aid clarity if people were always precise about what part of the balance of payments they were referring to when they spoke of a balance or imbalance. We will begin our discussion of the balance of payments with the current account.

Current account

The first main division that is conventionally made in balance of payments accounts is to separate the movement of current goods and services from other transactions. The current account is usually sub-divided into two main sections representing visible trade and invisible trade respectively.

TABLE 16.1 UK BALANCE OF PAYMENTS (MILLIONS OF POUNDS)

Row number	Relationship between rows		1977	1978	1979	1980	1981	1982
		Current account						
1		Visible trade: exports (f.o.b.)	31,728	35,063	40,687	47,415	50,977	55,546
2		imports (f.o.b.)	34,012	36,605	44,136	46,182	47,969	53,427
3 =	1 − 2	Visible balance	−2284	−1542	−3449	1233	3008	2119
		Invisibles:						
4		Services balance	3338	3816	4071	4267	4249	3844
5		Transfers balance	−1116	−1777	−2265	−2079	−1967	−2112
6		Interest, profits and dividends balance	116	661	990	−186	1257	1577
7 =	4 + 5 + 6	Invisible balance	2338	2700	2796	2002	3539	3309
8 =	3 + 7	Current balance	54	1158	−653	3235	6547	5428
		Currency flow and official financing						
9 =	8	Current balance	54	1158	−653	3235	6547	5428
10		Official long-term capital	−303	−336	−401	−91	−336	−337
11		Overseas investment in UK	4399	1877	4336	5240	3362	3459
12		UK private investment abroad	−2334	−4604	−6544	−8146	−10,671	−10,768
13		Foreign currency borrowing/lending by UK banks (net)	364	−433	1623	2054	1462	4173
14		Other capital flows	2040	−767	3338	−764	−1253	622
15 =	10 + 11 + 12 + 13 + 14	Total investment and other capital flows	4166	−4263	2352	−1707	−7436	−2851
16		Balancing item	3141	1979	206	−156	202	−3861
17 =	15 + 16 + 9	Total currency flow	7361	−1126	1905	1372	−687	−1284
		Financed as follows:						
18		Drawings on(+)/Additions to(−) official reserves	−9588	2329	−1059	−291	2419	1421
19		Other official financing	2227	−1203	−846	−1081	−1732	−137
20 =	18 + 19 = (−)17	Total official financing	−7361	1126	−1905	−1372	687	1284

Source: *Annual Abstract of Statistics*, Table 13.1, 1984.

Visible trade

As the name implies visible trade is trade in goods which we can actually see entering or leaving the country. These are ordinary imports and exports of raw materials, manufactured goods and consumer products. It can be seen from Table 16.1 that exports and imports of visibles are shown separately and that the visible balance is the difference between exports and imports. As exports are paid for with an inward flow of money they are treated as a positive value in striking the visible balance, and imports, which are paid for by an outward flow of money, are subtracted from exports in striking the visible balance. It may be noted that imports and exports are both valued f.o.b.–f.o.b. stands for free on board and means that the exports and imports are both valued loaded on the ship or other carrier at their country of origin. This means that the costs of shipping and insurance are not included in these figures. In some countries the figures are shown c.i.f. which means that the costs of shipping, insurance and freight are included in the total value rather than shown separately. It can be seen from the table that the visible balance was positive in 1980 to 1982 which of course means that the value of exports has exceeded the value of imports. It is more common in Britain for the visible balance to be negative. The positive visible balance in the early 1980s was due to two principal factors: North Sea oil has increased the value of British exports and the severe recession has reduced the value of British imports below what it would otherwise have been, particularly during 1980 and 1981 when severe de-stocking was taking place.

Invisibles

The invisible account presents current transactions which are not readily seen in the way that ordinary imports and exports are seen. In line 4 the services balance is shown. This represents the net balance from tourism and the activities of the City of London. Because of the strength of the City of London as a world financial centre this figure is almost always a significant positive figure. The transfers balance represents public and private transfers to governments and people in other countries and the interest, profits and dividends balance represents the net flow of these items in and out of Britain. Because Britain has been traditionally an exporter of capital this item is positive, showing the returns from this overseas investment. Line 7, the invisible balance, is the sum of lines 4, 5 and 6. It is always positive in the UK. The current balance is the sum of the visible balance and the invisible balance. That is to say that line 8 equals the sum of lines 3 and 7. As the invisible balance is always positive in Britain, and the sign of the current balance depends upon the sign of the visible balance and on the size of both balances.

When as in 1980, 1981 and 1982 the visible balance is positive then of course the current account as a whole will have a positive balance and it can be seen that in 1982 this was a very large positive balance (5.4 billion pounds). When the visible balance is negative as, for example, in 1978 and 1979 the visible balance may be positive when, as in 1978, the positive invisible balance exceeds the negative visible balance. The current balance may be negative, as in 1979, when the negative visible balance exceeded the positive invisible balance.

It is commonly thought that a positive current balance is desirable. Why should this be so? Leaving capital transactions to one side this would mean that visible plus invisible exports would exceed visible plus invisible imports and the country would be accumulating foreign exchange reserves – at least under a fixed exchange rate system. The view that this is desirable goes back to the eighteenth-century Mercantilist economists who believed that the accumulation of gold was good for a country's power and prestige. The gold or foreign exchange reserves are of course very desirable under a fixed exchange rate system to provide a cushion when the current account of the balance of payments is in deficit. There is, however, a limit to the amount of such protection that it is desirable to hold, particularly when it is remembered that a country is accumulating the reserves by having exports exceed imports. When exports exceed imports of course it means that people in other countries enjoy more of the goods produced in this country than people in this country enjoy goods that are produced abroad. It remains a mystery as to just why a positive current balance is almost always regarded as desirable while a negative current balance is almost always regarded as undesirable. Perhaps the fault lies with economists who are sufficiently under the influence of Mercantilists to refer to a positive balance as a 'favourable' balance and a negative balance as an 'unfavourable' balance.

Currency flow

The second major section of the balance of payments is the currency flow. The total currency flow consists of the sum of current balance (row 9 repeats row 8), investment and other capital flows, and the balancing item.

Investment and other capital flows

Capital transactions with the rest of the world are shown under investment and other capital flows. The total of these flows is shown in row 15 and the detail in rows 10 to 14. In row 10 there is the net long-term flow of official capital and then in row 11 overseas investment in the UK is shown. This was a large item during the period of heavy investment and development of the North Sea gas and oil fields. In row 12 UK private investment abroad is shown. This has been a very large item particularly since the removal of exchange controls in 1979. Rows 13 and 14 show net lending and borrowing by UK banks and other capital flows and the total of investment and other capital flows is shown in row 15.

Currency flow

The remaining item in this section is the balancing item. As the name implies this is the figure put in to ensure that the balance of payments in fact balances the way that it should in principle. Its significance is perhaps easier to see after we look at the final section of the table. Neglecting the balancing item the total currency flow shown in row 17 would be the sum of the current balance in row 9 and the total investment and capital flow in row 15. It can be seen for example that in 1982 total investment and other capital flows was minus 2.8 billion pounds. The sum of the minus 2.8 billion pounds in other capital flows and the current balance of plus 5.4 billion would mean a total currency flow of plus 2.6 billion. This currency flow has to be accommodated. Some people regard the total currency flow as the most important element in the balance of payments. Indeed when some people talk about the 'balance' in the balance of payments it is the total currency flow that they have in mind. The currency flow is the sum of the current account and the capital account and somehow or other must be accommodated.

In a clean float the accommodation will come by a change in the exchange rate.

If the exchange rate is fixed accommodation will involve a change in official financing.

It may of course be that the accommodation may involve a mixture of change in official financing and a change in the exchange rate. This is what happens with a 'dirty' or 'managed' float.

Official financing

The accommodation of the total currency flow is termed official financing. Official financing consists of changes in official reserves and other official financing which includes net foreign currency financing and net transactions with overseas monetary authorities including the IMF. It can be seen that in 1982 official reserves fell by 1.4 billion pounds. It can be momentarily confusing to see that a fall in the reserves is represented by a positive number whereas an addition to the reserves is represented by a negative number. It can also be seen that other official financing was minus 0.1 billion pounds in 1982.

The authorities can know with certainty what happens to official reserves and what happens to other official financing. Thus in 1982 it is clear that

M

reserves fell by 1.4 billion pounds and that other official financing was 0.1 billion pounds to overseas monetary transactions. The difference between these two sums is 1.3 billion. This represents an outflow of official financing. However we saw in the last paragraph that the sum of the current account and the total investment and other capital transactions was a currency flow of plus 2.6 billion pounds. We have an apparent contradiction. An *inflow* of 2.6 billion apparently financed by a *reduction* in the reserves! Something has clearly gone wrong. In fact what must have gone wrong is that there must have been an unrecorded outflow of 3.9 billion pounds. We know this because we know that the total currency flow must have equalled total official financing. This is then the figure that is required as the balancing item, i.e. it is the figure that is needed to make the balance of payments as a whole balance, as in principle it should. This huge balancing item in 1982 can be seen to have been very much bigger than the amounts in most years.

CONCEPTS FOR REVIEW

QUESTIONS FOR DISCUSSION

1   How is a floating exchange rate likely to be influenced by
   (a)   an increase in the price level in the home country (assuming foreign prices are constant)
   (b)   an increase in the level of aggregate demand in the home country
   (c)   a fall in the price of monetary assets in the home country
   (Consider each event separately.)

2   What would happen under the gold standard if the pound sterling were convertible into 0.257 ounces of gold, the dollar into 0.053 ounces of gold and the actual exchange rate depreciated to $4.50 = £1?

3   What are the advantages and disadvantages of the gold standard?

4   In what sense must the balance of payments always balance? In what sense may the balance of payments be out of balance?

5   If the currency flow in the balance of payments is positive what will happen (a) with a fixed exchange rate, (b) with a floating exchange rate?

17

Economic Policy
in an Open Economy

While we have recognized from the outset that exports are a component of injections and that imports are a component of leakages, the international impact of economic policy has been largely neglected. In a very open economy such as the British one this is clearly a major deficiency and it is the purpose of this chapter to remedy that deficiency. In section A the framework for economic policy in an open economy is considered, and in section B that framework is applied.

A   THE FRAMEWORK FOR ECONOMIC POLICY
IN AN OPEN ECONOMY

In this section we introduce the building blocks for the consideration of economic policy in an open economy beginning with a discussion of the effects of inflation.

Inflation

If prices are stable in all countries, or if prices were rising in all countries at the same rate, there are no special balance of payments problems caused by inflation. However if prices are rising it will generally not be the case that prices are rising at the same rate in all countries. Table 17.1 shows comparative rates of inflation in Britain and a number of her competitor countries. This makes the point that inflation rates are not uniform and, as can be seen, British rates tend to be higher than many of her competitors.

If inflation is higher in one country than another then relative prices between the two countries will change. We saw in the last chapter that the purchasing power parity theory predicts that in the long run this change in relative prices will lead to a compensating change in the exchange rate. It is, however, convenient to begin by assuming that the exchange rate is on an

TABLE 17.1 RATES OF INFLATION (PERCENTAGES), 1974–82 (1975 = 100)

Year	US	Canada	Japan	France	Germany*	Italy	UK†	OECD (Total)
1974	10.9	10.9	24.7	13.7	7.0	19.1	16.0	22.7
1975	9.2	10.7	11.7	11.7	5.9	17.0	24.2	11.4
1976	5.8	7.5	9.3	9.6	4.5	16.8	16.5	8.7
1977	6.4	8.0	8.1	9.4	3.7	18.4	15.9	8.9
1978	7.6	9.0	3.8	9.1	2.7	12.1	8.3	7.9
1979	11.3	9.2	3.6	10.7	4.1	14.8	13.4	9.7
1980	13.5	10.1	8.0	13.6	5.5	21.2	18.0	12.8
1981	10.4	12.4	4.9	13.4	5.9	19.5	11.9	10.6
1982	–	–	–	11.6	–	–	8.6	–

*All households
†Eighty-five per cent of households including almost all wage and small/medium salary earners.

Source: *National Institute Economic Review*, No. 103, February 1983.

adjustable peg system and is, for the time being, fixed. If prices in say Britain are rising faster than prices in Germany this means that the relative price of German goods is falling. So long as the exchange rate remains fixed this will tend to cause British exports to fall and British imports to rise. There will also be a slight reduction in inflationary pressures from the supply side. The argument is illustrated with the aid of Figure 17.1. Part (a) of Figure 17.1 shows leakages and injections curves with the initial level of prices in Germany. The fall in relative prices in Germany means that people in Germany who were previously indifferent between the purchase of German goods and the purchase of British goods will now find German goods more attractive because they are relatively cheaper. The result of this is that British exports to Germany will fall. As exports are one component of the injections function this implies a downward shift in the injections function from J_0 to J_1. In Britain people who were previously indifferent between the purchase of British goods and the purchase of German goods will now find German goods more attractive because they are relatively cheaper. This will cause an upward shift in the import function which is one component of the leakage function. Therefore leakages will shift upwards from L_0 to L_1. This shifts the equilibrium between leakages and injections from point A to point B; that is to say the equilibrium level of output would fall from Y_0 to Y_1 at the initial price level. Part (b) of the diagram shows the effect on output and prices. The initial position of equilibrium is shown by the aggregate demand curve AD_0 and the aggregate supply curve AS_0 which are drawn with the original level of German prices. The level of output is Y_0 and the price level is P_0. We have seen that at the original level of prices P_0 the aggregate demand curve shifts down from AD_0 to AD_1. This means that the new aggregate demand curve (AD_1) will pass through the point B in part (b) of the diagram. It will be noted that point B is at the original price level (P_0). The economy would not, however, move to point B because the aggregate supply curve has an upward slope. Assuming for the moment that the aggregate supply curve did not shift, the new equilibrium would be at point C where AD_1 and AS_0 intersect. However it seems likely that the aggregate supply curve will also shift as a result of the change in relative prices. Imports from Germany are somewhat less expensive than they would have been had German prices moved in line with British prices. This fall in the relative price of German imports would cause the aggregate supply curve to shift down from AS_0 to AS_1, because the costs of imported German raw materials and manufactured goods are lower reducing the average level of costs in the UK. In fact the new position of equilibrium is at point D with output at Y_2 and prices at P_2.

The effect of a fall in relative prices in Germany has been to reduce aggregate demand and hence to lead to a lower level of output. The fall in the level of aggregate demand coupled with lower import prices will reduce the

Figure 17.1

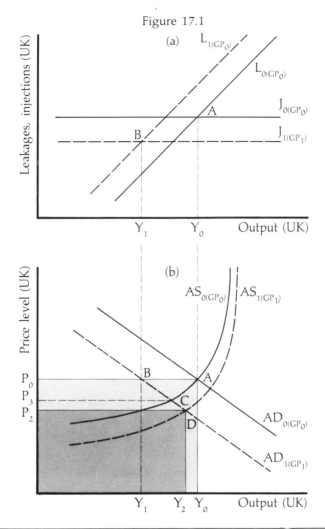

If prices in Germany fall relative to prices in the UK, people in Germany will buy fewer British exports causing $J_{0(GP_0)}$ to shift down to $J_{1(GP_1)}$. People in the UK would purchase more goods from Germany causing the leakage function to shift up to $L_{1(GP_1)}$. These factors thus decrease aggregate demand from $AD_{0(GP_0)}$ to $AD_{1(GP_1)}$ and the fall in the relative price of German imports increases aggregate supply from $AS_{0(GP_0)}$ to $AS_{1(GP_1)}$. The overall effect is a reduction in real output from Y_0 to Y_2.

extent of upward pressure on the price level in Britain.

The argument has been presented in terms of a stable exchange rate. The argument requires considerable modification if exchange rates are floating. Before doing this, however, it is helpful to look at the effect of the change in exchange rates in isolation.

Changes in exchange rates

The purpose of this subsection is to look at the effects of a change in exchange rates both on the balance of payments and on the domestic economy. The argument is presented in terms of a depreciation in the sterling exchange rate and the reader should, as an exercise, work through the effects of an appreciation in the sterling exchange rate. A depreciation in the exchange rate will normally raise both domestic demand and prices. It will also, under favourable circumstances, 'improve' the balance of payments – that is it will tend to reduce a balance of payments deficit.

Balance of payments effects

A fall in the exchange rate will increase the *volume* of exports and decrease the *volume* of imports. The impact on the *value* of exports and imports is less certain. It is convenient to illustrate the argument with reference to a specific example and I have chosen the automobile market for illustration. Suppose that as Table 17.2 shows we start from an exchange rate between the French franc and the pound sterling of 15 French francs equal to 1 pound sterling. Suppose that a British automobile exporter has a car which he is selling in France for the franc equivalent of £5000. That is to say the price in France would be 75,000FF. Suppose likewise that a French exporter is selling a car in Britain for the equivalent, in pounds sterling, of 75,000FF. That is the UK price of the French car is £5000. The cars are selling at the same price in the two countries and both French and British buyers will choose between the cars on some basis other than price. Suppose now that the exchange rate between the franc and the pound falls from 15FF = £1 to 10FF = £1. If, and this is a big if, the exporter of British cars maintains the price in pounds at £5000 then the new price in French francs will be 50,000. Likewise if the French car-exporting company maintains its price at 75,000FF then the price in pounds sterling will rise from £5000 to £7500.

TABLE 17.2

Exchange rate	Exports (UK car in France)	Imports (French car in UK)
15FF = £1	£5000 = 75,000FF	£5000 = 75,000FF
10FF = £1	£5000 = 50,000FF	£7500 = 75,000FF

Buyers of automobiles in France, seeing the price of British cars fall from 75,000FF to 50,000FF, will most certainly increase their purchases of British cars. What will happen to the value (i.e. price times quantity) of British cars sold will depend upon the elasticity of demand for British cars in France. Only if the elasticity of demand is greater than one will the value of British exports rise. In Britain the increase in the price of French cars from £5000 to £7500 will almost certainly result in a fall in the quantity of imports from France. Once again, however, the value of imports from France will depend upon the elasticity of demand in Britain for these imports. If the demand is elastic the value of imports will fall as their price rises.

The preceding argument has been based on the assumption that the change in the exchange rate does not affect the price, in pounds, charged by British exporters or the price, in francs, charged by French exporters. These might well change. Taking the British exporter first he might well argue that the price of £5000 was very low relative to his costs and left an inadequate profit margin. He may wish to increase his profit margin and would therefore take advantage of the fall in the exchange rate to do so. The extreme position would be for him to raise the price of the car from £5000 to £7500 thus leaving the price in French francs at 75,000. If this extreme position were adopted it does not necessarily mean that the exports of British cars would be unaffected. The enhanced profit margin might be used for more effective non-price competition: perhaps additional advertising, a better dealer network, larger stocks of new cars, larger stocks of spares, etc. In practice it seems likely that the exporter of British cars will desire enhanced profit margins and a lower French price. This will mean him setting the price of sterling somewhere between £5000 and £7500 and the price in francs somewhere between 75,000 and 50,000. The position for the French exporter is similar. If he maintains his profit margin he will have to raise the price of the car in Britain from £5000 to £7500. He is likely to feel that the impact of this much higher price would be to seriously reduce British sales of his cars. It seems entirely possible therefore that he will not increase the price of cars by as much as is indicated in the table. Again the extreme position would be for him to maintain the price of his cars in terms of pounds sterling at £5000 which would imply that he would have to cut the price in French francs to 50,000. Such an extreme cut in the French price would only be possible if profit margins were very high. It just happens that this has been true of many foreign cars selling in Britain. More generally the French importer will have to make a choice between raising his price and cutting sales or cutting his profit margin in an attempt to maintain his market share.

It has been argued that if elasticities are favourable a fall in the sterling exchange rate will 'improve' the balance of payments. Over what time period is this improvement likely to take place if the exchange rate depreciation is unexpected?[1] It has been suggested that the time pattern of the effect will look rather like the letter J as can be seen in Figure 17.2. Figure 17.2 measures time on the horizontal axis and the change in the balance of payments resulting from a fall in the exchange rate on the vertical axis. The origin represents balance of payments just before the fall in the exchange rate. It is

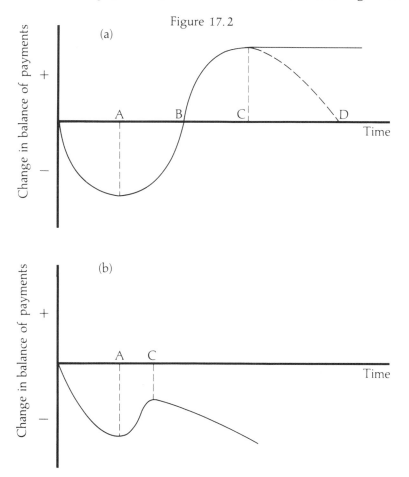

Figure 17.2

The 'J' curve shows the time patterns of the change in the balance of payments following a fall in the exchange rates. Because people in the home country are slow to adjust to dearer imports (by switching to home produced goods) and people abroad are slow to buy the new cheaper exports the balance of payments 'deteriorates' up to A. As people respond to the price changes the balance of payments 'improves' from A to C. Thereafter dearer imports raise domestic prices. In (a) the 'favourable' factors are relatively strong while in (b) the 'unfavourable' factors predominate.

1. If the fall is expected adjustment may be much quicker.

suggested that the initial effect of the fall in the exchange rate will cause the balance of payments to worsen. The argument is that if import prices rise in the short run it will take people time to change their pattern of purchases so that initially much the same quantity of goods will be imported but at higher prices, meaning that the value of imports will have risen. At this time very little will have happened to exports because potential buyers of exports in other countries will not have had time to adjust to the effects of lower prices of British goods. At time A this initial period ends. A occurs when people have had the chance to react to the change in prices. Reaction will take the form of people in Britain switching to domestically produced goods and people in other countries switching to British produced goods. These changes will boost export value and reduce import values and so the J curve begins to slope upwards. If elasticities are favourable it will cross the horizontal axis at B and rise up to a positive figure at time C. This new 'improved' balance of payments then may persist as is shown in the solid line. However we have to remember that one of the effects of the fall in the exchange rate has been to increase the price of imported goods. This includes imports of raw materials and semi-manufactured goods. In other words the fall has increased domestic costs. As these increased domestic costs begin to work their way through the system they will eventually lead to higher prices of exports and that will at least partially offset the lower export prices caused by the fall in the sterling exchange rate. A critical question is the extent to which export prices will rise as a result of the increase in import prices. The import content of goods which are exported is of course something that varies from product to product. But it is often quite a modest percentage and this on its own is unlikely to raise prices enough to offset the gains from the fall in the exchange rate. However the increase in import prices will not only raise the price of goods which are exported, it will also raise the price of goods for domestic consumption. This increase in the domestic price level may lead to pressures for higher wages in order to offset the decline in living standards which would otherwise occur. This means that the prices of exports will be increased (a) because of dearer imports,(b) because of the increase in labour costs and (c) because of a general increase in domestic prices. The resulting increase in domestic export prices means that instead of following the solid line after point C in Figure 17.2(a) the change in the balance of payments may follow the dashed line down to point D. If that happens there is no longer a favourable effect from the fall in the sterling exchange rate.

Opponents of falls in exchange rate suggest that the position may be more pessimistic than is shown in Figure 17.2(a). They would argue that the more likely pattern of events is as shown in Figure 17.2(b). As before, the initial effect is harmful. Then, however, because of low elasticities the improvement after point A is relatively weak. In addition the direct and induced effects of higher import prices work their way through the system quickly and strongly. As the diagram is drawn the peak effects on imports (at C) still leave the balance of payments in a worse position than it would have been had the exchange rate not fallen. The moral of the argument is that if the fall in the sterling exchange rate is to work steps must be taken to ensure that potential gains are not dissipated through higher domestic inflation.

Effects on the domestic economy

The effects of the fall in the exchange rate on the domestic economy are illustrated with the aid of Figure 17.3. The construction of Figure 17.3 is similar to the construction of Figure 17.1. The initial position prior to the fall in exchange rate is represented by the solid lines. We can illustrate the argument with the exchange rate between the French franc and the pound sterling. When the exchange rate against the French franc falls from 15FF to £1 to 10FF to £1 exports rise, shifting the injections upwards from J_0 to J_1. The fall in exchange rates also reduces imports from France causing the leakages function to shift downwards from L_0 to L_1. This causes the equilibrium level of output to rise from Y_0 to Y_1 at the initial price level P_0.

This increase in aggregate demand is represented by a shift in the aggregate demand curve in part (b) from AD_0 to the dashed line AD_1 (it should be noted that this change in aggregate demand is measured at the initial price level P_0). In addition to the shift in the aggregate demand curve, the increase in import prices will also cause the aggregate supply to shift upwards to AS_1. The overall effect of the fall in the exchange rate has thus been to raise the level of domestic output from Y_0 to Y_2 and to raise the level of domestic prices from P_0 to P_2. The extent of the changes in output and prices depends upon of course on how far the AS and AD curves shift. If import and exports elasticities are high, the aggregate demand curve will shift a long way to the right. If the effect on domestic prices is low the shift in the aggregate supply curve will be small. In this case the overall effect will be a large increase in domestic output and a small increase in prices. On the other hand if the elasticities of demand for imports and exports were low the aggregate demand curve would not shift very far to the right. If the effect of the increase in import prices was to start a round of cost-push inflation the aggregate supply curve could shift considerably up and to the left. It is thus possible that, as Figure 17.4 is drawn, the effect of the fall in the exchange rate would be to cause the level of real output to fall from Y_0 to Y_1 while the price level rose from P_0 to P_1. In those circumstances the fall in the exchange rate would clearly be disadvantageous.

Another example in which a fall in the exchange rate would be harmful is if the economy were already on the vertical segment of the aggregate supply

Figure 17.3

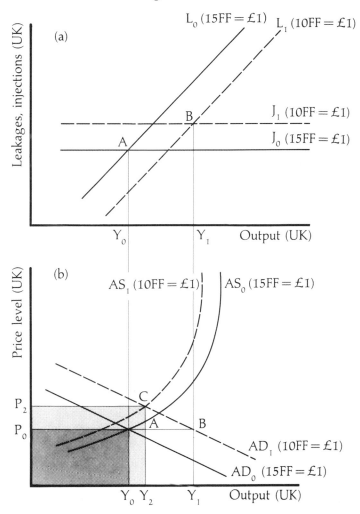

A fall in the exchange rate between the pound sterling and French franc from £1 = 15FF to £1 = 10FF will cause injections (export component) to rise from J_0 to J_1 and leakages (import component) to fall from L_0 to L_1. This increases aggregate demand from AD_0 to AD_1. The higher import prices decrease aggregate supply from AS_0 to AS_1. The effect of the fall in the exchange rate is thus to increase both output (from Y_0 to Y_2) and prices from (P_0 to P_2).

curve. In these circumstances, as is shown in Figure 17.5, the increase in aggregate demand caused by the increase in exports and by the replacement of home produced goods for imports would raise prices but, by assumption, not output. In these circumstances inflation might be further induced by the increase in import prices. This story has two morals. First the effects of a fall

Figure 17.4

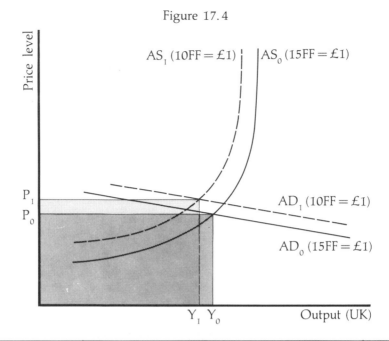

If elasticities for exports and imports are low a fall in the exchange rate will cause a small change in aggregate demand (from AD_0 to AD_1). If the increase in import prices is large and/or leads to higher wages the shift in the aggregate supply curve will be large (from AS_0 to AS_1). In these very adverse circumstances the fall in the exchange rate would have reduced output and increased prices.

in exchange rate will be much more beneficial when the aggregate supply curve is elastic than when it is inelastic. Second if one is at or near the vertical segment of the aggregate supply curve the fall in the exchange rate will not be successful unless it is accompanied by internal measures to reduce aggregate demand to make way for the extra exports and for the import substitution.

Inflation with a floating exchange rate

We have considered the effect of different rates of inflation between two countries when the exchange rate is fixed and we have considered the effect of a change in the exchange rate. What remains is for us to look at the two issues together. We have seen that if domestic inflation is higher than inflation in other countries there will be a tendency for exports to fall. This will reduce the foreign demand for local currency. The same differential rates of inflation will cause imports to rise which will mean that more domestic currency is sold to buy foreign currency. Thus both the demand curve and

Figure 17.5

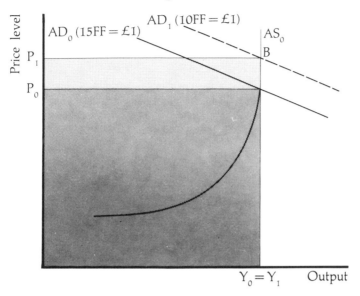

If an economy is at full employment and the aggregate supply curve is vertical, a fall in the exchange rate will increase aggregate demand and prices but not output unless domestic demand is reduced at the same time.

the supply curve for domestic currency will shift downwards (see Figure 16.2) which means that the exchange rate will depreciate. Thus if we have a floating exchange rate there will be a tendency for the exchange rate to fall whenever domestic inflation exceeds inflation in other countries. You should remember from the previous chapter that the purchasing power parity theory predicts that in the long run the exchange rate will change so as to just offset the effects of differential inflation.

Effects of a 'clean' float

If the currency float is completely 'clean' the exchange rate will adjust to whatever level is required to make the net currency flow equal zero. We have seen that when domestic inflation is higher than inflation abroad there is a tendency for aggregate demand to fall and for aggregate supply to rise (see Figure 17.1). A fall in the exchange rate on the other hand causes aggregate demand to rise and aggregate supply to fall. This means that if one country, say the United Kingdom, has a higher rate of inflation than other countries this will cause the exchange rate to depreciate and that fall in the exchange rate will tend to offset the effects of the inflation itself. If the float were clean and there were no other factors at work, the effects of the fall in exchange rate would precisely offset the effects of inflation on the price of imports leaving both aggregate supply and aggregate demand curves unaffected.

Effects of a 'dirty' float

It should also be noted that differences in inflation rates are not the only explanation for changes in exchange rates. In Britain in 1980 the foreign exchange rate actually rose at a time when Britain's inflation was very much higher than in many of her competitor countries (see Table 17.1). In part the reason for this was the low prices of monetary assets (high interest rates) caused by the tight monetary policy of the government. Another part of the reason for the rise in the exchange rate was the effect of North Sea oil. The high price of North Sea oil in 1980 led to the expectation that sterling to appreciate, and this expectation was self-fulfilling.

Another reason why differential inflation rates are not the only cause of changes in the exchange rates is that floats are often 'dirty' or 'managed'. If for whatever reason the exchange rate does not change by the full amount required to reflect differential inflation rates then aggregate supply and demand curves will shift in very much the way they would shift under an adjustable peg system.

B   ECONOMIC POLICY IN AN OPEN ECONOMY

We are now in a position to assemble arguments from various parts of the book and discuss economic policy in an open economy which is assumed to have a floating exchange rate.

Because the relationships can become very complex I wish to make certain simplifying assumptions, first about policy and second about the effects of policy. For policy I want to assume[2] that there are only two policy instruments: changes in the PSBR (showing the net effects of taxation and government expenditure) and changes in the price of monetary assets. I propose to define an expansionary fiscal policy as one which increases the PSBR and an expansionary monetary policy as one that increases the price of monetary assets. Contractionary fiscal and monetary policies are defined as reductions in the PSBR and the price of monetary assets and neutral fiscal and monetary policy as one that involves no changes in the PSBR or the price of monetary assets.

2.   This is by no means the only possible assumption. For example the stock of money or the exchange rate might be taken as a policy variable in which case the price of monetary assets and/or the PSBR would have to change to accommodate the other policy variable.

We know from the discussion in Chapter 12 that monetary and fiscal policy are not independent and in particular that there is a connection between the PSBR and the money stock. As we saw, that connection (see Table 12.1) depends first on government borrowing from the non-bank sector (which in turn depends on the price of monetary assets), second on bank lending to the private sector, and third, balance of payments changes. If the second and third factors are held constant it is possible to specify the relationships between the two policy variables: the PSBR and the price of monetary assets on the one hand, and the stock of money on the other hand. This is done in Table 17.3 which has nine cells determined by the possible combinations of monetary and fiscal policy. Each cell shows the consequent change in the rate of increase of the monetary stock (with ↑ for increase, ↓ for decrease and → for no change. Suppose we start with the central cell: if the PSBR is constant and if the prices of monetary assets are constant there is no need for the rate of growth of the monetary stock to change as a result of policy. Moving to the left along the middle row, if the PSBR is increased and security prices are held constant more monetary growth will be required. Conversely if the PSBR is reduced with prices of monetary assets unchanged then monetary growth will decline. Returning now to the central column it is possible to consider the effects of monetary policy given neutral fiscal policy. If the PSBR is constant and the authorities wished an expansionary monetary policy they would raise security prices (see the top row) by open market purchases which would increase the growth of the money supply. Conversely a contractionary monetary policy would mean lowering security prices (see bottom row central column) by open market sales. Having explained the central row and central column of Table 17.3 the four corners fall neatly into place. When both fiscal and monetary policy are expansionary there are substantial upward pressures in the money supply. When both are

TABLE 17.3

Monetary Policy	Price of monetary assets	PSBR:	Fiscal policy		
			Expansionary up	Neutral no change	Contractionary down
Expansionary	Up		M↑	M↑	M?
Neutral	No change		M↑	M→	M↓
Contractionary	Down		M?	M↓	M↓

contractionary there are downward pressures on monetary growth. When fiscal and monetary policy pull in opposite directions the effects on monetary growth depend on the relative strengths of the two sets of forces.

Expansionary fiscal policy

Having defined the policy variables (the PSBR and the price of monetary assets) and their effects on M, the remaining task is to examine their effects on the economy. The effects of a neutral monetary policy and an expansionary fiscal policy are summarized in Figure 17.6 where → means leads to, ER is the exchange rate, and IMP is the price of imports. Figure 17.6 is read as follows. An increase in the PSBR raises aggregate demand. This increases both domestic aggregate demand and increases imports. The rise in imports increases the demand for foreign currency (the supply of domestic currency) which lowers the exchange rate. The depreciation in the exchange rate has two effects: first it increases the price of imported goods which increases domestic prices (possibly initiating cost-push inflation) which means a reduction (a shift up and to the left) in aggregate supply. Second the fall in the exchange rate induced by the extra imports required for higher output increases exports and dampens the increase in imports. Import substitution and enhanced exports combine to increase aggregate demand further. The net result, as Figure 17.7 shows, is an increase in both prices and output. As a result of the higher price level the purchasing power parity predicts that there will be a further fall in the exchange rate. We saw in section A of this chapter (in the subsection on inflation with a floating exchange rate) that if the float is 'clean' this will have no further effects on aggregate demand or supply.

Expansionary monetary policy

The effects of an expansionary monetary policy, which has been defined to mean higher prices of monetary assets is shown in Figure 17.8 where PMA stands for the price of monetary asets and CX stands for capital exports. The increase in the price of monetary assets increases investment. This increase in investment increases aggregate supply (sometimes after a lag). Although not shown separately in the figure higher security prices further increase aggregate supply by reducing the cost of holding inventories. Increased

Figure 17.6

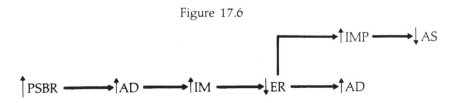

Figure 17.7

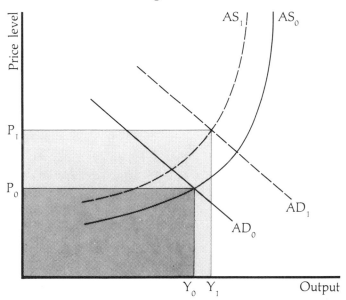

Expansionary fiscal policy increases domestic aggregate demand. It also increases imports which reduces the exchange rate, stimulating aggregate demand further. Higher import prices decrease aggregate supply. The net result is higher output (Y_1 less Y_0) and higher prices (P_1 less P_0).

Figure 17.8

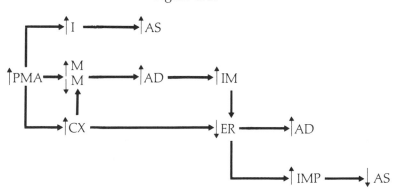

prices of monetary assets are achieved by open market purchases which increase the stock of money. Higher security prices at home make it more attractive to send funds abroad so that the increase in the domestic money supply is smaller than it would have been in a closed economy. The net growth in the money stock increases real wealth which leads to higher aggregate demand, higher imports and a fall in the exchange rate. The

Figure 17.9

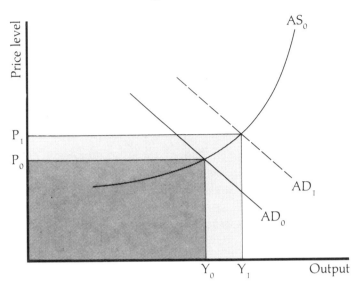

Expansionary monetary policy increases domestic aggregate demand. There will be downward pressure on the exchange rate which will increase import prices and hence reduce aggregate supply. However higher security prices increase aggregate supply by reducing costs of inventories and by stimulating investment. It is assumed in the figure that the two forces in aggregate supply cancel each other out. The overall effect is higher prices and higher output.

downward pressure on the exchange rate is increased by the capital exports. The fall in the exchange rate increases aggregate demand and reduces aggregate supply. Diagrammatically the effects are shown in Figure 17.9 where it is assumed that the aggregate supply curve does not change because it is assumed that the increase in supply from extra investment will just cancel out the decrease in supply from higher import prices. This assumption might not be correct and the AS curve might shift up or down. As the figure is drawn prices and output both increase.

As an exercise the reader should work through the implications of other policy combinations.

Expansionary monetary policy – the monetarist view

The monetarist view of the effects of an expansionary monetary policy follow from (1) their view of the domestic effects of monetary policy and (2) the purchasing power parity theorem.

It will be recalled from Chapter 11 that the monetarists believe that prices will change in proportion to any change in the money stock. Furthermore they believe this to be true for all countries. International differences in rates of inflation will be due to international differences in rates of growth of the stock of money.

You should remember that the purchasing power parity theory predicts that the exchange rate adjusts to compensate for differences in rates of inflation. Thus if the inflation rate in Britain were 10% and the average inflation rate abroad were 5%, the exchange rate would depreciate by 5% a year. It follows from this (1) that higher domestic monetary growth causes the exchange rate to depreciate faster and (2) that higher foreign monetary growth causes the exchange rate to depreciate more slowly – or to appreciate.

Clearly the international monetarist position depends on the domestic monetarist position. We have seen (in Chapter 11) that this is highly controversial. It also depends on the purchasing power parity theory which, as we have seen (in Chapter 16), is a long run theory of the exchange rate.

Policy options for the 1980s

What then are the implications of our analysis for the conduct of economic policy in Britain? We end with a look at policy options for the mid-1980s. The view of the Conservative government in the period 1979–83 was to have a contractionary fiscal policy coupled with a monetary policy that was at first contractionary and later expansionary. Aggregate demand was reduced and there were consequential falls in output, imports, employment and the rate of increase in prices. Most critics of the government's policy believe that recovery will require increased demand. With increases in the PSBR being ruled out by the government, possibilities for a stimulus in demand include the effects of

(1)   a fall in the exchange rate
(2)   a rise in world trade
(3)   higher security prices
(4)   a fall in the savings ratio.

While (1) and (4) have happened in the early 1980s, most critics of government policy think these possibilities are too uncertain and too small to offer substantial prospects for output to increase by enough to offer a realistic hope of falling unemployment.

It is perhaps not surprising that critics of the government's policy are not united in their alternative policy proposals although most do agree that fiscal policy should be used to provide some stimulus to demand and would welcome, or at least not worry about, the fall in the exchange rate that this would generate. Two of the major worries about this policy are

   (1)   the presence of structural unemployment and the reduction in the
         capital stock that have occurred in the recession may mean that the
         short-run aggregate supply curve will prove quite inelastic;
   (2)   higher import costs and higher demand for labour could raise money
         wages substantially and shift the aggregate supply curve sharply
         upwards.

These critics have no real answer to (1) and hope that agreement with the
unions, perhaps in the form of a national economic assessment, would
provide the answer to (2).

The other critics would go for a more moderate increase in demand thus,
at least in part, avoiding the two objections noted above.

Readers of this book will not be surprised to learn that my view is that
both the government and many of its critics have put far too little emphasis
on sensible measures to increase aggregate supply. This criticism of government is not restricted to the present Conservative government but is a
criticism of post-war economic policy generally. Indeed in some ways recent
policy has been an improvement with some steps being taken to make it
easier to start up in business, to increase labour mobility and to stimulate
investment. All are laudable objectives – all need to be pushed further.
Unfortunately the major supply-increasing idea of government seems to be
to cut income taxes. This is unfortunate because there is little evidence that it
will work. The major effects of cuts in income tax appear to be in increasing
aggregate demand. Demand needs to be stimulated but supply needs
stimulation as well. When demand is expanded government needs to ask
itself which method of expanding demand will have the largest simultaneous
effects in expanding aggregate supply. Sweeping general measures like
income tax cuts are unlikely to be the answer. Some general measures like
increases in prices of monetary assets and Meade's income policy may help
but what is really required is the hard detailed slog of sorting out structural
problems.

QUESTIONS FOR DISCUSSION

1   Draw diagrams to illustrate the effects on the German economy if
    German prices rise less than British prices.
2   How will a fall in the exchange rate affect (a) the volume, (b) the value of
    exports and imports?
3   What effects will a fall in the exchange rate have on domestic output and
    prices?

4   What would be the effect of a fall in government spending on output and the price level in an open economy with a floating exchange rate (a) when the price of monetary assets is not changed and (b) when the price of monetary assets rises?

5   What would be the effects of a fall in the price of monetary assets on output and the price level in an open economy with a floating exchange rate assuming the PSBR did not change?

6   How would a cut in taxation affect output and the price level (a) with fixed exchange rate, (b) with a floating exchange rate?

Index